FAILING

ROSA FREEDMAN

Failing to Protect

*The UN and the Politicisation
of Human Rights*

HURST & COMPANY, LONDON

First published in the United Kingdom in 2014 by
C. Hurst & Co. (Publishers) Ltd.,
41 Great Russell Street, London, WC1B 3PL
© Rosa Freedman, 2014
All rights reserved.

A Cataloguing-in-Publication data record for this book
is available from the British Library.

978-1-84904-410-3 *hardback*
978-1-84904-409-7 *paperback*

www.hurstpublishers.com

This book is printed using paper from registered sustainable
and managed sources.

For Andrew
(and Alfie)

CONTENTS

ACKNOWLEDGEMENTS

I am deeply grateful to Michael Dwyer for encouraging me to write this book. Michael and Jon de Peyer have both been incredibly patient throughout this project, as have Andrew and Alfie. I am also very appreciative of the friends (Antonia Mitchell, Ed Perchick, Fiona de Londras, Hannah Simon, John Baldwin and Sorah Grossman) and family (Gill, Jeremy, Seth and Sophie) who read drafts or parts of the book and provided such insightful and honest comments. I am similarly grateful to the two anonymous peer-reviewers. Finally—because I do not believe that the acknowledgements section ought to read like an Oscars acceptance speech—I want to thank Olivia Klevan who, despite refusing to read a word I write, always goes above and beyond in terms of her support, advice and encouragement.

AUTHOR'S NOTE

The United Nations does many good things around the world: from health to labour, from refugees to financial aid, from humanitarianism to diplomacy. I do not aim to provide an overall assessment of the Organisation. *Au contraire*. This book is focused on one area that the UN covers, and one aspect of that area in which the UN fails to accomplish the duties with which it has been entrusted. It is about the UN's work on international human rights and its failure to protect individuals from grave violations and abuses. The aim of this work is to explain why the UN fails to protect human rights. It is not aimed at the specialist reader, although s/he may be interested in the examples and analysis. The specialist reader might wonder why I have not covered humanitarian intervention, Responsibility to Protect ('R2P'), or any one of a number of other interrelated topics. Those issues are discussed in other works, although there clearly is a need to disseminate that information to a non-specialist audience. But in order to make this book readable, accessible, and to remain focused on the task at hand, I have not deviated from international human rights other than where it is necessary to explain the overlap with other international laws and legal mechanisms. This book is intended to start a conversation amongst the wider public. It is time that we start asking questions: about how our money is being spent at the UN, about the nature of the bodies contained therein, and about how the UN can be reformed to ensure that it is able effectively to undertake its duties. I hope that this book will provide a spark that will ignite.

PROLOGUE

On 17 March 2008, I witnessed Mr Gibreil Hamid, a refugee from Darfur, addressing the United Nations Human Rights Council. Mr Hamid's statement to the Council was brief. He mentioned three incidents within a conflict that had already claimed 200,000 lives and displaced two million people.[1] Mr Hamid's hands remained steady as he talked, but his eyes flickered nervously as he addressed people who were supposed to hold power to end such atrocities. Concisely and precisely, he told the Council how a report delivered earlier in the day demonstrated that 'the Government of Sudan is violating human rights and international humanitarian law, with physical assaults, abductions and rape'.

He described how government forces rounded up and killed 48 civilians praying in a mosque in Muhajiriya; how, after government planes had dropped bombs on Habila, those same soldiers entered the village to steal animals, shoot inhabitants and set fire to the houses. He went on to recount that in West Darfur armed men had attacked a group of ten women and girls. A sixteen-year-old girl from the group had been gang raped, and at least three other women were whipped and beaten with axes. Police and soldiers refused to intervene.

Nestled in the heart of the UN's compound in Geneva, the Human Rights Council and its adjoining meeting rooms span three floors of a rather drab-looking building tucked away towards the back end of the UN compound. The Serpentine Bar, next to the Council Chamber, allows delegates to sip their lattes while looking out across a stunning view of Lake Geneva. Government delegates, human rights activists and

UN staff mill around the building during Council sessions. Many wander in and out of the Chamber itself, even when victims who may have travelled halfway across the world are delivering statements or entering into dialogues.

The meeting rooms around the Chamber are filled with formal meetings, bringing together government delegates, regional groups and political blocs, and with informal meetings organised by non-governmental organisations (NGOs). The atmosphere is relaxed, particularly amongst state representatives, with much of the 'real' work being done behind the scenes prior to the Council's official session. Diplomats and their teams keep to themselves, although the Serpentine Bar and the outdoor smoking areas are places where everyone intermingles. Even in those areas, however, the hierarchies remain obvious. The dress codes vary according to the individual's role. The more expensive the clothes, the more likely it is that the delegate holds significant power. But power does not necessarily equate to knowledge or understanding of human rights. Indeed, the opposite often is true. The men and women holding power tend not to be based in Geneva, or if they are they tend not to attend Council sessions other than on days designated for top-level delegates. On the High Level Segment days, when ambassadors and other key state government officials attend the Council's session, the clothes and briefcases in and around the Council signify money and importance. All too often, that is a signal that the individual has flown in for the occasion; knows little about human rights; and has required in-depth briefings from his or her human rights team the previous evening.

While Mr Hamid portrayed these events, delegates within the Council continued their conversations. People wandered around the Chamber, talking on mobile phones, rustling papers or gathering up their belongings. The webcast of his statement shows people walking into and out of the row directly behind the speaker; the hum of voices accompanies Mr Hamid's words.

This brave man, who had survived unspeakable atrocities, had made the long journey from Africa to Geneva to tell his story, to speak of the suffering of his people, to 'tell the truth of what is happening' in Darfur. Almost incredibly, his words were ignored by the very people in whom he had put his faith and hope. Government delegates, for whom human rights violations exist in numbers, in theory, in the abstract, simply ignored the man standing before them who had witnessed those horrors with his own eyes and whose words begged the world to stop the suffering of his people.

Mr Hamid's message was clear. He asked 'this Council to please stop praising Sudan for its "cooperation". Mr President, attacking little girls is not "cooperation".' Later, at the very same session, Council members ignored the pleas of this survivor. The Council passed yet another resolution that called for the end to abuses in Darfur, but that also commended Sudan's government for its efforts and called for it to receive further assistance and support. By ignoring Mr Hamid's words, the Council was choosing to ignore every victim in Darfur.

The UN first discussed the horrors in Darfur in March 2003, thirteen months after the war began; thirteen months that had seen deaths, rapes, burning villages, beatings and displacements; thirteen months of 'business as usual' at the UN, with no formal discussion about the atrocities in Darfur; thirteen months after the Organisation first discussed the situation in Darfur, the UN Humanitarian Coordinator for Sudan, Mukesh Kapila, said that attacks against civilians were 'close to ethnic cleansing'.[2] He claimed that 'the only difference between Rwanda [1994] and Darfur is the numbers involved of dead, tortured and raped'.[3] The following month, UN Secretary General Kofi Annan insisted that '...the international community cannot stand idle [but] must be prepared to take swift and appropriate action. By "action" ... I mean a continuum of steps, which may include military action.'[4]

That action never materialised.

In the three years between 2004 and 2007, the UN Security Council passed 20 resolutions on Darfur. Some set up UN missions[5] and others called for a peace agreement.[6] None set out concrete steps for protecting individuals from rape, displacement, beatings or death. They were all passed unanimously. The same cannot be said of the resolutions that blamed Sudan's government;[7] or threatened to impose sanctions;[8] or took action such as imposing travel bans, asset freezing, and preventing the sale of military equipment;[9] or referred Sudan to the International Criminal Court.[10] Set against the individual and collective suffering in Darfur, those resolutions were hardly robust; but they were nevertheless contentious, with Algeria, Brazil, China, Pakistan and Russia abstaining during the votes.

Sudan had powerful allies in China and Russia, who both hold veto powers at the Security Council. China[11] and Russia[12] were also supplying weapons to Sudan's government. Sudan was also protected by its regional allies in Africa and its political allies in the Organisation of Islamic Cooperation (OIC). The African Group and the OIC ensured that criticism of Sudan's government was muted at the Human Rights Council[13] and lacked unanimity at the Security Council.[14] Not only did the UN fail to protect individuals in Darfur, the efforts of some of its major constituents ensured that those violations were able to continue.

The UN is failing to protect people from grave human rights abuses. It is failing to deal with the conflicts that give rise to wide-scale atrocities. But why is it failing to confront these horrors? Although the UN may protect some human rights in some situations, there are vastly more failures than successes. This book explores what is possible in law, what is possible politically, and why the UN is failing to protect human rights.

Many books by eyewitnesses, victims, child soldiers and activists detail individual and collective suffering. I am not well-placed to tell those stories, nor are they my stories to tell. I was not there. I did not experience abuses nor bear witness to atrocities. Each story is one of unbearable anguish. But each story is a personal account that cannot go beyond its own particular conflict and context. My aim in this book is to tell a different story: the story of why the international community allows conflicts to continue and human rights to be violated. It is a story of UN inaction.

1

INTERNATIONAL LAW

WHAT LAW?

On 23 February 2009, a passenger called Binyam Mohamed landed at RAF Northolt. With the world's media waiting for his exit from the plane, an undernourished man emerged with his head bowed.[1] Visibly nervous, and with his shaking hand holding on to the staircase rail, Mr Mohamed climbed out of the plane and descended the short flight of stairs onto the tarmac below. His lawyer, Clive Stafford Smith, a man who had fought tirelessly for his release, waited to greet him at the bottom of those stairs.[2] Mr Mohamed had been arrested in Pakistan, then taken via Morocco and Afghanistan to Guantanamo Bay in Cuba.[3] Tortured, beaten, chained and 'disappeared', Mr Mohamed was flown against his will and without due process from country to country, from prison to prison.[4] His captors and interrogators were of various nationalities, but it was clear that American and British intelligence agencies were involved throughout.[5] Seven years after he was first arrested, Mr Mohamed, an Ethiopian national and a British resident, finally returned home.

Mr Mohamed was shackled, and spent weeks at a time chained to his cell wall. He was deprived of sleep, kept awake by constant loud noises ranging from Dr Dre rap music to ghost sounds and Halloween noises—all played at decibels that made 'many men lose their minds'.

He was beaten, tortured and scalded. He had his genitals cut with a scalpel. In Pakistan, British intelligence agents met with Mr Mohamed before colluding with his captors to ensure that he did not have access to lawyers or legal process. The Moroccan authorities placed Mr Mohamed in a facility where he was tortured and interrogated for 18 months. He was then moved to a prison in Kabul, before being forcibly taken first into US custody in a military base in Afghanistan and then to Guantanamo Bay. At each stopover he was subjected to horrors and ordeals designed to break his body and mind.

'Before this ordeal, torture was an abstract word to me. I could never have imagined that I would be its victim. It is still difficult for me to believe that I was abducted, hauled from one country to the next, and tortured in medieval ways—all orchestrated by the United States government.'[6]

Enforced disappearances, indefinite detention without trial, extraordinary renditions, torture—these abuses of human rights have all been used in the 'War on Terror'. Countries involved may physically arrest or abduct an individual; torture and interrogate that person; allow extraordinary rendition flights to use their airspace or refuel at their airstrips; or knowingly collude on any other aspect of the process. More than a quarter of the world's countries have been complicit in these practices during the 'War on Terror'.[7] Afghanistan, Albania,[8] Algeria, Australia, Austria,[9] Azerbaijan, Belgium, Bosnia and Herzegovina,[10] Canada,[11] Croatia, Cyprus,[12] Czech Republic, Denmark,[13] Djibouti, Egypt, Ethiopia, Finland, France,[14] Gambia, Georgia, Germany,[15] Greece,[16] Hong Kong, Iceland, Indonesia, Iran, Ireland, Italy,[17] Jordan, Kenya, Libya, Lithuania, Macedonia, Malawi, Malaysia, Mauritania, Morocco, Netherlands,[18] Norway, Pakistan, Poland,[19] Portugal, Romania, Saudi Arabia, Somalia, South Africa, Spain,[20] Sri Lanka, Sweden,[21] Syria, Thailand, Turkey, the United Arab Emirates, the United Kingdom,[22] the United States, Uzbekistan, Yemen, Zimbabwe; all of these countries have in some way been involved in extraordinary renditions.[23] That list is worthy of attention.

An extradition is the forced removal of a person from one country to another in accordance with a pre-existing agreement between the two countries. Renditions involve physically moving a person from one country to another for the purpose of bringing them to justice in the second country. An extraordinary rendition is one that does not occur in accordance with legal processes. It does not occur in order to bring the person to justice. In some cases it occurs without the knowledge or consent of the country from which the person is moved. Extraordinary renditions violate international law.[24]

Extraordinary rendition may involve the following multiple violations of international law: (a) illegal arrest and indefinite detention; (b) abduction; (c) denial of access to any legal process; (d) enforced disappearance; and (e) torture and other ill treatment. Mr Mohamed was indefinitely detained in Pakistan, Morocco and Afghanistan, as he was in Guantanamo Bay. He was originally abducted from Pakistan and that abduction continued throughout his detention. Mr Mohamed was denied access to any legal process in Pakistan, Morocco and Afghanistan. His disappearance was brought about by force and he suffered torture and other ill treatment.

The prohibition against torture is one of such fundamental importance that it applies to every country in the world.[25] It cannot be breached in any circumstances. There may be times when a country can legitimately not comply with its legal obligations; for example, limiting freedom of expression during times of war.[26] But torture does not fall into that category.[27] There is no legal excuse or justification for torture. Treaties on international human rights and on international humanitarian law prohibit torture.[28] They prohibit *refoulement*—transferring individuals to countries where they will be in danger or at risk of torture.[29] They also require countries to prevent, criminalise, investigate and punish torture. This includes the acts of torture themselves, conspiracy to torture, and aiding and abetting torture.

Every country that colluded in Mr Mohamed's extraordinary rendition was guilty of violating at least one of these laws. Whether he was tortured in a particular state; or by agents of that state; or with those agents' knowledge; or transferred to a country where he was at risk of torture; or even if his flight passed through the airspace of a country that suspected the plane was carrying a detainee to be tortured—all of these violate the laws prohibiting torture.

Collusion and involvement with extraordinary rendition at any level breach countries' legal obligations.[30] But the 'War on Terror' is used as a justification, an excuse, a rationale for ignoring the law. The US says this explicitly. At the UN, the US insists that different laws ought to be applied during the 'War on Terror'. Other countries are less brazen about their involvement. Many European countries have faced internal back-lash for allowing rendition flights to refuel in their territory or to use their airspace; while others, like the UK, have paid significant sums of compensation to victims in whose torture and detention they colluded.[31] But still, the question remains, why did any countries, let alone so many, simply ignore the law and become involved with these illegal actions?

In theory, international law is binding upon countries. But in practice countries do not have to follow laws and, unlike individuals, cannot be coerced into doing so. They cannot be forced to follow international law. Countries can be encouraged, but they cannot be *made* to do anything. Countries cannot be placed in prison. They cannot be removed from global society in the way that a murderer or paedophile can be contained and restrained. Countries can join an organisation, but they cannot be coerced into keeping their pledges and fulfilling their commitments.

A person living in England is subject to the laws of the land. If a woman steals, or kills, or drives drunk, she can expect to be arrested by the police, tried by a judge and jury, and sent to prison, be fined, receive community service, or some other penal sanction. If a man buys faulty goods and the shop refuses to provide a refund, he can access the civil courts and pursue a claim for compensation. If a woman is a member of a trade union and that union neglects to ballot her in accordance with its constitution, she can bring an internal action which, if unsuccessful, can be brought before the national courts. The law governs every area of our lives, our interpersonal relationships, our employment, access to services, and so on. We know that if the law is broken, there are courts, tribunals, mediators and other mechanisms which exist to resolve any and all legal issues.

The same cannot be said for world affairs. Law does not govern every area. There are no world police forces that hold power over countries. International courts and tribunals do not rule over all states, and their judgements cannot be legally enforced. A country that invades another country will not be arrested. It may be criticised at international organ-isations; it may experience other nations calling off diplomatic relations; it may be ostracised by all or part of the international community. But then again, as with Russia's invasion of Chechnya or China's occupation of Tibet, it may be that none of these events come to pass. A country that sells faulty goods to another country will not have the bailiffs knocking at its door. It may find that other countries do not want to continue to trade with it or that it is criticised within an international forum, but those are calculated risks that it chooses to take. Ultimately, international law is little more than a series of guidelines that depends entirely on international relations and diplomacy.

There are, of course, some measures that may be used against a country that fails to follow international law. These include travel bans, asset-freezing, sanctions, prohibiting sale of weapons and even military invasions. But these are used infrequently and, where they are, it is only after a lengthy (and ultimately fruitless) diplomatic process. Often significant aid, peacekeeping missions, fact-finding and investigative work, as well as political dialogue, have occurred over a long period prior to any enforcement measure. If those measures do not work, it is unlikely that anything short of military action will coerce a country into complying with a particular law.[32] States, organisations and alliances are all reluctant to intervene militarily. Countries do not want to risk the lives of their soldiers. Often those that are prepared to invade are already fighting wars on more than one front. States are also reluctant to set precedents that may later adversely impact upon them or their allies. Political interests are crucial to these decisions and the law is only one factor to be considered. Thus the diplomatic games continue.

People born in England, or indeed any country, are not able to choose which laws govern over them. They do not come of age and then decide which laws they will accept. They cannot lodge a formal declaration that the laws of theft or libel simply do not apply to them. They may be able to choose to remain outside part of the legal framework. For example by choosing not to drive they choose not to be governed by the laws that relate to driving. Or by not being an employer, they are not governed by laws relating to how they can fire an employee. But those choices are lifestyle choices; they are not formal declarations of opting out of national laws that govern over every individual. Of course, people could choose to break a law and risk dealing with the consequences. But they cannot elect that a particular law simply does not apply to them.

Countries, on the other hand, are able to invoke the underlying principle of 'state sovereignty'.[33] This rather grandiose term simply means that all countries are equal, that all countries govern themselves and that, generally, no country may be bound by a rule unless it voluntarily consents to be bound. The exceptions to this rule are those international laws which are stated to be of universal application. Laws against genocide, torture,[34] aggressive use of force and slavery are all examples of *jus cogens* rules[35]—or 'peremptory norms'—from which no country may excuse itself.[36] However, in the absence of a world police force, countries can choose to break these laws with far less risk than an individual in England who rapes or murders. But, ignoring those peremptory norms for the time being, observance of all other international laws is voluntary. Countries can choose to opt in or to opt out. Even where they opt in they can declare that they only consent to part of a particular rule.

The US has decided, tacitly at least, that it does not want to be bound by the United Nations Convention on the Rights of the Child.[37] So, whether or not it follows the rules contained in that treaty, it has not formally consented to be bound by those rules. The US is also not bound by the Kyoto Protocol. Again, it chooses not to be bound.[38] Despite climate change being a global issue, despite America being one of the top carbon dioxide emitters, the US remains outside the laws set out in that protocol. Whether America then chooses to respect the rights of the child or to cut its carbon emissions is irrelevant—it is not legally bound to either of those regimes. The US is known for its unilateralist and exceptionalist approach to international law.[39] It believes that the law ought to exist, and spends vast resources ensuring that law is created and generally accepted by other countries. Viewing itself as the world's policeman, however, means that the US then chooses not to consent to be bound by those very laws that it promotes. The same occurs irrespective of the law's subject matter—the environment, human rights, international criminal law, trade agreements, the list goes on.

Countries have their own reasons for not consenting to certain rules of international law. Those reasons may be viewed as valid by some, or even by many, but the ultimate result is a system where different countries are bound by different rules. Not only is that confusing for countries and international organisations, but it means that people are afforded different guarantees and protections depending on where they are situated in the world. That undermines two crucial foundations of most legal systems: the need for law to have certainty and for it to be applied consistently.

One good example is the Convention on the Elimination of All Forms of Discrimination against Women (CEDAW).[40] CEDAW essentially provides an international bill of rights for women. Altogether 187 countries have voluntarily consented to CEDAW. But 22 of those countries have opted out of some of its rules. The UK's acceptance of CEDAW does not require it to eliminate gender discrimination vis-à-vis the monarchy, religious bodies or combat troops. As it happens, gender discrimination for succession to the throne was recently abandoned.[41] In 2012, the Church of England attempted—albeit unsuccessfully—to remove gender discrimination in its own ranks. But the UK's position shows that it wished to go at its own pace in those areas. Australia also does not accept the application of CEDAW with regard to women and combat units. Rightly or wrongly, Australia views such discrimination as necessary for its defence policy. Who is to say whether Australia's position is any more or less valid than that of Algeria, which refuses to apply CEDAW provisions that conflict with its national Family Code? Or than that of the United Arab Emirates, which refuses to be bound by a provision that violates Shariah rules of inheritance? Or that of the many Muslim countries that opt not to be bound by any provision which conflicts with Shariah law? Why should any country be able to duck and weave out of obligations in a treaty by which it voluntarily consented to be bound? Is it better to have a system whereby most states sign up to most rules? Or ought the system to be one size fits all, but allow many countries not to commit to many of the obligations? The general consensus seems to be that it is better to enable the maximum number of states to agree to be bound by as many rules as possible[42]—an interesting twist on utilitarianism.

National laws are made by governments. Individuals may have some input, whether through democratic processes or consultations. Generally, laws are written by legal advisers and enacted by the government. Every country has its own processes for creating new laws, repealing unwanted laws, and amending existing laws. International law is rather different. The entities that create the law are also subject to those very same laws. That would be like everyone in England sitting down together to write the laws. Countries write the rules, then decide whether to be bound by those rules, and finally decide whether to ignore them altogether. There are obvious flaws in that system.

Treaties are the strongest method for creating international law. A treaty is an agreement between countries whatever the subject matter, which can range from shipping to trade, from postal agreements to transnational crime. Countries may first choose whether to sign a treaty to indicate their willingness to be bound by it. Later they may choose whether to ratify the treaty, and if they do so, whether they will be bound by its provisions. It is not unheard of for a country at the heart of treaty negotiations later to decide not to ratify it. A country may see the general good in a treaty being created, but think that *it* does not need to be bound by its laws. Unsurprisingly, the US is pretty good at that tactic.[43] States are more likely to ratify a treaty for political gain than because they recognise the inherent good in its provisions. That is not to say that some countries do not have altruistic or idealistic motivations, but many more countries ratify treaties for political reasons. Treaties offer protection to countries seeking to avoid ill-treatment at the hands of other states. They are also useful for countries wishing, for example, to demonstrate their commitment to human rights, environmental protection, or safer military weapons, especially if development aid or trade agreements are contingent upon showing those commitments. Countries may also wish to enter into relations with other states. Joining a treaty gives rise to that opportunity. The more countries are party to a treaty, the greater the level of protection afforded by that instrument. Treaties are like parties—it is as much about who else shows up as it is about the reason for the event.[44]

The more powerful a country, the less likely it is to consent to be bound by treaties, because its need for any political gains that ratification may bring is less important than its domestic interests. China, for example, has not signed the Rome Statute establishing the International Criminal Court, signifying that country's lack of interest in—or even outright objection to—the Court. Russia has taken the first step in terms of signing the Rome Statute but has not yet ratified the treaty, so it remains outside the Court's direct jurisdiction. Those countries, consequently, are not bound by the rules or competence of that court. At the opposite end of the spectrum, the more politically isolated countries are also less likely to ratify a treaty; political gains are unlikely either to motivate that state or to be forthcoming from other countries. The Democratic People's Republic of Korea (North Korea) is yet to sign the International Convention on the Elimination of All Forms of Racial Discrimination. Nor has it or Zimbabwe signed the Convention against Torture and Other Cruel, Inhuman or Degrading Treatment or Punishment. Treaties, then, are a powerful tool yet they result in different countries being bound by different laws, in a vast interconnected spider's web of rules and whom they bind.

Other methods of creating international law are of less interest for understanding the UN and its failure to protect human rights. Suffice to say that international law may also be created by 'custom' and by 'soft law'. Customary international law does exactly what it says on the tin. Rules which are generally practised and which countries view as binding then become law through custom. Countries tacitly 'consent' to these rules by following them, and it is only when sufficient countries follow the rules that they become law. It is all a little bit 'chicken and egg'. The more intrusive a law, the greater the need for widespread practice and acceptance of a 'rule' before it is viewed as 'law'. Customary law may only affect a few countries—for example, if there is customary practice about who has the right to use a river that runs along the boundary between countries—or it may affect all countries in the world. The customary law prohibiting torture binds all countries. Therefore, even North Korea and Zimbabwe are bound by the obligation not to torture, despite not being party to the Convention against Torture and Other Cruel, Inhuman or Degrading Treatment or Punishment. However, those two countries will be bound by fewer rules on torture than countries which have consented to be bound by all of the rules found within that treaty.

When the methods of creating laws are compared, the international legal system seems to fall short of being a system of law. That view is supported by comparing national and international courts and tribunals. Anyone within England can be summoned to court, and that individual cannot say, for instance, that they do not recognise Stratford Magistrates Court; no man can lodge a declaration that the Old Bailey cannot try him for murders of women with blue eyes; no woman can assert that she refuses to recognise that the High Court is able to resolve a libel case.

The International Court of Justice is the UN's main court. It only hears cases between countries. Nicaragua brought a case against the US in 1986.[45] Nicaragua's government supported armed groups in El Salvador. The US responded by laying mines in Nicaragua's ports, infringing its airspace and placing economic sanctions against that country. All of this was done in the name of collective self-defence. Nicaragua brought a case to the International Court of Justice. The US insisted that the Court did not have the power to try the case, claiming that the matters could not be heard by the Court. Even though the US had accepted the Court's power generally, it argued that those powers did not apply to these events. The US refused to engage with the Court. It refused to hand over documents to the Court. It even refused to send representatives to the Court during the hearings. Even though the Court passed judgement against it, the US refused to comply with the Court's findings. The US then used its veto power at the Security Council to stop the Council from enforcing the judgement.[46] Opting in and out of courts is not something an individual can do, yet countries, or at least those with sufficient political power, are able to so do.

As this discussion has indicated, international law cannot be viewed through the lens of national law. It is a wholly different legal system; it relies as much on politics as it does on law. Countries are concerned about retaining power over their own destinies. Retaining control is seen as more important than having a legal system that governs over all states. Realism defeats idealism.

2

THE UN

A BRIEF EXPLANATION

The UN compound in Geneva is built on a hill overlooking the lake. As you walk down the winding road leading to the UN, each gated embassy seems bigger than the last. The biggest and most powerful countries own buildings nearest to the UN. There are also the schools for diplomats' children, the private university of Diplomacy and International Relations and offices at the bottom of the road where well-funded NGOs can position themselves close to the UN compound. Wandering down that road, every now and then you might see a banner or even an actual protester holding a placard. Human rights abuses occur across the world, under the media spotlights and in the most forgotten, dusty corners of the earth. Protesters seek to remind UN staff, government delegates, diplomats, activists, locals, tourists and any other passers-by about the plight of their people or their cause. Most people simply walk on by. Millions of protesters in many countries marched about the Iraq War; but the 'Coalition of the Willing'—or at least Australia, Poland, the UK and the US—marched into Iraq regardless. Protests around the world about the plight of the Tamils did nothing to rescue them from the atrocities in Sri Lanka. One-man (or even one-banner) shows stand little chance of being noticed, let alone remembered.

La Place des Nations is a large and splendid square outside the main entrance to the UN in Geneva. The three main features are its fountains, the imposing statue of a broken chair[1] and flags of every nation flutter-ing in the breeze. Tramlines pass in every direction; the square is a noisy hub of activity for locals, tourists and people working at the UN. Everyone crosses, circles or camps out at this central point. Often, espe-cially when the Human Rights Council is in session, protestors gather in this square outside the UN's official gates. They stand and sit, they sing, dance and pray, they talk and shout, they hang posters and hand out leaflets. Darfur, the DRC, the Iraq War, Myanmar, Palestine, Sri Lanka, Tibet: stories of occupation, violations, oppressive regimes and subjugation. Their causes are worthy and their stories heart-breaking; their eyes are filled with hope and expectation that someone, somewhere might hear their plight.

Men and women dressed in suits and formal attire walk swiftly through these crowds, eyes fixed on the gates and hands clamping mobile phones to their ears. Others are deep in conversation, walking step by step through groups of people whose words are falling upon their deaf ears. The hearts of these men and women are closed, their minds focused on the day of work ahead. The protesters are nothing more to them than obstacles to navigate on their way to the office. Except that those offices are the UN buildings. These men and women are UN staff, government delegates or NGO activists. The really impor-tant people drive in via the side entrance—their diplomatic plates allow-ing them to avoid the inconvenience even of seeing the protesters. The scene is like an up-market version of the streets of Calcutta or Johannesburg. But in Geneva the outstretched hands are not begging for alms; rather for attention, for someone to care, to do something to change the world. Yet the people simply walk—or drive—on by.

We know that protests *can* work. The Arab Spring protests were suc-cessful, as were the marches against the Poll Tax and the Suffragettes' campaign. But protests can also be ignored regardless of their size and their political cause. CND failed in its campaign to ban the bomb. And whatever we wear, wherever we go, 'yes' might mean yes but many people do not recognise 'no' as meaning no. A number of questions need to be asked here. Does the UN simply ignore the protests outside its gates? Or is it simply unable to do anything to help? Does the UN hold the power to make a difference or to change the world? Do the UN officials in their expensive suits care?

The United Nations was supposed to bring a fresh start for the world. Two World Wars had each resulted in millions of deaths and countless atrocities. The League of Nations had failed. It failed to prevent the Second World War. It failed to prevent the march of colonial powers. It failed to ensure that countries followed the rules and stopped invading one another. The time had come to start anew.

The League of Nations was disbanded and the United Nations created. But the end product remains an international organisation that is state-led and state-run. The UN cannot be separated from its members. It does not exist other than to serve as an arena for those same countries it seeks to control. The United Nations is financed and led by countries, meaning that they hold the power even if not the control. Although the UN Secretariat consists of paid employees, it is the member states that pay the wages and provide the job descriptions. Ultimately, when we talk of 'the UN', we are talking about the collective will of its members. This is important because there is a misconception that the UN can 'take action'; the reality is that states determine whether action is taken. Following a line that can be traced back to 1648 and the beginning of international law,[2] the UN's underlying principles are that (i) all countries are equal and (ii) countries are only bound by rules to which they consent.[3] Those crucial foundations demonstrate little movement away from the League of Nations. The King is dead, long live the King.[4]

There are three pillars of the UN: firstly and most importantly, to maintain peace and security; secondly, to ensure self-determination and development; and thirdly, to protect and promote human rights. The three pillars are interlinked, and to some extent interdependent. Wars are waged for many reasons, but a main one arises when people seek to overthrow occupying powers. Self-governance is a primary aim of guerrilla fighters across every region in the world. Development stems from the need to ensure that newly self-governing states, and less developed countries, are given support. Underdevelopment leads to instability, as is clearly the case in Somalia and Haiti.

The need to 'reaffirm faith in fundamental human rights'[5] stemmed directly from the horrors perpetrated by Nazi Germany. Genocide, war crimes, crimes against humanity—none of these words comes close to describing the sheer horrors of the Holocaust or the Second World War. Human rights violations frequently are either a precursor to war or perpetrated during armed conflicts. The Democratic Republic of Congo, the former Yugoslavia, Libya, Sudan and Syria are just some recent examples. Colonialism, occupation, administration and other forms of governance over indigenous populations also give rise to violations of human rights. The pillars, then, are clearly intertwined.

It seems so simple: create an international organisation to maintain peace and security; to enable development; and to protect and promote human rights. Yet the UN has not fully achieved those aims. Indeed, in some areas it is all but failing to fulfil its duties. The question is 'why?' The following sections set out some of the main problems the UN faces. They also provide foundations for later chapters on why and how the UN fails to protect human rights.

Membership

The starting point is the Charter of the United Nations[6] which established that membership would be open to 'peace-loving states'.[7] It was clearly envisaged that some countries would not be members of the organisation.[8] The UN, then, was not supposed to be an organisation open to all countries. Instead, it was designed to consist of states that wished to pursue and enforce international peace and security. However, that principle seems to have been lost by the wayside. UN membership can in no way be seen as including only peace-loving countries. Too many UN members have started wars or committed acts of aggression. The most obvious example is the Cold War when the two superpowers, both with permanent seats on the Security Council, engaged in war or provided the power behind wars across the world. Neither the US nor the USSR at that time, not to mention many other countries across the world, could claim to be 'peace-loving'.

Where it comes to human rights, UN members have also perpetrated atrocities against their own people. Such countries cannot be described as 'peace-loving'. Human rights abuses do not only occur within the context of wars. South Africa retained its UN membership throughout the era of apartheid. China, the Democratic People's Republic of Korea and Russia (formerly as the Soviet Union and now as the Russian Federation) commit grave human rights violations within their own territories. Bahrain, Egypt, Libya, Syria and Tunisia repress and subjugate their own people, despite great hopes that the Arab Spring uprisings would bring about change in those countries. Iran, Qatar, Saudi Arabia, the United Arab Emirates and Yemen continue to deny human rights to their own citizens. All of those countries, and more, have faced little

THE UN: A BRIEF EXPLANATION

more than gentle rebuke at the UN despite widespread knowledge of their human rights abuses.

It is easy to point to the Democratic People's Republic of Korea (North Korea), Iran, Sri Lanka, Zimbabwe, or any number of states that threaten international peace and security, internally or externally, through words or actions. But the better starting point is to look at three of the five 'Great Powers'[9] who defeated the Nazis, set up the UN and hold significant global power, all of whom have threatened international peace and security at different stages of the UN's existence.

Since 1945 the United States has either indirectly or directly, including threats of using nuclear weapons, attacked 44 countries.[10] Since the end of the Cold War, most notably, the US has invaded Iraq and Afghanistan. The US-waged 'War on Terror' has involved a range of war crimes and human rights violations that threaten international peace and security, including renditions, torture and detention without charge. Those abuses have been well documented, and include secret flights carrying terrorism suspects; complicity in torture in other countries; Guantanamo Bay; and CIA agents or their counterparts from other countries interrogating individuals in cells in Pakistan, Egypt and Ethiopia. The 'War on Terror' has continued since 2001 with countless victims, some of whose stories are well known and others of whom are faceless, nameless and sometimes yet to return to their homes and families. The US position in the global order has been seriously weakened by the tactics it has used in this pseudo 'war'. No longer can it claim the moral high ground; no longer can it criticise other states for failure to respect fundamental human rights. The 'War on Terror' has contributed to global insecurity, with many young men citing it as the direct cause of their heeding a call to arms against the West and specifically against the US. From bombings of embassies to terror attacks on marathons; from the resurgence of the Taliban in parts of Afghanistan and Pakistan to the support for the Muslim Brotherhood in Egypt; and of course the influx of Al-Qaeda cells in internal uprisings across the Arab world and in parts of the former Soviet bloc, all of these are in no small part down to the anger caused by US tactics in its 'War on Terror'.

The USSR was also directly or indirectly involved in many threats to international peace and security during the Cold War period. Since then, the Russian Federation has been implicated in conflicts such as that currently occurring in Syria, as well as conducting its own systematic war crimes and human rights abuses nearer to home, for example in Chechnya, South Ossetia and Georgia. Russia's involvement in conflicts has played as significant a role in global insecurity as that of the US. It is not just Russia's role in military conflicts close to home in the former Soviet bloc that threatens international peace and security. Russia has continued to play out the Cold War throughout the Middle East. It provides weapons to rogue states that threaten the US's main ally within that region—Israel. While the US protects Israel—the only democratic state within the Middle East and an occupying power that subjugates and oppresses the indigenous Palestinian population—from action by the international community, Russia supports those countries that threaten Israel's very existence. Its close links with Iran and Syria have become clearer since the internal war between President Bashar Al-Assad and the rebel factions seeking to overthrow that dictator. Russia has not only blocked international action that would have assisted the millions of civilians caught up in that horrific war,[11] but it has continued to supply weapons to Assad's regime despite clear evidence of the abuses being perpetrated by the government against its own people in Syria. A senior Russian lawmaker warned that if any action were taken against Assad, Russia would increase its sale of arms to Iran in order to ensure that weapons would reach the dictatorial regime.[12] Iran is another country that threatens international peace and security, not least through its development of nuclear weapons. Russia's close ties with that regime, including financial and military support, speaks volumes about that country's approach to international peace and security.

China, the world's fifth largest arms exporter,[13] has directly or indirectly been involved in wars and conflicts in South East Asia, Africa and the Middle East in recent decades, coming on the back of its own long and bloody internal civil war. China continues to occupy Tibet, oppressing and violating the rights of the people who live in that region. China too remains involved in internal and international armed conflicts. Despite the embargo against selling weapons and military equipment to Sudan during its genocide in Darfur, China continued to do exactly those things.[14] As Sudan's closest economic and military partner, China was in a position to pressure that government into ending the atrocities in Darfur. Instead, while millions of people were displaced, raped, tortured or killed, China continued to fuel the conflict by trading with and selling military equipment to Sudan. The horrors of that conflict will be explored in more detail in Chapter 7, but China's role in that conflict should not be underestimated. The 'oil for guns' scenario has occurred time and again, with China placing economic growth above its responsibilities of ensuring international peace and security.

If those founder members who hold so much power at the Security Council are themselves not peace-loving, then how can we insist that other countries, even those who wage war, abuse human rights or create nuclear weapons, be denied UN membership?

Powers

A key flaw of the UN is that it has very few teeth to *do* anything about threats to international security. The Security Council was designed to prevent or respond to threats to world peace.[15] The five Great Powers that defeated Nazi Germany wanted to ensure that the UN would fulfil this role. They designed the Security Council in such a way as to ensure that acts of aggression could swiftly be neutralised. It seems clear that if the most powerful states in the world are enabled to uphold those aims through the UN's apparatus, then there ought to be no more wars.

The Security Council holds the greatest powers and least democratic structures of all UN bodies. China, France, Russia, the US and the UK were each granted a permanent seat on the Security Council and the power to veto any of its resolutions. The Council's ten non-permanent members are elected for two-year terms. None of those members has a veto power. The five permanent members, then, are the first among equals, or like the pigs in *Animal Farm*:

'No one believes more firmly than Comrade Napoleon that all animals are equal. He would be only too happy to let you make your decisions for yourselves. But sometimes you might make the wrong decisions, comrades, and then where should we be?'[16]

When looking at voting records of the Security Council, it swiftly becomes apparent that the five permanent members as well as their closest political allies can and will be protected by the veto. China has blocked every resolution on Tibet that has been proposed at the Security Council. The US vetoes any action against Israel. And, most recently, Russia has ensured that the Security Council takes no action against the Syrian regime.

Where the Security Council does act upon a threat to international peace and security, the parameters for such action are markedly different from those originally envisaged. The United Nations Charter Chapters 6 and 7 set out ways that the UN can respond when peace and security are threatened. Crucially, Chapter 7 outlines the mechanics for a UN standing army. That army was supposed to fill the shoes of the armies of the most powerful nations, ensuring that coalitions—of the willing, or otherwise—need not be created to take action on threats to international peace and security. That army has never existed, however.[17] Whether because countries were reluctant to cede control of their own soldiers, or because the Cold War undermined any potential collaboration between East and West, the UN has been left all but toothless. Instead, the UN relies on methods for pacific settlements of disputes, under Chapter 6 of the UN Charter, and on non-military actions under Chapter 7.[18] Clearly, these have not been sufficient.

The Security Council nonetheless remains the UN's most powerful body. It is the only one of the UN's main bodies with the power to take action on the ground. The Security Council may use whatever measures it deems necessary[19] before using military action to ensure the continuance of international peace and security. A non-exhaustive list is included in the UN Charter Article 41. To date, the Security Council has used sanctions,[20] arms embargoes,[21] weapons inspections[22] and imposing no-fly zones,[23] amongst others. The Security Council has used those powers to address situations that threaten international peace and security, with varying degrees of success.

Those powers, while significantly reduced from the original vision of the UN's creators, do mean that the Council's five permanent members hold very significant political clout across the UN. They sit in on every Security Council debate. They can veto any Security Council resolution. They hold many of the political cards. But France and the UK can no longer claim to be amongst the five most powerful nations in the world. Brazil, Germany, India and Japan are far more credible candidates. France and the UK have not exercised their veto rights since they lost their world power, yet France and the UK will not in the foreseeable future be giving up their seats, their vetoes or the political clout all this brings.

The UN's other bodies are granted far less far-reaching or effective powers, at least in terms of immediate and practical impact on the ground, than those held by the Security Council. As they are not mandated to deal with international peace and security, it was seen as unnecessary or perhaps too dangerous to grant them binding or enforceable powers. With the exception of the International Court of Justice, the most significant power held by other UN bodies is that of passing resolutions or decisions. But the resolutions or decisions are not binding. While they may, and often do, carry political weight, they only provide results on the ground if countries choose to take heed of their substance. The General Assembly passed more than 500 resolutions and decisions condemning apartheid in Southern Africa. While those documents delivered a strong political message, they did nothing to change the facts on the ground. It was the Security Council's actions that actually *did* something to impact on the apartheid-era regime.

A lack of enforcement powers undermines attempts to achieve anything other than through political and diplomatic processes. Essentially, most of the UN's work focuses on politics and on information-sharing. Many UN bodies have powers to fact-find, investigate and hold discussions with national experts and individuals on the ground, all of which provides platforms for disseminating information and providing recommendations to states regarding compliance with human rights obligations. These are soft powers, but they are crucial for the UN's work. UN-appointed independent experts have been tasked with gathering information on, for example, Myanmar (Burma), Democratic People's Republic of Korea (North Korea), Guantanamo Bay, torture in Russia, human rights defenders in China, elections in Zimbabwe, the genocide in Darfur, and a vast range of other issues where information has been almost impossible to gather through other sources. The resulting reports have been invaluable for understanding security and human rights within those regions. Indeed, many form the basis for political, diplomatic and even Security Council action. However, they do nothing to protect individuals 'on the ground'—from war and from gross and systemic violations of their human rights. And that comes back to the UN's lack of teeth and the failure to set up mechanisms envisaged in Chapter 7 of the UN Charter.

Politicisation

The UN's lack of teeth is not the only reason why it frequently fails to take much-needed action. The UN's main bodies are often hampered, and at times paralysed, by politicisation. Countries use UN bodies to achieve political objectives. Many of those aims are not connected to the work being done within that particular body.[24] Politicisation is partly explained by flaws with UN membership and partly by the UN being state-led, which makes it a slave to the international political environment.

The most obvious example of politicisation occurs within the General Assembly.[25] On first glance, this appears to be a wonderfully democratic body: one country, one vote. Marvellous; except that we cannot draw a true analogy to the idea of 'one person, one vote'. Some countries have tens of millions of people, perhaps even a billion. Others have a few thousand. So, 'one country, one vote' clearly is not equal when thinking about the individuals represented by each vote. Unlike the European Union, where the number of votes is roughly proportionate to the size of a country, the UN's version of democracy fails to take states' populations into account. What the General Assembly does is to give unrepresentative bargaining power to smaller or weaker states. Little wonder, then, that political blocs dominate the body's proceedings. Vote-trading and political games are rife, frequently undermining the General Assembly's credibility. States, self-interested creatures that many of them are, regularly prefer to focus on national objectives than on the altruistic nature of fulfilling the UN's purposes. Those national aims often involve supporting or protecting allied states—creating a body that often seems to be involved in a large-scale, real-life, modern version of the board game 'Diplomacy'.[26]

Little wonder, then, that the General Assembly is great at taking up populist causes such as ending apartheid in South Africa and returning occupied land to the Palestinian people, but rarely discusses less fashionable conflicts. Between 1946 and 1992 the General Assembly adopted 569 resolutions on Southern Africa[27]—approximately one fifth of the total recorded votes.[28] On average, the General Assembly passed between five and ten resolutions annually on apartheid policies. By contrast, during that time the Assembly passed five resolutions on China's abuses against indigenous peoples: three on Tibet and two on Burma. Four resolutions were passed on the grave abuses committed by the USSR, despite ongoing oppression and subjugation of the Chechens, Ingush, Balkars, Baltic peoples, Roma, Jews, Muslims, Romanian ethnic Hungarians, Tibetans or Uighurs by the USSR and other communist states.[29] Violations against Native Americans were ignored altogether, as were similar practices and policies against the Aborigines in Australia and the Maoris in New Zealand. More recently, the 5 million dead and millions more displaced in the Democratic Republic of Congo since the turn of the millennium have resulted in an average of two resolutions[30] at each annual General Assembly session. That can be compared with the nearly 300 resolutions (on average, twenty-three per session) passed about Israel during that same period of time.

Why the discrepancies? The answer is 'politicisation'.

Intergovernmental bodies, like the UN, are by their very nature political. But when an institution is grossly selective, disproportionately scrutinises some countries and altogether ignores others, and demonstrates a complete lack of even-handedness, then politicisation undermines the body's credibility and ability to fulfil its mandate. A body's roles and functions, such as information-sharing and being a platform for discussion, and the political weight of its resolutions, are weakened when some countries are ignored altogether and others may simultaneously claim that they have received disproportionate scrutiny and a lack of even-handedness in their treatment. But politicisation is rife across the UN system, not just within its intergovernmental bodies but even permeating the greatly respected system of UN-appointed independent experts.[31] As we shall see in later chapters, politicisation is a significant factor in the UN's failure to protect human rights.

Regionalism and Politics

The UN is divided into five regional groups: the African Group, Asian Group, Eastern European Group, Group of Latin American and Caribbean countries (GRULAC) and Western Europe and Others Group (WEOG).[32] All UN members have a seat in the General Assembly. In the other bodies, membership is limited and countries are elected for fixed terms. A certain number of seats are allocated to each of the five regional groups, often on a proportionate basis.

Countries often have more in common with their regional allies than with other states. Grouping countries according to their regions allows for a few states to sit on a body and to represent their neighbours' interests. This allows the UN to have smaller bodies, which tend to work more efficiently, without excluding countries from having their interests represented. Much of the behind-the-scenes work at the UN occurs within meetings of the regional groups. Often they will discuss and negotiate internally before entering into informal and formal cross-regional dialogues.

There are significant problems with the regional group system.[33] Not all countries are adequately represented by their regional groups. At the extreme end of the spectrum, Israel is not a member of its natural regional group. Arab states[34] within the Asian Group block Israel from membership, despite its geographic location within that region.[35] Israel has been afforded WEOG membership in New York since 2000 on condition that it does not seek election to UN bodies. In 2013 an announcement was made that Israel would be afforded WEOG membership in Geneva, but the terms of that membership are not the same as for all other member states. This is an extreme example of a country being failed by the regional groups system. Other countries may be sidelined by being lumped together with regional neighbours. Japan is an obvious example of a country that often aligns itself with a different regional group (WEOG) than its own (Asian Group). The bigger a region, the less likely it is that homogeneity will exist across the group. There are also the internal dynamics within regional groups. Japan and China have their own history of tensions, as do Iran and Iraq, North and South Korea, and the Balkan states. Just because these countries are connected geographically does not mean that their interests are in any way aligned. Dominant members and even subgroups within a region undermine the aim of representing all countries' interests. It is naïve—even idealistic—to think that regional groups will operate upon Marxist principles.

Regional groups encourage entrenched positions and significantly contribute to the politicisation of UN bodies. In order to further their collective objectives, or to protect a member's interests, regional groups often adopt bloc tactics to further their aims. These include voting together *en masse* and repeating statements made on behalf of the regional group in order to emphasise the internally negotiated position. The system encourages countries to lobby one another, internally within the regional group and externally using the group's power as a bargaining tool. Often countries or groups will trade support for unrelated matters in order to ensure support for their own objectives—thus undermining the UN's mandate and work. Regional groups are also adept at protecting their members, even when they are doing things that ought to be criticised and when action ought to be taken. One harrowing example that will be fully explored in Chapter 7 is the African Group shielding Sudan from scrutiny during the genocide in Darfur.

The imperfect system of regional groups is then compounded by political alliances. Countries cannot be told *not* to have alliances with states from other regions. Geographic location is not the only factor in determining countries' natural groupings. Religion, forms of governance and political outlook are also common bonds between countries. Cuba and Venezuela have natural alliances with some Eastern European countries, owing to their similar political outlooks and forms of governance. Islamic countries from across Asia, Africa and Eastern Europe have much in common with each other; often they share more political aims with one another than they do with their regional neighbours. Those blocs have become increasingly important—perhaps even as important as regional groups[36]—as they allow countries to flex their collective muscles in order to achieve joint objectives.

Political blocs started with the polarised East and West during the Cold War. Countries that did not fall squarely within one or other camp eventually joined together to create the Non-Aligned Movement[37] to do exactly what its name suggests. The collective strength of those countries, many of which were newly decolonised and/or developing states, was far superior to the sum of its parts. That political bloc enabled those countries to further their own political objectives at a time when the Cold War dominated the international arena.[38] Since the dissolution of the USSR, new political blocs have developed into significant players at the UN. The UN holds out that it is like communism in action. Except that it is more like *Animal Farm*. All countries are created equal, but the pigs will assert their superior equality. Of course, the identity of those pigs changes from time to time.

The European Union, with its 'common position' that all members negotiate and then are expected to promote *en masse*, is a striking example of how political blocs undermine the notion of 'one country, one vote'.[39] The Organisation of Islamic Cooperation, which spans three of the five regional groups and has allies in Latin America, is the most powerful of all the political blocs. Not only does it have strength in numbers—fifty-three member states[40]—but many countries within the bloc also have significant economic, military or political power.[41] The OIC typically operates as a bloc in promoting its collective aims and shielding its member states from action. While some chinks have appeared in its armour, owing to the Arab Spring uprisings, the bloc is still *the* force to be reckoned with at the UN. The OIC ensures that Israel receives disproportionate scrutiny within UN bodies, whilst simultaneously shielding members such as Sudan, Iran, Saudi Arabia and Egypt from much needed action at most bodies. However, with no OIC member holding a permanent seat at the Security Council, that bloc relies on Russia and China to exercise their veto power to protect OIC countries. This has been a key method for blocking Security Council action on Syria during the recent conflict.

So, when the suited and booted men and women stride across la Place des Nations; when the cars with tinted windows roll through the Pregny gate; when the casual observer sees the shattered hopes of the protesters—perhaps it is because those who work in the UN understand that the UN's capacity cannot, rather than will not, meet such expectations.

3

INTERNATIONAL HUMANITARIAN LAW, CRIMINAL LAW, HUMAN RIGHTS LAW

Walk out of the Palais des Nations, through the tunnel of flags repre-senting each member state, and head across the square towards the busy intersections bustling with cars, trams and buses. In a quiet spot over to your right, in the shade of a leafy green tree, there is a small stone monu-ment with the simple inscription:

Bosna
i
Hercegovina
1992.–1995.
Srebrenica
11. Juli 1995.

The horrors and atrocities committed during the break-up of the former Yugoslavia were televised across the world. Concentration camps with skeletal victims peering out from behind barbed wire. Massacres in forests, with the dead buried in shallow pits. Women and children flee-ing their homes with possessions strapped to their backs. The world watched as people cowered in burnt-out buildings, bombs falling around them, cities under siege. Those film reels and photos evoked memories of Nazi Germany, half a century earlier. The world had said 'never again', yet here was history repeating itself only fifty years later and a few hundred miles down the road.

FAILING TO PROTECT

In primary school, my classmates and I were encouraged to collect food and clothes to send to the war victims in the former Yugoslavia. Photos of crying children, refugees in a war-torn land, reminded us of how fortunate we were to have a bed, a home, a family. When we asked our teachers 'who will rescue those children?', there was no response. The UN had failed. Failed to prevent the war. Failed to protect the people. Failed to rescue the victims. *Plus ça change, plus c'est la même chose.*

What tools does the UN—a collective of countries from across the world—have in its arsenal? What laws bind countries, and people, in their treatment of others? How can individuals be protected from abuses, violations, atrocities and arbitrary or summary killings? Are there any ways of ensuring that we can make real the cry of 'never again'?

After the horrors perpetrated by Nazi Germany and its collaborators, three separate but interconnected areas of international law developed in order to protect people from such atrocities as had been perpetrated during the Second World War: international humanitarian law; international criminal law; and international human rights law. This chapter explains each discrete area of the law, their overlap and when it is appropriate for one, two or all three to be used.

International Humanitarian Law

The purpose of international humanitarian law[1] is to protect people during times of war. It is aimed at the specific risks to soldiers and civilians that arise from armed conflicts. The first thing to understand, then, is that international humanitarian law never applies during peacetime. It is a set of rules that kicks in only during wartime. Therefore, it excludes many of the worst abuses in recent history such as Stalin's purges, South Africa's apartheid policies and Mao's forced collectivisations. In this way, international humanitarian law is different from international human rights law and international criminal law, which apply all of the time.

There are very specific rules about what counts as a conflict for the purposes of international humanitarian law. Even when all the factors are in place, the protection it provides differs depending on the type of conflict that occurs. Internal conflicts, such as civil wars or uprisings, have different international humanitarian rules from those concerning international conflicts.

INTERNATIONAL LAWS

International humanitarian law traces its roots back to the creation of the Red Cross in 1863[2] and the first Geneva Convention in 1864.[3] Prior to those events, there had been growing recognition of the need to have rules governing war as well as to protect civilians during conflicts. The creation of an international organisation and an international treaty demonstrated the wide acceptance of those aims. Most of international humanitarian law is codified, but many of those treaties represent rules of customary international law. This means that countries are bound by the laws of customary international law even if they have not consented to be bound by the treaties. States cannot avoid those particular obligations, then, simply by not signing up to a treaty.

The laws of armed conflict traditionally only applied to international wars. Countries were reluctant to accept any international supervision, through laws or otherwise, of events occurring within their own territories. The notion of state sovereignty—that a country rules over itself and determines what happens within its borders—was sacrosanct, even where internal conflicts impacted upon the people living in those places. The international community was not concerned with what happened to individuals, whether insurgents or civilians, during internal uprisings or wars. Instead, it was solely concerned with the way countries conducted wars with one another and the threat posed by states to each other's citizens.

Since the horrors of Nazi Germany, and the atrocities committed against German citizens, there has been an increasing movement towards ensuring that similar rules apply to internal and international armed conflicts. Over the past 60 years, conflicts have become internationalised even where they predominantly occur on the soil of one country. Some wars spill into neighbouring states, as happened when the conflict in Darfur went beyond Sudan's borders and into Chad. Others are difficult to categorise as internal or international, such as the break-up of the former Yugoslavia where the war started within one country which then broke down into a number of independent states. There are conflicts that remain within one country, such as the genocide in Rwanda, but even then there was an international impact as it threatened regional peace and security. And whenever UN peacekeepers are involved, there is an obvious international element to any war. The need to harmonise the law of international humanitarian law has widely been accepted and steps continue to be taken in that direction.

Laws governing armed conflict provide *obligations* on the warring parties rather than *rights* for individuals within the war zone. This is a crucial distinction that sets international humanitarian law apart from international human rights law. Obligations vary according to the type of conflict, the people involved and the scenarios in which issues arise. There are laws governing the treatment of the wounded and sick,[4] prisoners of war,[5] targets of bombs and shells, weapons used, and protecting refugees. All parties to a conflict are obligated to 'respect' and to 'ensure respect' for international humanitarian law.[6]

Individuals are protected by law either as: (1) 'protected persons', who have a high level of protection; or (2) people in the power of a party to an armed conflict, who enjoy minimum guarantees.[7] Protected persons are divided into combatants who have fallen into enemy hands and civilians. Different rules apply to both categories, and they provide stronger protection than the minimum guarantees afforded to persons under the power of a party to the conflict.

Unlike international human rights law, individuals cannot directly enforce humanitarian obligations. The obligations bind the parties to a conflict rather than creating individual rights. As importantly, the relevant treaties do not create mechanisms for enforcing the law. The international community can take action to implement the laws or remedy violations. The International Committee of the Red Cross does invaluable work to implement international humanitarian law during armed conflicts.[8] Where individuals break humanitarian laws in ways that also constitute an international crime, they may be prosecuted under the related area of international criminal law. If a violation of international humanitarian law does not fall under international criminal law, then states are required to ensure that they are offences punishable by their national courts.

International human rights law and international humanitarian law both seek to protect individuals. Although they focus on different aspects of protection, there is a strong argument that both form part of a broader system of human rights protection.[9] The two legal regimes complement and overlap with one another. The International Court of Justice has differentiated between: (a) rights that fall within the scope of international humanitarian law, such as those of soldiers; (b) those guaranteed by international human rights law, such as rights to marriage or family life; (c) and those coming under both regimes.[10]

INTERNATIONAL LAWS

International Criminal Law

National courts are mandated to prosecute persons who commit criminal offences and international criminal courts and tribunals are required to hold accountable individuals who violate international criminal law. That area of law traces its origins back to the same starting point as international humanitarian law. The Tokyo and Nuremberg trials, after the Second World War, heralded the birth of international criminal law whereby individuals are prosecuted for international crimes before international courts and tribunals. The four core international crimes are genocide, crimes against humanity, war crimes, and aggression.

Military commanders in Nazi Germany were guilty of all four core crimes. The scale of the atrocities shocked the world to its core. Those crimes had to be prosecuted and punished. The military tribunals in Tokyo and Nuremberg were necessary for justice to be seen to be done. The fact that those crimes did not exist as international criminal law when the acts were perpetrated was incidental. The invention of international criminal law and its retroactive application to Nazi leaders were justified on moral grounds. Arguments that such justice was 'victor's justice' were drowned out by stories of the systematic atrocities perpetrated by that regime.

There were, I suppose, three possible courses: to let the atrocities which had been committed go unpunished; to put the perpetrators to death or punish them by executive action; or to try them. Which was it to be? Was it possible to let such atrocities go unpunished? Could France, could Russia, could Holland, Belgium, Norway, Czechoslovakia, Poland or Yugoslavia be expected to consent to such a course? […] It will be remembered that after the First World War alleged criminals were handed over to be tried by Germany, and what a farce that was! The majority got off and such sentences as were inflicted were derisory and were soon remitted.[11]

Since 1945, international criminal law has become codified and enshrined in international, regional and national law. International criminal tribunals were created to prosecute individuals after the wars and mass killings in Cambodia,[12] the former Yugoslavia,[13] Rwanda[14] and Sierra Leone.[15] The International Criminal Court was created in 1998 in order to provide a permanent court in which to prosecute individuals violating the core crimes in any conflict. There has been growing recognition that war criminals must be prosecuted and punished, whether by international courts and tribunals or by national courts acting upon international law.

The most culpable are the ones prosecuted under international criminal law—commanders, military leaders and those who give the orders or hatch the plans for war crimes. Otherwise, the international criminal courts and tribunals would be overflowing with prosecutions. The idea is that soldiers and others who commit crimes on the ground will be prosecuted and punished at the national level. But those who bear the most responsibility, who shoulder the most blame, will be tried as criminals at the international level. This ensures that justice is seen to be done and that corruption cannot occur within national courts in countries where many war criminals still have supporters. It also ensures that appropriate sentences can be handed out to those found guilty of the most heinous crimes.

The core international crimes frequently involve violations of human rights and/or humanitarian law. Genocide—the destruction of a people, in whole or in part—includes violations of the right to life and of the requirement of non-discrimination and, frequently, minority rights. Crimes against humanity and war crimes include grave breaches of the Geneva Convention, torture, enforced disappearances, and outrages on personal dignity. The overlap between international human rights law and international humanitarian law is clear. But international humanitarian law only applies during times of armed conflicts and not during times of peace. International criminal law does cover acts committed outside of war, but some international crimes can only be committed during armed conflicts.

The International Criminal Court[16] has been heralded as a new way forward for prosecuting international criminals, but a main problem is that states are not required to submit to the Court's jurisdiction. It all comes back again to state sovereignty, and a country's right to choose the laws and legal mechanisms by which it is bound. If a state is not party to the International Criminal Court, then its citizens can only be arrested and prosecuted if they step into a country that has signed the Rome Statute. George W. Bush, for example, can remain in the United States and ensure that he is never arrested and prosecuted for war crimes or crimes against humanity. The US is not party to the International Criminal Court and is unlikely to sign up any time soon. The Court has issued arrest warrants for various Sudanese persons allegedly responsible for the genocide and atrocities in Darfur. But those persons remain at large.[17] Sudan is not party to the Court, so none of the individuals will be arrested unless they enter a country that has signed the Rome Statute; or until the international community places political pressure on Sudan's government to hand over the identified people to the Court. The Court's arrest warrants seem little more than an exercise in public relations, even if they send a signal of condemning the atrocities and massacres in Darfur.

So, even where mechanisms exist for protecting individuals and punishing abusers under international law, much still depends on state sovereignty and international politics.

International Human Rights Law

The modern era of international human rights law has widely been accepted as being a direct response to the atrocities committed by Nazi Germany. The world bore witness to a country systematically oppressing, subjugating and then slaughtering its own citizens. Nazi Germany violated the basic rights of German citizens who were also Jews, gypsies, homosexuals, disabled, political opponents of the Nazi party, and many more. International humanitarian law dictated how a country must treat foreign nationals, but not how to deal with its own non-combatant civilians. Moreover, the Nuremberg Laws and widespread oppression and abuses from 1933 to 1939 fell outside of an armed conflict and thus would not have been governed by international humanitarian law. After the defeat of Nazi Germany, when the concentration and extermination camps were publicly exposed, there was an obvious need to ensure that such acts could never happen again.

A first step towards 'never again' was the Universal Declaration of Human Rights.[18] In 1948, countries from across the world boldly and loudly set out the rights of all humans, all persons, all men, women and children irrespective of race, religion or the colour of their skin.

What is a declaration? It is to say something, to pronounce it, to make it known formally or officially. But to make a Universal Declaration of Human Rights does not mean that every human has every one of the 48 rights, nor that they are universally adhered to or even accepted. Indeed, many of the countries that wrote and supported the declaration were simultaneously governing over empires, occupying land, subjugating and oppressing people—the same people that they declared were holders of these universal rights.

Thus was born the modern era of international human rights law. Those laws trace their roots back to religious texts and teachings, to ancient societies and cultures. They have foundations in the US and French Declarations, and in the growth of the international system both before and after the First World War. But the system that we call international human rights law began on 10 December 1948.

Of course, a declaration is not a treaty. States did not consent to the Universal Declaration of Human Rights. Nor were they bound by it, at least not at that early stage. But it was and is crucial to international human rights law. Within two years, Europe had created the first international human rights law treaty—the European Convention on Human Rights (1950)[19]—which codified and created binding law about many aspects of the Universal Declaration. The United Nations ought similarly to have codified the Declaration and created binding law swiftly and decisively. Global politics, however, swiftly got in the way of that aim. The West and the East—the US and the USSR—reached a deadlock on international human rights law in much the same way that they did about other international matters during that time. Nearly two decades after the Universal Declaration on Human Rights, two separate treaties were created to codify those rights at the universal level. The International Covenant on Civil and Political Rights[20] enshrined one type of right found in the Universal Declaration; the International Covenant on Economic, Social and Cultural Rights[21] did the same for the other rights. There are some common articles such as on non-discrimination[22] and the right of self-determination.[23] Largely, however, the two treaties reflected two different ideologies on international human rights law. The West promoted rights of individuals, protecting them from state interference. The East promoted rights of individuals to have certain things guaranteed by the state. Many countries are party to both treaties, but even today, long after the end of the Cold War and with far more human rights treaties in existence, some countries remain tied solely to one or other ideology.

The two broad human rights ideologies that underpin the Universal Declaration are joined by a third category of rights that has developed significantly since the 1970s.[24] Third Generation Rights focus on peoples' rights.[25] They protect collective rights to things such as a clean and healthy environment, to development and to peace. Those rights are broad and have been criticised for being vague and bringing tangential subject matters into the human rights arena. Critics argue that those rights would fit better in environmental, financial or other bodies.[26] Many of the criticisms levelled at Third Generation Rights were previously made in relation to Economic, Social and Cultural Rights.[27] A main argument is that it is difficult to bring a case to court alleging that one of those rights has been violated. What would be the evidence for such a case? Allegations of abuse of the right to adequate housing or to health, let alone to peace, would require courts to examine state policies and budgets. But that does not mean that cases cannot be and have not been heard. Where such rights are protected by a country's constitution, courts have issued judgements. In India[28] and South Africa[29] cases have focused on the right to health and adequate housing. In Japan[30] and Costa Rica[31] courts have ruled on the right to peace. Discussions about the divisions or indivisibility of the three categories of rights go beyond the scope of this book. Throughout this work I shall focus predominantly on Civil and Political Rights as they are the least contentious and the easiest in which to demonstrate abuses. But that is not to say that violations of other types of rights are not just as serious a problem.

International human rights law provides rights for individuals as well as obligations for states. Those rights and obligations exist at all times, although they may be limited within exceptional circumstances where proportionate and necessary for aims such as national security. Any such limitation is governed and scrutinised by international law. Some human rights are easier to implement than others. To comply with an individual's right not to be tortured, countries simply must refrain from torturing or from being complicit in torture abroad. An individual's right to adequate housing is more tricky, particularly for economically weaker countries or ones experiencing natural or man-made disasters. For those rights, there are minimum core obligations[32] that all countries must implement. After that, countries are required progressively to realise rights[33] and each state is judged according to its resources.[34] Sweden cannot be compared with Somalia.

Countries party to human rights treaties are required to provide protection and remedies under national law. Some human rights, such as the prohibition against torture, form part of customary international law; therefore states cannot choose whether or not to be bound by those rules. There exist regional and international mechanisms for individuals to seek remedy for human rights violations. Nine UN human rights treaties have their own treaty-bodies that monitor compliance with the obligations and provide recommendations for states party to each treaty.[35] Some of those have mechanisms for individuals to report violations of their rights. The UN Human Rights Council also has a mechanism for individuals to submit complaints about human rights abuses. Europe, the Americas and Africa have human rights commissions and courts that perform similar functions. Unlike international humanitarian law and international criminal law, there are mechanisms which enable individuals to bring complaints of violations of the law.

Protection Problems

Enforcement is the biggest problem across all three of these areas of law. All parties to the treaties know their obligations, and as Louis Henkin famously said: 'It is probably the case that almost all nations observe almost all principles of international law and almost all of their obligations almost all of the time.'[36]

But that does not mean that all laws are obeyed all of the time. And when international humanitarian law, international criminal law or international human rights law are not observed, atrocities and horrors are perpetrated. Despite the availability of some courts, tribunals or other bodies for adjudicating on alleged violations of the law, enforcement remains a key problem. With international criminal law, where the ICC has jurisdiction both over the crime committed and the individual concerned, then enforcement can take place. But this is the exception rather than the norm. The lack of enforcement mechanisms across all three areas means that the system relies upon international relations, diplomatic processes and—in extreme situations—Security Council action.

Of course, that does not mean that the law does not exist; nor that the law is not binding. But it does mean that countries can be forced to comply with the law. The more obligations there are, and the more they rely upon state consent through the form of treaty ratification, the harder they are to enforce. Where a law is universally accepted as customary international law, then there is more likely to be political pressure to enforce. National courts might also be willing to prosecute and punish their own citizens and/or foreign nationals for violating those norms. In terms of international human rights law, one main problem for enforcement—and indeed for individuals' certainty about their rights—is that the vast majority of the obligations are not universally binding and that there are so many variations in terms of which states are bound by which laws. Enforcement, then, becomes a difficult and complex diplomatic game.

4

UNIVERSAL RIGHTS OR CULTURAL RELATIVISM?

Mama positioned me on the rock. She sat behind me and pulled my head against her chest, her legs straddling my body. I circled my arms around her thighs. She placed a piece of root from an old tree between my teeth. 'Bite on this.'

Mama leaned over and whispered, 'Try to be a good girl, baby. Be brave for Mama, and it'll go fast.'

I peered between my legs and saw the gypsy. The old woman looked at me sternly, a dead look in her eyes, then foraged through an old carpet-bag. She reached inside with her long fingers and fished out a broken razor blade. I saw dried blood on the jagged edge. She spit on it and wiped it on her dress. While she was scrubbing, my world went dark as Mama tied a blindfold over my eyes.

The next thing I felt was my flesh being cut away. I heard the blade sawing back and forth through my skin. The feeling was indescribable. I didn't move, telling myself the more I did, the longer the torture would take. Unfortunately, my legs began to quiver and shake uncontrollably of their own accord, and I prayed, Please, God, let it be over quickly. Soon it was, because I passed out.

When I woke up, my blindfold was off and I saw the gypsy woman had piled a stack of thorns from an acacia tree next to her. She used these to puncture holes in my skin, then poked a strong white thread through the holes to sew me up. My legs were completely numb, but the pain between them was so intense that I wished I would die.[1]

Waris Dirie was five years old when she was mutilated by a 'Gypsy woman' brought to the house by her father.[2] Her description of that life-defining event is harrowing. In 1996 Ms Dirie, by then a supermodel, actress and author, was appointed UN Special Ambassador for the elimination of Female Genital Mutilation. She has used her position to continue her ongoing campaign for an end to that ritual. Opponents of female genital mutilation[3] point to the rights of the child,[4] the right not to be tortured,[5] the right to life, the right to health, and many others.[6] Defenders of the ritual claim that it is a cultural practice and invoke arguments of cultural relativity.[7]

The notion of cultural relativism is one of the main obstacles to universal human rights protection and promotion. The world is not made up of homogeneous states. Indeed, even within fairly homogeneous regions there are different cultures and identities that emphasise very different values and norms. Cultural relativism acknowledges the need to allow states with different identities to commit to human rights obligations in ways that do not undermine their own values and cultures. That enables countries to manage the tension between engaging with the international human rights system and retaining their own identities and interests. And it works where those values and norms do not contradict fundamental aspects of international human rights law. But there are plenty of times when the tension between universality and cultural relativism[8] results in grave, systemic human rights abuses.

Nawal El Saadawi wrote about oppression and subjugation of women in Arab societies. Her books were the first openly to discuss female genital mutilation in a way accessible to the Arab and Western worlds.[9] Women are widely recognised as a vulnerable group in many societies and their human rights, therefore, require specific protection. The Convention on the Elimination of All Forms of Discrimination against Women[10] aimed to provide such protection. However, there are two main problems with that treaty. Firstly, not all countries have become party to the Convention and therefore not all are bound by its provisions. Secondly, many states have made reservations to the treaty, thus limiting the extent to which they are bound. The cause of both of those issues, or at least the justification made by many countries, is 'cultural relativism'.

Do universal rights undermine cultural or religious practices? Are universal norms simply an imposition of Western values on other countries?[11] Can there be exceptions to the most basic human rights? Do cultural differences really supersede universal norms? These questions are not merely theoretical.[12] They have very real consequences for people, often women, across the world. Do females have the right to work? The right to health? The right to an education? Or are those rights dependent on the culture and norms of the society into which a person is born?

Cultural relativists[13] do have a point. The notion that international human rights represent universal values fails to take into account that those norms predominantly stem from the powerful countries that created the law. Just because the language is couched as universal, with grandiose statements about the rights applying to 'everyone' and 'all human beings', does not mean that this is actually the case. Firstly, insisting on universality means that the rights are not context-specific. No account is taken of cultures, religions, traditions or heritages. Secondly, many so-called universal rights are not fully recognised, understood or applied in many countries, or indeed regions, around the world. Thirdly, rights may be in tension with existing norms and values in states which were unable to have their voices heard during the creation and development of international human rights law. Fourthly, most universal norms stem from Western ideologies, and those that do not come largely from the former Soviet Union. As such, they are seen as a neo-imperialist method for imposing values on former colonial countries. Lastly, there is a wide gulf between how these universal rights are upheld in different countries—usually impacted as much by economics and resources as by forms of governance and ideologies.

Critics of universality argue therefore that countries, societies and cultures have different notions of rights, responsibilities, obligations, and the nature of human beings and social relationships.[14] The Western focus on the individual as central and protected is not replicated within other regions. The African Charter on Human and People's Rights[15] sets out the rights of families, communities, societies and countries. Focus on the collective nature of rights, and the need to limit or restrict individuals' rights where they clash with those of the group, is anathema to traditional notions of international human rights law.[16] The modern era of human rights largely centres on the individual. Civil and Political Rights protect a person from interference by the state. Economic, Social and Cultural Rights provide individuals with the freedom to be granted certain things by the state. Of course, there are some collective or group rights. The right of people to self-determine, to choose who will govern over them, that played a central role in decolonisation, and protection of minorities gives rights to individuals based on their group identities. But these are the exceptions. Cultural relativists criticise the human rights system because it fails to take into account that many countries, particularly in Africa and Asia, have their own ideologies and values that are not person-centred.

Cultural relativists argue that universal rights fail to take into account the context within which those rights operate. It would be easy to say that these arguments are abstract and that all people ought to have all rights at all times. But what about when those rights contradict the norms and values of a society? This is an argument that does not just occur within countries that did not have a voice during the creation of international human rights law.

The US insists that all individuals have absolute freedom of expression. Hate speech, despite being morally repugnant, is protected by that right. The US was founded by immigrants, many of whom had been persecuted in Europe owing to their beliefs. The right to express oneself freely forms a central part of that shared heritage. Countries in Europe have different interpretations. Germany and France ban some forms of hate speech. Why? Because of the context within which the right to freedom of expression operates.[17] Those countries have strong contingents of neo-Nazi groups. Recent history has shown what may occur when the far Right rises to power in Germany and in Vichy France. Upholding an absolute right to freedom of expression by allowing individuals to promote hate speech can, and indeed did, lead to the worst forms of human rights violations against many millions of Nazi Germany's victims. It seems obvious why the context impacts upon the understanding of human rights. In some countries, the rights of the individual might be tempered by the rights of society.

Prisoner voting rights is another controversial issue within Western countries. Do all individuals have an absolute right to political participation? Or does that right require a person to fulfil certain societal responsibilities, such as obeying the law? The lengthy debate in the UK has demonstrated that even in a Western country which has played a leading role in creating international human rights law, there is an understanding that rights can give rise to responsibilities. In some countries, the rights of the individual might be dependent on the fulfilment of corollary duties to society.

Both of those examples, however, focus on limiting rights rather than removing them altogether. Cultural relativists have made out a strong case for promoting development of rights and norms that are context-specific not artificially universal. They are also correct in insisting that different countries may limit rights in circumstances that depend on their culture, history and heritage.

The problem is that there are basic, fundamental rights that cannot be removed or compromised on the basis that they contradict traditions within a country or region. The right to life, and the right not to have one's life arbitrarily or summarily taken away by the state, is a fundamental right with which every individual is born. It cannot apply only to those people born into countries that view life as sacred. The right not to be tortured is an absolute right that can no more be viewed as context-specific in terms of the 'War on Terror' than it can in terms of traditions of female genital mutilation. Non-discrimination must apply to everyone, regardless of gender, race, religion or colour of their skin—it cannot be granted to some but not all. While one might concede that some rights must be limited within some contexts, the notion that there is no such thing as a universal right ignores the fact that all people are born with basic, fundamental human rights.

Another argument put forward by some cultural relativists is that universal rights are of little practical value or use within countries and cultures where those ideas either are misunderstood or clash with local norms. That argument demonstrates the difference between idealism and realism. If a right might not be upheld, ought it no longer to be viewed as a right? International human rights law is built upon idealism.[18] It is idealistic to expect that all individuals will realise all of their rights all of the time. But that idealism provides the benchmark for what occurs in reality. Lower the benchmark, and you will lower what happens in practice. Lawyers typically are idealists—they set out what ought to occur, in a perfect world, and expect the best possible outcomes. Practitioners, activists, politicians, workers, individuals on the ground, all have to strive to achieve those aims. No country has a perfect human rights record. All countries, from Sweden to Somalia, Norway to North Korea, have human rights abuses occurring on their soil. The annual reports of Amnesty International demonstrate—year upon year—that no country is perfect. Far from it. But what international human rights law expects is that all countries will do their best, within their available resources, to respect, protect and promote all rights for all individuals within their control.

The universality debate encompasses the discourse that human rights are a form of neo-imperialism. Some proponents of cultural relativism view international human rights law as an imposition of Western values, under the guise of universality, which may clash with the norms and values found in other parts of the world. That mantra has been picked up by a number of states, including China and Cuba who have referred to international human rights law as 'a neo-colonial tool of oppression'. Strong and emotive language, indeed. But we ought not to forget that the modern system of international human rights was created by countries that occupied vast areas of the world. This was often done through colonialism, but also through international mandates and illegal occupations. Those states, whether from the Western or Soviet blocs, had spent the preceding centuries actively seeking to dominate, subjugate and colonise countries across Africa, Asia, Eastern Europe and Latin America, imposing their ideologies on the people who inhabited those conquered lands. Little wonder, then, that decolonised states are reluctant to be bound by laws created by their former imperial masters. Even more so, when those powerful countries criticise newer nations for failing adequately to respect, protect or promote human rights. Those criticisms might be viewed as a new method for subjugating or oppressing formerly-colonised people, particularly where they are accompanied by threats to withhold aid or have other financial or trade implications.

A further problem is that resources are required in order for a state to comply within its human rights obligations. That includes, but is not limited to, financial resources. Countries also require human resources, such as doctors for the right to health, teachers for the right to education, and lawyers for the right to gain access to courts. It also includes natural resources and technology.[19] Countries are required to make the most of their resources to ensure that human rights are respected, protected and promoted. But the huge disparity in resources between countries such as Sweden and Somalia, Norway and North Korea, means that human rights will more effectively be realised in some states than others. Universality of rights might be understood to imply that all countries will be judged according to one standard. That would be unfair, however, and is not actually the case in practice. States are judged according to core minimum standards, and after that are judged according to their own resources and capacity for implementing and ensuring human rights.[20] Universal rights are a benchmark, and the core minimum obligation is the lowest common standard that is required for each right. If a country has used its available resources and still cannot meet those standards, for example after a natural disaster like a tsunami or earthquake, or during times of armed conflict, then the international community has an obligation to step in and assist with the protection of human rights. Countries experiencing problems with implementing human rights rightly call for capacity-building and technical assistance. Problems arise, however, when those calls are made in order to avoid having to use available resources—or as a smokescreen for a country's failure—to protect and promote human rights.

A main problem for proponents of cultural relativism is that their cause has been hijacked by countries, cultures or people who seek to justify human rights abuses. Universalists insist that religion, culture or tradition cannot be invoked to disfigure (or even disable) children through female genital mutilation or to oppress, criminalise or kill men and women on the grounds of their sexuality. It seems difficult to counter those arguments. Individuals, by virtue of being human, have certain rights that cannot depend on the place of birth. The charge of ethnocentrism does not ring true where we are discussing a young girl's right not to be forced into marriage before puberty. Cultural relativism cannot be used to deny a child the basic right not to be born into slavery. Yet there are many who seek to justify such violations on the basis of heritage, tradition or religion.

One argument for criminalising homosexual acts in many African or Islamic countries is based on religion.[21] That argument is derailed, before it can even be debated, by the oppression, subjugation and violation of the rights of individuals based solely on their sexual orientation or gender identity.[22] Cultural relativists who insist on a context-specific approach to sexual acts are undermined by the systematic violations of the human rights—such as to life, liberty and expression—of lesbian, gay, bisexual and transgender people living within such countries.

Oil-rich countries like Sudan that call for capacity-building and technical assistance give a bad name to those states who do require resources from the international community. During the massacres in Darfur, Sudan sought to avoid its human rights obligations by frequently asking for assistance in implementing those rights.[23] It is one thing for Haiti or Somalia to stretch out its hand for assistance, but quite another for one of the world's largest oil-producing countries to pretend that it could not stop state-sponsored violence, deaths, displacements, looting, pillaging and rapes owing to a lack of resources and capacity.

Discrimination against women might be legitimate within certain contexts. Countries may choose to limit jobs, such as combat roles within the armed forces, available to women. Others may require women to wear specific types of clothing on religious or traditional grounds. Girls might be expected to attend female-only places of education. But where a country seeks to subjugate women, to allow legal violence against women, to enable girls to enter into forced marriage long before adulthood, and then seeks to justify it on 'cultural' or 'religious' grounds, the argument for cultural relativism is once again undermined.

The debate on universality and cultural relativism is complicated. As with so many things in life, if it was simply black or white then the debate would not have lasted for so long. The problem is that the shades of grey at the theoretical level have an impact on individuals' lives on the ground. The World Health Organisation estimates that 140 million women and girls live with the effects of female genital mutilation.[24] When thinking and discussing these issues, we ought never to lose sight of those females and the individual story that each one tells.

To understand whether female genital mutilation violates universal rights or whether there might be context-specific limitations acceptable within certain cultures, we must first understand the practice. According to the World Health Organisation, there are four types of female genital mutilation:

1. Clitoridectomy: partial or total removal of the clitoris (a small, sensitive and erectile part of the female genitals) and, in very rare cases, only the prepuce (the fold of skin surrounding the clitoris).
2. Excision: partial or total removal of the clitoris and the labia minora, with or without excision of the labia majora (the labia are 'the lips' that surround the vagina).
3. Infibulation: narrowing of the vaginal opening through the creation of a covering seal. The seal is formed by cutting and repositioning the inner, or outer, labia, with or without removal of the clitoris.
4. Other: all other harmful procedures to the female genitalia for non-medical purposes, e.g. pricking, piercing, incising, scraping and cauterising the genital area.[25]

Each type involves different procedures and has a different impact on a woman's health, sexual experiences and ability safely to give birth. Each type carries greater or lesser risks of death, whether at that time or later in life. Does that matter? From a human rights standpoint, is there any difference between cutting a flap of skin away from a child's vagina and removing all of the outer parts of her genitalia? Does it make a difference if the mutilation is performed by a doctor with the child under anaesthetic or by an unlicensed person wielding unsterilised implements?

Unlike male circumcision, there are no known medical benefits to any type of female genital mutilation. Therefore, even if performed by a doctor, all types violate the prohibition of all forms of physical violence against a child[26] and the right of a child to the highest attainable standard of health.[27] There can be no medical justification for limiting those rights through female genital mutilation.

Types 2 and 3 clearly violate the prohibition against torture or inhuman or degrading treatment. The effects of those types, more so than types 1 and 4, impact on a woman's health to the extent that they can and do threaten her right to life. This is particularly true during pregnancy and childbirth. Women with types 2 and 3 are likely to experience tears, internal and external, in the vaginal and anal areas, as well as severe complications that frequently lead to death.

Bearing all that in mind, the question arises as to how female genital mutilation can be justified by so many people and why so many millions of parents mutilate their daughters every year. Heritage, tradition, religion, culture, shame, guilt, marriage, societal pressure, virginity, purity: these are some of the justifications bandied around. And some of them may be true. A woman who has not been mutilated might have problems finding a spouse within some societies. There may be some religious sects that advocate mutilation as a religious practice. There may be long-standing traditions of mutilations stretching back throughout centuries. None of those allow a person to violate anyone's absolute right not to be tortured.

But do any of those reasons justify limitations on other rights? Is there a difference between the types of mutilation when answering the questions set out above? Can the mutilation of a child be justified by claiming that failing to carry out the procedure would result in that child being ostracised by the community and denied membership of, and identity within, their religious or cultural group? There are no easy answers to these questions, not least when written about within a country that criminalises all forms of female genital mutilation but allows male circumcision by doctors and by unlicensed religious practitioners

Of course, female genital mutilation is only one of many examples of practices or actions that are 'justified' under the guise of cultural relativism. In many ways it is an extreme example in terms of the action itself, but it is practised widely across countries and regions around the world. The tension between universality and cultural relativism is well illustrated by exploring the debate on female genital mutilation and, more broadly, the treatment of women in many societies. But the same discussions apply to treatment of LGBT persons, religious or racial minorities, children, or other vulnerable groups. The same also is true of other specific practices that form part of a culture within individual states or more broadly across a region.

Debates on universality and cultural relativism go to the heart of the practical application of international human rights law. They cannot be ignored. But there needs to be a greater understanding that political correctness, cultural sensitivity, dialogue and engagement do not have to result in the end of universal rights. Rights can be universal with acceptable context-specific limitations. A balancing act can be achieved between the basic, fundamental nature of human rights and the need to protect societal, cultural, religious or other public policy concerns. But these can only be done for the *right* reasons. They ought never to be used as a way of justifying violations and oppression or avoiding obligations.

5

UN HUMAN RIGHTS MACHINERY

The first day of all UN Human Rights Council sessions presents an enormous task for the kind-but-firm security staff who provide passes for people wishing to enter the compound. That is no small task; anyone without a permanent pass must arrange pre-authorisation, fill in the required forms and have their photograph taken and printed onto a security badge. Men and women—very occasionally accompanied by small children—queue at the Pregny Gate, up the hill from the Place des Nations, patiently waiting their turn. Government delegates, UN staff and some NGO activists based in Geneva avoid the queues by flashing their permanent passes at the main entrance. The rest—academics, occasional delegates, visitors, specialist speakers, and many others—form an orderly line at the side entrance. On many occasions, I have seen individuals turned away for not having the correct paperwork or identification documents. The saddest case was a Kurdish Iraqi who had come to make a statement on behalf of an NGO, but was turned away for presenting a refugee passport. Only a permanent passport will suffice. That man, who was there to share his personal experiences of systematic human rights abuses, whom the Council is required to protect, was rejected for not owning a document that had been denied to him by a government hell-bent on persecuting him and oppressing his people.

On Wednesday 7 March 2012, in a bid to avoid hours of queuing on the first day of the Council session, I entered the Pregny Gate to collect my UN pass. A handful of people were queuing at the same time, and we nodded and smiled at one another. I was drawn to a man and woman nearby who, unusually for delegates, were radiating excitement and optimism through their enthusiastic smiles and body language. As we collected our badges and walked through the security gates the man, who was bald and rather stocky, turned to me and asked which building housed the Council chamber. We fell into step and started talking as we walked together across the compound, with the angular woman, who towered over both of us, following a couple of paces behind. Upon reaching the building, I showed them where to go and watched them cheerily wave goodbye. It was an unusual encounter, since the UN is often a rather formal and unfriendly arena. I thought little more of it as I wandered upstairs and sat down to listen to the Council's proceedings.

On that day the Human Rights Council facilitated its first panel on Lesbian, Gay, Bisexual and Transgender (LGBT) rights.[1] This was heralded as a milestone for the Council. The previous year, five years after the Council's creation, it had passed its first resolution on LGBT rights.[2] The resolution set out that the Council would host the panel, and it took place at the 19th Session. The resolution and panel were landmark events. Until then, discussions on LGBT rights had been blocked by the Organisation of Islamic Cooperation and by many African countries.[3]

In 2010, 76 of 192 UN member states criminalised homosexual acts.[4] Almost half of the countries around the world fined, imprisoned, corporally punished or even imposed the death penalty on individuals who chose to have consensual sexual relations with people of the same gender.

To be clear, Lesbian, Gay, Bisexual and Transgender rights do not simply relate to the sexual activities of LGBT individuals. Arguments about cultural relativism and the criminalisation of homosexual acts only address one aspect of LGBT rights.[5] Those rights are not just about sexual relations. They are also about basic and fundamental human rights. The LGBT resolution and panel were focused on ensuring that all sexual orientation and gender minority individuals have their human rights protected from systematic abuse and violations perpetrated, or tacitly approved of, by states. It was aimed at those states that empower police and other authorities to abuse, harass, extort, imprison and execute individuals on grounds of sexual orientation and gender identity. Countries around the world systematically violate the rights not to be tortured, arbitrarily arrested, or discriminated against in the workplaces, hospitals and schools, and indeed not to be killed, based solely on a person's identity rather than their acts.

All people are born equal. International human rights law provides protection for all individuals. That protection extends to everyone regardless of race, religion, age, sexual orientation and gender identity. So, when countries systematically violate those rights, we would expect the UN human rights machinery to step in and protect those persons. Just as human rights bodies focus on other categories of vulnerable people, including women, children, indigenous populations and persons with disabilities, so too those institutions ought to protect sexual orientation and gender identity minorities. It seems obvious that the Human Rights Council, which discusses all other vulnerable minorities, ought to debate and take action on LGBT rights. Obvious, perhaps, but that does not take into account *Realpolitik* at the Council.

On Wednesday 7 March 2012 as the UN Secretary-General Ban Ki-Moon delivered a video address opening the Panel on LGBT Rights, every delegate from OIC member states in attendance stood up and filed out of the Council Chamber. As Ban Ki-Moon boldly stated that attacks on LGBT persons are attacks on universal values, OIC countries' government delegates to the UN's principal human rights bodies turned their backs on the Secretary-General and walked out of the room.[6] So much for universal values and fundamental rights. The OIC political bloc refused to hear that LGBT individuals are people born equal and with basic human rights.

It took five years and 17 sessions before the Council passed a resolution on sexual orientation and human rights.[7] Resolution 17/19 was a seminal moment, heralded as a milestone both for the Council and for LGBT rights. But that resolution was an anomaly. The OIC's internal rifts at that time meant that the bloc did not vote *en masse* to prevent the resolution from being passed.

Resolution 17/19 on LGBT rights was passed during the Arab Spring uprisings. The OIC was experiencing internal divisions based on ongoing national conflicts. South Africa, who tabled the resolution, faced significant opposition from many of its regional neighbours in the African Group. The strength of that opposition, and the bravery of South Africa, Mauritius, Zambia and Burkina Faso in voting for the resolution, ought not to be underestimated. But it is crucial to understand that OIC members were conspicuously absent from the negotiating process. By the time it was tabled at the Council, it was too late for OIC states to block the resolution.

A year later, when the Panel took place, the OIC was almost fully reunified. The bloc flexed its collective muscles to undermine discussions on LGBT rights. That decision seems to have been designed to undermine the panel's legitimacy. Islamic states were reported as saying that the panel had 'nothing to do with fundamental human rights'. OIC members, including the Ambassador of Pakistan, registered their 'concern' and 'opposition' to 'controversial notions like sexual orientation and gender identity'. So much for universal values. So much for human rights for all. So much for the UN's principal human rights body protecting people from systematic violations.

That afternoon, sitting in the Serpentine Bar, I once again saw the man and woman who had been so excited and optimistic upon entering the UN compound in Geneva. They sat with activists from a well-known NGO. This time they looked less happy, less enthusiastic. Here were two people who had changed their external gender despite knowing that they could and probably would face oppression for those actions. Here were two people who had faced a world of prejudice and abuses aimed at their gender identities, and had walked tall and proud. Here were two people who had come to the UN expecting the Council to recognise and pronounce the need to protect their human rights. Here were two people who watched an entire political bloc turn its back on the notion that all people, including gender minorities, have basic and fundamental human rights. Their expressions said it all. But why do so many people place such expectations on that one institution?

The Human Rights Council is the UN's principal human rights body.[8] There are many others that fall within the 'UN Human Rights Machinery',[9] an umbrella term for specialist human rights bodies and the more general UN institutions that cover human rights as part of their mandates. Each body is governed by its own rules, has its own roles and functions to fulfil, has a unique composition, and is able to perform different tasks. Some bodies are interconnected; others have a relationship with one another; while some are disparate and isolated. The term 'machinery', then, is rather misleading.

All of the bodies contribute to the UN's third pillar of human rights. Individually or collectively, they are tasked with promoting, protecting and developing international human rights law.[10] While the UN generally is good at promoting and developing human rights, it largely fails to fulfil its protection duties. Promoting rights occurs through education, capacity-building, technical assistance, developing human right resources, providing recommendations to countries, amongst others. Human rights are developed through the legal and political processes within UN bodies. Protection requires very different types of actions, ones which the UN is ill-equipped to undertake. Protection includes political processes but also entails binding powers and enforcement activities—things that we know are sorely lacking at almost all UN bodies. The specialist human rights bodies have a range of powers, but none are able to bind states through enforcement activities. All rely upon countries adhering to resolutions and recommendations, either because they believe they are required to so do or because of political pressures. The only other recourse for enforcement is to enlist the Security Council to help and assist in that regard—something that only occurs in the most extreme instances of gross and systemic human rights violations.[11]

Henkin's point about almost all nations observing almost all of their international obligations almost all of the time[12] does not really help in terms of protecting human rights. It is precisely those countries that are the exception to that general rule who routinely ignore the UN human rights bodies and, indeed, systematically abuse individuals' rights. The lack of binding powers means that the least protection occurs in the places that need it most. But that does not mean that no protection occurs at all. Far from it.

The Human Rights Council was created in 2006 after its predecessor, the UN Commission on Human Rights, had failed.[13] The Council is an intergovernmental body[14] whose 47 elected members[15] send government delegates to sit at the Council. Based in Geneva, the Council meets for at least ten weeks per year over the course of at least three sessions.[16] During its regular sessions it discusses its permanent agenda and holds interactive dialogues with human rights experts. The Council may also convene special sessions to discuss crisis human rights situations. All countries can participate in Council discussions, but those which have not been elected as members do so as observers. Those observers are not given a vote but their voices are heard. Civil society groups may also observe and participate in Council proceedings.

The UN in Geneva includes many specialised agencies concerned with disparate matters such as labour,[17] health[18] and refugees.[19] Some countries can afford permanent delegations in Geneva with specialist advisers for the broad range of organisations. Others rely solely on one delegate to attend meetings of all of those bodies. The bigger the delegation, the more it is likely to include a human rights specialist. Many of the men and women who sit at the Council representing smaller or economically weaker countries have no prior knowledge of or expertise on human rights.

The Human Rights Council has never been too concerned about whether its members respect human rights within their own countries. Prior to the Council's creation, there were proposals that members be required to demonstrate concrete steps taken to implement, promote and protect human rights within their own territories.[20] However, those proposals were diluted to 'soft criteria' requiring countries standing for membership to demonstrate a commitment to human rights.[21] As a result, states known for systematic and grave abuses have been elected to the Council. Apparently oblivious to the irony, those countries send delegates to discuss and negotiate how best to protect and promote human rights across the world. Nothing quite compares to seeing the contrast between NGO activists and victims of abuses sitting in the same room as well-dressed and well-fed government delegates from known abuser states like Bahrain, Ethiopia and Saudi Arabia. The irony increases when those delegates criticise Israel and the United States for violating human rights. That is not to say that Israel and the United States do not commit human rights abuses—they do, and often with impunity. But listening to Egypt and Pakistan criticise others for violating human rights is a somewhat galling spectacle.

In 2013, Council members elected Poland to be its President.[22] Switzerland and Ecuador became Vice-Presidents alongside Mauritania and the Maldives. Mauritania is a North African Islamic state where conversion to any other faith is punishable by death. The country's criminal code provides for a three-day period of reflection and repentance for any Muslim found guilty of apostasy. 'If he does not repent within this time limit … he is to be condemned to death as an apostate and his property will be confiscated by the Treasury.' Anyone found to have practised a homosexual act also faces the death penalty in Mauritania.[23] Black Africans have long been used as slaves in Mauritanian society, with estimates that up to 18 per cent of the population are still in slavery.[24] Female genital mutilation is formally illegal but 'widely practiced' according to Freedom House.[25] Women's rights are low on the agenda, as evidenced by a World Economic Forum that placed Mauritania as 106th out of 115 countries in terms of the gender gap.[26] As is apparent, Mauritania does not do well in the human rights league tables. The Maldives does not do much better. That Indian Ocean island requires all of its citizens to be Sunni Muslims. Freedom of speech is limited, particularly where it is 'contrary to the tenets of Islam'. Foreign workers *may* practise non-Muslim faiths, but only if they do so in private. Homosexual acts are criminalised, punishable with banishment and flogging rather than death. Women's rights are not afforded much weight either, for example females alone face corporal punishment for extramarital sex.[27] Clearly, when electing its vice-presidents, Council members were not particularly concerned with being led by example.

The Council's leadership and even its membership make a mockery of the UN's human rights system. For the principal human rights body to include known abuser states appears absurd. After all, how can the Council have credibility and legitimacy if it is comprised of countries that themselves systematically violate human rights?

There is another way of looking at the Council. The body is universal—it includes countries from across the world and its work applies to all UN member states. Clearly, that gives it credibility. If the UN dictated which countries could be elected, then the Council would no longer be able to claim the same degree of legitimacy. Inclusiveness leads to cooperation, dialogue and state engagement. Those are not factors lightly dismissed. Countries must come to the table in order to hear recommendations on human rights. States must allow fact-finders into their national territory to gather and share information. Countries must attend Council sessions in order to request and accept capacity-building and technical assistance. The body's universality depends upon and requires all states to actively participate in Council proceedings and processes.

There are other specialist institutions, including the treaty-based bodies,[28] the Special Procedures system[29] and the Office of the High Commissioner for Human Rights. The treaty-based bodies, as their name suggests, deal only with the human rights obligations arising under a specific human rights treaty. Unlike the Council, then, which addresses all rights within all countries, the treaty bodies have a very limited scope and application. They only examine human rights compliance within countries that are party to the particular treaty in question. Treaty bodies are staffed by independent experts as opposed to government delegates. The system of independent experts works where countries have already chosen to participate by being party to a treaty. Yet the treaty bodies have no greater binding powers or enforcement mechanisms than the Human Rights Council. Their main role is to monitor states' compliance with human rights, to provide recommendations, to develop and expand upon human rights obligations. Some have a complaints procedure for individuals who allege violations. Treaty bodies, like the Council, are far better equipped for promotion and development roles than for protection duties.

Independent experts are also used within the Special Procdures system. Each mandate deals with a different human rights theme or examines all rights within one specific country. Mandates are created by the Human Rights Council or, exceptionally, the General Assembly. Inevitably, there are political objectives behind the creation of mandates, particularly those that are country-specific. Special Procedures mandates are political, but the system itself is not politicised because it is comprised of experts who operate independently of their own governments and of the UN. Mandate-holders undertake country visits, provide reports and recommendations, and engage with local actors and civil society. Their work is crucial for information gathering and sharing, promoting rights and ensuring technical assistance and capacity-building. Mandate-holders have been given unprecedented access to places where human rights are systematically violated. The impact of their work ought not to be underestimated. Once again, however, that system is political and relies upon the goodwill of states for its recommendations to be implemented.

When one investigates the human rights apparatus, it quickly becomes apparent that it focuses on political and diplomatic processes. That works well for promoting and developing human rights, but is ineffective in protecting rights in situations where countries choose to ignore those bodies' work. It is one thing to offer time and resources in a non-confrontational manner in order to assist countries with implementing human rights obligations. But it is very different to intervene in order to protect individuals from human rights abuses.

Dialogue and cooperation are not useful or appropriate tools in grave or crisis situations. They encourage talk rather than action and are aimed at long-term change rather than short-term intervention. Ultimately, where political pressure and diplomatic channels fail to persuade a country to cease violations and uphold its obligations, it falls to the Security Council to take action to protect human rights. That brings us right back to the problems at the Security Council, particularly the veto power; the lack of enforcement mechanisms; and the UN's over-reliance on that one body. For all the billions of dollars spent each year on the UN Human Rights Machinery, the system is powerless to protect individuals in situations where states are happy to ignore world political pressures to cease violations. As we shall see, the UN human rights bodies have failed time and again to protect individuals from gross and systemic human rights violations.

The following six chapters explore different reasons why the UN fails to protect human rights. At the heart of each type of failure is the politicisation of human rights. The chapters examine different forms of politicisation, using illustrative rather than exhaustive case studies. While each chapter presents examples of how politicisation undermines the UN's protection role, taken together these help to explain why the UN is unable to protect individuals from human rights abuses. It is only through such analysis that we can then think about moving forward from the current position.

6

LOOK! WE DID SOMETHING

SOUTH AFRICA AND ISRAEL

On 9 May 2004, two unmarked vehicles drove down into the village of Goi-Chu, located within the Urus-Martanovski region of Chechnya. Zelimkhan Isaev was at his home in Sverdlov Street when gunmen burst into his house. Mr Isaev was dragged out of his house and taken away in the cars shortly after 9 p.m. The next day, federal armed forces returned to the Isaev family home to conduct a search. Witnesses say that after three hours nothing illegal had been found, and that before leaving one of the soldiers placed a hand grenade under the pillow in the bed where Mr Isaev slept. On 11 May, it became known that Mr Isaev's health was deteriorating after being severely beaten and tortured in order to extract his signed confession that he had sabotaged military equipment in Grozny. He was not admitted to hospital until 12 May, by which point he had three broken ribs and badly damaged internal organs sustained during beatings as well as numerous traces of electric burns. He remained under armed guard in the hospital for four days until Mr Isaev's relatives were allowed to take him to a hospital in Ingushetia on 16 May. The young man died that night. Doctors established that his death was caused by the beatings and torture sustained since 9 May. He was 26 years old.[1]

Zelimkhan Isaev was abducted, tortured and beaten to death during the fifth year of armed conflict in Chechnya. His is just one of the tens of thousands of stories of abduction, displacement, torture or killing that took place during the second Chechen war. A month prior to Mr Isaev's death, the United Nations Commission on Human Rights considered whether to pass a resolution condemning human rights abuses in that region. The draft resolution called on Russia to cease violations of international humanitarian law and human rights and to investigate and punish all incidents committed by its agents. In particular, the resolutions expressed concern about 'forced disappearances, extrajudicial, summary or arbitrary executions, torture, ill-treatment, arbitrary detentions, attacks against humanitarian workers, continued abuses and harassment at checkpoints'.

By 2004 tens of thousands of people had been killed during the armed conflict in Chechnya.[2] Arbitrary detention, torture and forced disappearance had become the norm within that region. Gross and systemic human right violations were committed by Russian agents with impunity. Local officials acknowledged the discovery of 49 mass graves where nearly 3,000 civilians were buried.[3] Hundreds of thousands of people were displaced during the war, and in 2004 there remained 65,000 displaced persons in Ingushetia alone.[4]

At that time, the Commission was the main UN human rights body. Two years later, it was disbanded and replaced with the Human Rights Council.[5] The Commission's failure was attributed to its excessive politicisation and its lack of action on many grave human rights situations.[6] But that is not to say that it did nothing; far from it. One thing the Commission did was focus on Israel and the Occupied Palestinian Territories.[7] Some scrutiny was necessary, but the Commission focused disproportionate and excessive attention on Israel compared with similar or even worse abuses elsewhere.[8]

The 2004 draft resolution on human rights abuses in Chechnya[9] was defeated by a vote of 23 against[10] to 12 in favour,[11] with 18 abstentions.[12] Despite the ongoing armed conflict and grave human rights violations, the Commission had similarly voted against taking action on Chechnya in the previous two years. The European Union tabled the resolution, and all 12 votes in favour came from Western states who were members of the Commission. Unsurprisingly, Russia voted against the resolution. Of greater interest are the countries from two political blocs that might have been expected to support Chechnya.

A number of decolonised countries voted against the resolution despite Chechnya clearly trying to throw off the yoke of its former imperial master. The political pay-off for a state supporting the resolution on Chechnya would be damaging its own relationship with Russia. It is clear why many states would be reluctant to stoke the flames of Russia's ire. While the Cold War has ended, Russia remains a powerful ally and a dangerous enemy. Russia's economic and military might remain a crucial factor in international and diplomatic relations. Countries take this into account when determining whether or how to act. The more reliant a country is on a powerful ally—for trade, diplomatic protection or even military backing—the more likely it is to place national political objectives in front of the subject matter of any tabled resolution at a UN body.

OIC members would usually be expected to support a Muslim state, such as Chechnya. However, those countries also either abstained or blocked the resolution on Chechnya. In 2003, Russian President Vladimir Putin attended the OIC summit in order to discuss his country becoming an observer member of that bloc.[13] Islam is an official religion in Russia and the Muslim population in that country is one of the largest in the world. Russia's links not only with individual OIC members but also with the bloc itself undoubtedly played a significant, if not primary, role in those states abstaining or voting against the resolution on Chechnya.

The lesson is clear: national and regional political objectives supersede concerns about human rights.

Even Western countries—usually at the fore of promoting democracy and human rights—were not as proactive as one might have hoped. The US refused to sponsor the resolution. Having caused significant tensions within the Security Council by invading Iraq, the US was wary of worsening its relationships with Russia and China and its stance at the UN immediately after the invasion was to avoid antagonising them.[14]

While states used the draft resolution on Chechnya to further their own unrelated political objectives, human rights abuses in that region continued to be perpetrated with impunity. And it is not just Chechnya that flew under the UN's radar. Other crises or ongoing situations were afforded scant attention within UN human rights bodies. The armed conflict in the Democratic Republic of Congo has claimed over 6 million lives since 2000.[15] Women continue to be raped and tortured by government forces, rebels and militia, all acting with impunity. Tens of millions of people have been displaced, with many having fled their villages before they were looted and burned to the ground.[16] Occupation and systematic human rights abuses have occurred in, for example, Kashmir, Northern Cyprus, Tibet and Western Sahara. Minority groups like the Kurds are displaced for generations, stateless and continual refugees. Yet the UN, particularly its main human rights bodies, almost always fails to take action and frequently declines even to discuss those human rights situations.

In the modern, globalised world with constant media scrutiny, attention is being increasingly drawn to the UN's lack of action on human rights situations. States cannot simply sweep that lack of action under the carpet. Instead, they rely on telling success stories in order to mask the failure to act.

When the UN focuses excessive and disproportionate attention on a particular state, it creates an ostensible 'success story'.[17] It can then point to its action on that situation in order to show that it is successfully protecting human rights. Often excessive scrutiny provides significant political and diplomatic pressure that forces a country to cease abusing human rights. The point here is not that the states under the spotlight do not merit attention but rather that the UN's constant focus on one grave human rights situation masks its failures elsewhere.

Questions must be asked: Why are some countries excessively scrutinised while others avoid any attention whatsoever? How are those countries selected? What are the political motivations for disproportionate attention? And what is the impact on human rights protection across the world? The easiest way to answer those questions is to examine two cases of disproportionate scrutiny and ostensible 'success stories'—South Africa and Israel.

South Africa

The UN's greatest human rights 'success story' is the ending of apartheid in South Africa.

Abuses in apartheid-era South Africa were grave, gross and systemic. Government policies of racial segregation and subjugation meant that there were state-sponsored, systematic human rights violations. It was absolutely right that the UN focused attention and took action on South Africa.

At the same time as apartheid in South Africa, other countries had similar policies of state-sponsored racial oppression and human rights abuses. The Soviet Union had apartheid-type policies that systematically abused the rights of Chechens, Ingush, Balkars, Baltic peoples, Roma, Jews, Muslims, Romanian ethnic Hungarians, Tibetans and Uighurs.[18] A clear parallel can be drawn between the oppression of millions of non-Russian, indigenous peoples within the USSR[19] and the apartheid policy which oppressed non-white peoples in South Africa. China adopted similar policies against Tibetans; the US against Native Americans; Australia against the Aborigines; Canadians against the First Nations people. Yet, while the UN focused excessive efforts of ending apartheid in South Africa, it took no action—and almost nothing was even discussed—about similar abuses elsewhere.

Why was so much attention devoted to South Africa and so little to other similar situations? The answer is simple. The political set-up during the Cold War enabled South Africa to be the pariah state whilst simultaneously shielding other countries from scrutiny.

Countries were neither willing nor able to take on the two superpowers—Russia and the US. Nor were they willing to criticise China, which led the Non-Aligned Movement of developing and decolonised states. But it went further than that. Countries closely allied with one of those three states were also protected by Cold War politics.[20] The only country without political protection was South Africa. Decolonised countries tried to keep the spotlight on South Africa—a country that still practised racist policies and human rights abuses that had been widespread during colonial times.[21] Apartheid also provided a unifying issue on which developing countries spoke with one voice. Their allies in the Non-Aligned Movement—led by China—supported those endeavours. European states were distancing themselves from the recent human rights violations that they had perpetrated as imperial powers. South Africa was a stark reminder of imperialist atrocities. Western states, then, were not prepared to protect South Africa from scrutiny. Russia supported decolonisation as part of its supposedly Marxist approach to world affairs, but also because it wanted newly independent countries to take its side in Cold War politics. It, too, had no interest in shielding South Africa from scrutiny.

No states, then, had to choose sides between the superpowers, because every country accepted that the spotlight be placed on South Africa.[22] Of course, many of those countries were themselves abusing rights at home,[23] and excessive scrutiny of South Africa ensured that attention was deflected away from their own human rights records.[24]

The UN's lack of even-handedness on South Africa was particularly apparent at the General Assembly. Between 1946 and 1992 the General Assembly adopted 234 resolutions on apartheid, 111 on Namibia, and 224 on other issues regarding Southern Africa. Those 569 resolutions totalled approximately one fifth of the total recorded votes. On average, the General Assembly passed between five and ten resolutions annually on apartheid policies. Some sessions saw almost double that number.[25] By contrast, during that 46-year period the General Assembly passed five resolutions regarding gross and systemic violations by China against indigenous peoples: three on Tibet[26] and two on Burma.[27] Only four resolutions that were passed concerned grave abuses committed by the USSR: one general resolution[28] and three on violations in Hungary.[29] Violations against Native Americans were ignored altogether, as were similar abuses against the Aborigines in Australia, the Maoris in New Zealand and First Nations in Canada.

From 1965, states regularly challenged South Africa's credentials at the General Assembly. Countries objected to South Africa's delegation because its members were sent by a non-representative and illegitimate government.[30] States insisted that the exclusively white government represented less than 20 per cent of the population, and was therefore not legitimate. In 1974 the General Assembly effectively expelled South Africa.

The UN's focus on South Africa was successful. Political pressure and UN action meant that South Africa eventually withdrew from Namibia, ended the apartheid policy and ceased to be a pariah state. Beyond the success story, focus on South Africa deflected attention away from other countries which were abusing human rights. No one would argue that the UN was wrong to focus on South Africa. The problem is that ending apartheid in South Africa is held up as the great success of that generation, while no regard is given to the many millions of victims that the UN ignored.

Israel

Another stark example of the UN's lack of even-handedness is its treatment of Israel. A microcosm of the excessive scrutiny of Israel can be seen if we return to the Commission on Human Rights' 2004 session. At the same time as the Commission voted against taking action on Chechnya, it passed five resolutions about Israel.[31] That disparity cannot be explained by the gravity of the two conflicts.

LOOK! WE DID SOMETHING

The second *intifada* ('uprising') in Israel and the Occupied Palestinian Territories took place at the same time as the second Chechen war. Amnesty International reported that by 2004 the 'spiralling' violence had resulted in the deaths of 3,200 Palestinians and over 1,000 Israelis.[32] While tragic, that is far fewer than the deaths in Chechnya. Tens of thousands of Palestinians were made homeless during that period. Again, many more Chechens were displaced. Both armed conflicts involved gross and systemic human rights violations. Individuals within the weaker territories were subjugated, oppressed and killed. The UN's mandate to protect human rights involves taking action on such situations. While the graver situation in Chechnya was all but ignored, excessive scrutiny was given to the Israel–Palestine conflict.

That pattern has been repeated across the UN. The obvious question is 'Why Israel?' Israel commits grave human rights abuses, but it is by no means the worst offender. So, why does it receive such disproportionate attention at the UN? Why were a quarter of all Commission on Human Rights country-resolutions about Israel while not a single one focused on China? Why does the UN General Assembly discuss and pass resolutions about Israel at almost every session yet fails to devote even a fraction of that time to countries such as India, Sri Lanka and Turkey? Why does Israel merit disproportionate scrutiny while other abusers fly under the radar?

The answer is the same as it was for South Africa. The UN focuses on Israel because most states support or tacitly accept such scrutiny.

The General Assembly, in particular, has lacked even-handedness on Israel. A stark example is Resolution 3379 (1975), entitled 'Zionism is Racism'.[33] Resolution 3379 reflected international politics and diplomatic relations at that time. Arab countries had gained significant strength and influence largely owing to 'the oil weapon'.[34] Many Arab states had participated in or supported the wars against Israel in 1948, 1967 and 1973. Those countries used the General Assembly to focus attention on the Palestinian cause. They went further than denouncing Israeli treatment of the Palestinians.[35] Resolution 3379, which equated Zionism with racism, challenged the state of Israel's right to exist.

The USSR supported the Arab states. Israel had once been viewed as a potentially socialist state but was increasingly allied with the US. Decolonised states lent their support, perhaps because of alliances with the USSR or on anti-imperialist grounds. The Palestinians' predicament raised grave questions about human rights but the dictatorial regimes in the Arab and Soviet blocs raised equally serious questions. Global action against Israel deflected attention from those countries' own human rights abuses. Many Western states might have supported criticism of Israel if there had been even-handed scrutiny of human rights throughout the Middle East. But the singling out of Israel was manipulation of human rights for political ends.

Resolution 3379 was repealed[36] in 1991.[37] But that is not the end of the story of disproportionate attention on Israel. Far from it. Resolution 3379 is just one of many ways in which the UN has lacked even-handedness on Israel, and the Human Rights Council has become a main vehicle for that disproportionate attention. Although it is mandated to protect rights across the world, the Council has devoted vastly disproportionate attention to Israel.

Israel does commit violations against Palestinians and Israeli Arabs, although it is a democratic state that is formally committed to international human rights law obligations. It grants wide access to human rights organisations and provides legal recourse for human rights violations through domestic and international courts. Yet, of all the human rights situations across the globe—including those states under despotic rulers who provide almost no access to the outside world to ascertain severity of the situation[38]—Israel is the only country that appears on the Human Rights Council's permanent agenda.[39] Israel has been the sole focus of six of the Council's 19 Special Sessions convened on grave or crisis situations. Compare this with Darfur, the Democratic Republic of Congo, Libya, Myanmar and Sri Lanka, each of which has been the subject of only a single special session.

It is interesting briefly to examine the situations in two of those countries in order to understand the disproportionate scrutiny afforded to Israel in comparison with other human rights abusers.

In February 2008 the *Guardian* newspaper reported on the village of Ninja in the Walungu region of the Democratic Republic of Congo.[40] The village is populated almost exclusively by women and children because almost all the men have been killed by armed militias. Virtually all women in the village have been raped by the militias—'some countless times'.

'Mirindi Euprazi was at home with her family when the rebels attacked. They broke into her home and took all her possessions, before torturing her, her husband and their teenage children. Then the horror began.

"They forced my son to have sex with me, and when he'd finished they killed him. Then they raped me in front of my husband and then they killed him too. Then they took away my three daughters."

She hasn't heard of the three girls, 13, 14 and 17, since. A small woman, she speaks softly and without visible emotion, but as she describes being left naked while her house burned, she raises a hand to cover her face.'

Heartbreakingly, what happened to Ms Euprazi is so common that it no longer shocks or even surprises people with knowledge of the conflict. Millions of people—men, women and children—have been killed in the Congo since the turn of the millennium. Rape, displacement, torture, looting, pillaging, were all so widespread as to make it almost impossible accurately to record the figures.

In the final days of the 2009 civil war in Sri Lanka, some 20,000 people were killed,[41] four times the number of Palestinians killed during the eight years of the second *intifada* between 2000 and 2008.[42] Near the end of the conflict in Sri Lanka, 'hundreds of thousands of Tamil civilians were penned into a tiny spit of sandy land along the eastern coast, living in squalid makeshift encampments, starving, exhausted and under fire from the Sri Lankan military'.[43] The corpses 'started mounting up as the army shelled a safe zone it had demarcated for civilians and hundreds of thousands of people fled'.[44] In one small village of Puttumattalan, 700 people were killed by the army as they tried to flee to safety. 'It took five or six days to dispose of all the corpses.'[45] One man described the process to a former employee of Amnesty International:

'We just dropped the bodies in ditches because there were so many. It was the worst thing in the world. They were all sorts—men, women and kids. More women than men, but children of all ages. Sometimes even now I think of committing suicide. It was terrible. It was like a crematorium, bodies and more bodies and blood everywhere. Till I die I will never forget what I saw there.'[46]

At least the Council devoted some time to Congo and Sri Lanka, even if it was only a fraction of the time and resources devoted to Israel. Many other situations were altogether ignored. No special sessions were called on Chechnya, Egypt, Kenya, Tibet or Zimbabwe, despite the crises that have taken place since the Council's creation. Beatings, torture and killings in the run-up to Zimbabwe's 2008 elections were not even discussed at the Council. Kenya's ethnic violence, which has subsequently led to accusations of crimes against humanity,[47] flew under the body's radar. Violence in Egypt, during the Arab Spring and beyond, did not concern Council members sufficiently for them to convene a special session. The list goes on. And throughout that time, Israel has been given vastly disproportionate time and resources.

Excessive scrutiny of Israel has not gone unnoticed. It was so obvious during the Council's first year that the then Secretary-General Kofi Annan called on it to stop focusing on Israel while being silent on other grave situations.[48] But little notice was taken.[49] OIC members dominate at the Council. They are the drivers behind the excessive focus on Israel. Their objectives include political, religious, cultural and regional ties with the Palestinians and with affected neighbouring states. Crucially, those countries also use Israel to divert attention away from systemic violations within influential OIC members such as Pakistan, Algeria and Egypt.

Another reason that some countries overtly politicise the UN in relation to Israel is because of its ties with the US. Israel is seen as the US foothold in the Middle East. That relationship encourages anti-US states, such as Cuba, China, Venezuela and Russia, to use Israel as a way of attacking US hegemony and interference. The Cold War might long be over, but the practices learnt during those times still persist.

Israel is also viewed by some as a remnant of colonialism. Israel occupies Palestinian lands and has racist and discriminatory practices towards the indigenous people. That is then used as justification for Israel receiving excessive scrutiny. But that justification does not stand up when thinking about the lack of focus on other similar occupations. Tibet and Kashmir are obvious examples that receive some media attention but almost no scrutiny at the UN. And what about Turkey's occupation of Northern Cyprus since 1974? That self-declared state has been an occupied territory for four decades and yet has flown under the radar at UN human rights bodies.

Of course, decolonised states identify with the Palestinian cause. The political links between many African and Asian states and the Organisation of Islamic Cooperation—and historically with the former Soviet bloc—have resulted in Israel becoming a *cause célèbre* amongst decolonised countries from those regions. What is striking is that many of the states that propose or support excessive action on Israel themselves commit as grave human rights abuses within their own territories. History, it seems, does repeat itself. It is likely that the UN will have another 'success story' when Israel finally ceases to violate Palestinians' rights. But at what price will the UN claim that success?

LOOK! WE DID SOMETHING

One lesson learnt from the UN's treatment of South Africa and Israel is that it can do something to protect human rights violations. But it seems that only one such situation can be focused upon at any one time. And there is no direct link between the gravity of the situation and the decision to focus attention on that country. No one would suggest that attention ought not to have been devoted to the ending of apartheid in South Africa or to the occupation of Palestinian land. The fundamental problem is that those two situations are held up as UN successes when really they mask abject and abysmal failures elsewhere. Tens of millions of people have been forgotten. Why? Because politics trumps human rights each and every time.

7

STOP SHOUTING, START HELPING

POST-COLONIALISM, HUMAN RIGHTS AND DEVELOPMENT

Darfur

Dr Halima Bashir worked in Darfur, tending to the victims of government-sanctioned atrocities. She was sent to work in Darfur because of the horrors that were perpetrated in that region and the lack of medical care available for victims. Dr Bashir treated victims of rape, beatings and torture. Her clinic provided medical attention to women and girls who had been sexually abused and raped during the armed conflict in Darfur. Then, one day, the government-backed militias came for her. Three soldiers hauled Dr Bashir out of her clinic, abducted her and took her to a military camp.

'She was thrown into a cell … and beaten. She was kicked in the stomach and hit repeatedly on the legs, hips and shoulders.

"I fell to the floor and tried to cover my head with my arms. A boot made contact with my face, a searing white light shooting through my eye socket. Another kick to the head, this one smashing into the fingers of my hand with the crunch of breaking bone."

The beating continued, and then she was moved to a detention hut and painfully bound and gagged. That night, government soldiers and members of

Sudan's dreaded Janjaweed militia came and raped her repeatedly …. The gang rapes continued for the next three days.'[1]

And what made Dr Bashir a target for those violations? Why did government-backed militias single her out for abuses? Dr Bashir had informed a United Nations fact-finding team about an attack on a girls' primary school where militias had raped students as young as eight years old. Dr Bashir had treated those victims for horrific injuries that they had sustained during that attack. Her punishment for passing that information to the UN was to be tortured, beaten and raped.

Reports from Darfur throughout the Council's existence showed that rape and sexual violence were being used as a weapon of war. Women and children were systematically raped by militias in Darfur. The stigma attached to those attacks led to women abandoning babies conceived through rape. Yet Sudan's government claimed that rape was not an issue. Aid workers reported that if they spoke out about sexual violence then they would be removed from the country.[2] Little wonder, then, that the government-backed militias sought to silence Dr Bashir.

Unlike other grave human rights situations, UN bodies focused significant attention on the conflict in Darfur. Violations were well-documented. The Human Rights Council discussed the conflict at all of its early sessions. It even paused from its focus on Israel to convene a Special Session on Darfur. Resolutions and decisions on Darfur were tabled at Council sessions. The body ensured that fact-finding missions were sent to the region. It provided a forum in which the European Union and African Union brokered a deal to send in a group of experts to monitor and provide recommendations on Darfur. The UN peacekeeping mission (UNAMID)[3] was supported by the UN's human rights machinery.

Yet UN human rights bodies took almost no meaningful action on Darfur. In 2005 the UN appointed Sima Samar[4] as Special Rapporteur on Sudan.[5] Samar had reported on the situation to the Council since its creation. Despite her efforts, no progress was made. While NGOs documented the gross and systemic violations, the Council's resolutions only weakly called for action on Darfur. That action rarely materialised. It provided only broad, general recommendations and frequently did not follow up on the implementation of its recommendations. The Council failed to take steps to protect individuals in that region. The facts on the ground showed little improvement. It was mainly the Security Council's action that protected human rights in Darfur.[6] The question is why?

What precludes action being taken on situations that receive significant and necessary attention at UN human rights bodies?

The armed conflict in Darfur started in 2003. Sudan's government armed and backed militias who attacked ethnic groups that supported the rebels. Amnesty International's report from the year of the Council's creation paints a depressing picture of the human rights situation in Darfur in 2006:

A Darfur Peace Agreement negotiated in Abuja, Nigeria, was signed in May by the government and one faction of the opposition armed groups in Darfur, but conflict, displacement and killings increased. The government failed to disarm the armed militias known as the Janjawid, who continued to attack civilians in Darfur and launched cross-border raids into Chad. Hundreds of civilians were killed in Darfur and Chad, and some 300,000 more were displaced during the year, many of them repeatedly. Displaced people in Darfur and Darfuri refugees in Chad were unable to return to their villages because of the lack of security. In August government forces launched a major offensive in North Darfur and Jebel Marra, which was accompanied by Janjawid raids on villages and continued at the end of 2006. The air force frequently bombed civilians. The African Union Mission in Sudan (AMIS) was unable to stop killings, rapes and displacement of civilians or looting. Government security services arbitrarily detained suspected opponents incommunicado and for prolonged periods. Torture was widespread and in some areas, including Darfur, systematic. Human rights defenders and foreign humanitarian organizations were harassed. Freedom of expression was curtailed. The authorities forcibly evicted displaced people in poor areas of Khartoum and people in the Hamdab area where a dam was being built. Armed opposition groups also carried out human rights abuses.[7]

Grave violations continued throughout the Council's early years. Millions of people were displaced from their homes. Hundreds of villages were destroyed. Rape and sexual violence continued to be used as a weapon of war. This chapter does not detail the conflict in Darfur. There are many, broader studies on Darfur. Totten examines the human rights violations in that region.[8] Hassan and Ray give a history and analysis of the conflict.[9] This chapter focuses on why the UN human rights bodies failed to protect individuals in Darfur despite the even-handed scrutiny of the abuses.

Sudan is a member both of the African Group and of the OIC. That regional group is one of the two strongest at the Human Rights Council. The OIC is the dominant political bloc at the body. Sudan therefore received significant support from allied states. But that support was not sufficient to shield it from attention. The sheer weight of evidence meant that the violations could not be swept under the carpet. Regional and political support for Sudan's government could not keep Darfur off the Council's agenda but its allies ensured that the Council did not blame the government for those human rights abuses.

Sudan and its allies deflected responsibility for the violations by claiming that the government lacked the resources necessary to protect individuals in Darfur. Sudan's government claimed to cooperate with peacekeeping efforts.[10] UN bodies, independent experts and NGOs constantly documented the government's links with systemic human rights violations. When challenged about its role in the abuses, the government claimed that it lacked capacity to protect human rights.

Sudan became adept at asking the UN to provide technical assistance, capacity-building and other resources. The government insisted that it needed 'support, especially financial support, from the international community. We would require 200 billion dollars to settle the problem in Darfur.'[11] The African Group backed this assertion, saying that '[t]he international community at large, and donor countries in particular, [must] provide financial and technical assistance to Sudan'.[12] The OIC called on the international community 'to strengthen the Sudanese government' and 'provide moral support and technical assistance'.[13]

The language used appealed to decolonised and developing states. Sudan and its allies adopted a post-colonial discourse. They even blamed the West for trying to 'undermine the sovereignty of an African government'.[14] Such statements are almost a 'call to arms' for decolonised states.

One aspect of the post-colonial approach to human rights is that former imperial powers should not criticise other states for human rights abuses. Those countries should instead be assisted in creating human rights mechanisms. This position is not wholly contentious. Many decolonised states lack the capacity fully to implement and protect human rights. Decades, if not centuries, of subjugation have resulted in fragile or developing legal systems. The onus is therefore shifted to the former-colonial powers to assist those countries that they previously oppressed.

A main problem with this approach is that it is used as a tactic to deflect attention away from state-sponsored abuses. Calls to support Sudan's government were a method for shielding Sudan. They did not acknowledge, let alone deal with, the government's responsibility for those violations. Instead, they provided a smokescreen that allowed Sudan to continue to collude in the atrocities within Darfur.

By adopting a post-colonial discourse, Sudan aligned itself with countries that lack capacity for implementing fundamental rights. But many of those countries do not arm militias or soldiers and enable them to systematically abuse the rights of their citizens. Haiti, for example, clearly requires support to protect individuals from human rights abuses. It is a fragile state with very limited resources, facing natural and man-made disasters. Protecting human rights within Haiti requires resources, technical assistance and support from the UN and its member states. Similarly, Somalia and Timor Leste need help from the international community. The UN and international aid agencies have been at the fore in protecting human rights in those states. But there is one big difference between those countries and Sudan: the governments, no matter how fragile and unstable, are not arming and backing militias that perpetrate crimes against humanity and genocide within their own territories.

Although claims of lack of capacity may be true in fragile states, they are increasingly being used by many countries that have the resources but lack the political will to implement rights. Those calls for assistance are taken up by countries' political and regional allies. That stops UN bodies taking meaningful action on grave abuses within those states. Instead, pressure is placed on the UN and aid agencies to support governments that are actually perpetrating gross and systemic violations.

Sudan's tactics worked. They created a smokescreen for continuing to perpetrate abuses. All the while, the government continued to arm and support militias that systematically raped, tortured and killed civilians, burnt down their houses and forced them to leave their villages. The situation in Darfur was one of the gravest human rights situations[15] during the Council's early years. It required more attention and resources than situations in Myanmar, Israel or even Sri Lanka.[16] Many have labelled events in Darfur as 'a genocide'.[17] In July 2010, the International Criminal Court's second arrest warrant for Sudan's President—Omar Al-Bashir—added genocide to its original list of charges.[18] Sudan's claims that it lacked the capacity to implement human rights were nothing more than an attempt to deflect attention from its violations.

But it is not just post-colonial discourses that are relied upon to avoid responsibility for human rights abuses. Countries also play on an anti-West sentiment. They claim that human rights are a neo-colonial tool of oppression.[19] International human rights law is portrayed as a Western construct imposed on all other states. This stems from the idea that human rights represent norms and values belonging to the countries that originally created that system. Many of those countries were colonial powers at the time of the Universal Declaration of Human Rights. The tension between creating the modern era of international human rights law and systematically violating rights within colonies remains a bone of contention nearly seven decades later. Decolonised states, and their allies from across the Global South, allege that the West uses human rights as a stick to beat less developed countries. Among the countries at the fore of making these accusations are China, Cuba, Iran and Venezuela, all of which have long adopted an anti-West discourse to provide a smokescreen for their own abuses.

Those countries use UN human rights bodies to criticise Western states, particularly the US and the UK for abuses during the 'War on Terror', whilst simultaneously claiming that international human rights law is a fundamentally flawed system. And those statements are strongly supported by countries that also share an anti-West sentiment. They provide a unifying theme for states that have their own issues with the Global North. Some rail against perceived US hegemony while others seek to attack former-colonisers from Europe. Of course, that anti-West feeling provides a good reason for rejecting 'Western' notions of rights. They are also used to demand that those same, wealthy countries provide resources and technical assistance for implementing human rights across the world.

Cuba

Orlando Zapata Tamayo was arrested during Cuba's 'Black Spring'[20] in March 2003.[21] A former plumber and a political activist, Mr Zapata Tamayo was a member of the Alternative Republican Movement National Civic Resistance Committee. He was arrested along with 75 other political dissidents, all of whom were subjected to 'summary trials' and lengthy prison sentences.[22] Mr Zapata Tamayo was originally sentenced to three years' imprisonment, but that was later increased to 36 years.

Despite repeated calls for his release, alongside other political prisoners, Mr Zapata Tamayo remained in prison until his death in 2010. He went on hunger strike 'to protest against what he said were repeated beatings by guards and other abuses at Kilo 7 Prison in the eastern province of Camagüey. His back was "tattooed with blows" from beatings, according to his mother.'[23] Two weeks before his death, his mother said that 'he was "skin and bones, his stomach is just a hole" and that bedsores covered his legs. He was so gaunt that nurses were unable to get intravenous lines for fluids into his arms and used veins on his neck instead.'[24] Although Mr Zapata Tamayo was moved to a hospital, Cuban authorities 'did not try to force feed him'.[25] Elizardo Sanchez, from the Cuban Human Rights Commission, said that 'his death shows the totalitarian arrogance that is not measuring the human impact of its acts.'

Amnesty International has long campaigned against Cuba's 'prisoners of conscience'. But it is not just political dissidents who face prison sentences, harassment and beatings in Cuba. Journalists and human rights defenders are also routinely persecuted by the government and subjected to gross and systemic human rights abuses.[26] As with Darfur, the abuses in Cuba are so well-documented that it is impossible for the government to deny them.

Like Sudan, Cuba appeals to decolonised and developing states in order to dodge criticism at UN human rights bodies. It does not claim that it lacks capacity for human rights. Nor does it use post-colonial language and themes. Instead it harnesses a broader, anti-West point of view. Although Cuba may have valid concerns about Western countries, many of those are based upon political rather than human rights concerns. Yet it uses human rights as a mechanism for attacking the West, usually the US. Support for its position is easily garnered because so many states share Cuba's resentments against Western countries. A main problem with airing those grievances within the UN human rights machinery is that it is often unrelated to the discussion at hand. As a result, time and resources are withheld from situations that cry out for the UN's attention. And that is a primary motivating factor for states, like Cuba, that wish to duck and weave their way out of having their human rights records scrutinised.

Cuba manipulates Human Rights Council discussions by focusing attention on the US.[27] Firstly, that undermines US efforts to focus on Cuba's human rights violations. Secondly, it ensures that discussions are diverted from human rights abuses within other states. During a Council discussion on torture, Cuba announced that the CIA was training and developing terrorist groups to attack Latin American countries and that it was plotting to kill the Cuban head of state.[28] Of course,

Cuba did not draw any link to issues of torture—the topic being discussed at the Council. And it failed to provide any evidence to support its allegations.

But Cuba was not content with diverting the Council's attention from other situations. It used the Council to blame the US for violations occurring within Cuba. At one point it accused the US of having a 'policy of hostility' and 'coercive measures' that 'has had a serious impact on Cuba. Humanitarian damage has occurred especially in areas of public health and education.'[29] That accusation has links with the type of blame set out within post-colonial discourses.

Cuba's statements were picked up by other countries. They were either political or regional allies, or states that simply aligned with the anti-West rhetoric. Those semi-alliances smack of the old adage that 'my enemy's enemy is my friend'. Syria is but example of a non-regional or political ally that supported Cuba's attacks.[30]

Venezuela picked up on and supported Cuba's statements. It told the Council that 'we denounce those that protect and foster terrorism, specifically our neighbour to the north—America'.[31] Like Cuba, Venezuela failed to provide context or evidence to support its assertions. Both countries have a history of bad relations with the US. The Council was by no means the first UN body that those states used to attack the US. Targeting the US at the Council gave Cuba and Venezuela the opportunity to attack the US and divert attention from other countries' human rights records.

DPRK (North Korea) echoed the anti-West propaganda. It said that the US sought to 'destroy' its 'socialist system' through 'hostile policies' and referred to 'conspiracies with the EU and Japan'.[32] North Korea insisted, somewhat absurdly, that 'it is a well-known fact that the US is the worst human rights violator in the world'.[33] The fact that North Korea felt comfortable using the UN's human rights machinery to accuse Western states of being 'the worst' violators shows just how far off-course the Human Rights Council had veered. Since its creation, North Korea has systematically violated its citizens' fundamental rights. Indeed, and as will be explored in Chapter 10, it may be the worst human rights abuser and most repressive regime in the world.

Clearly the US, which has long-standing tensions with Cuba, played a role in keeping the spotlight on that country. But the US cannot shoulder the responsibility for Cuba's human rights record. Cuba is known systematically to abuse civil and political rights. Freedoms of expression, assembly, association and movement are systematically violated within Cuba. Individuals are denied fundamental rights, such as due process, within Cuba's judicial system.[34]

However, Cuba's tactics worked. Cuba skilfully used its anti-West rhetoric to harness support in its drive to avoid scrutiny of its human rights record. At the Human Rights Council, Cuba utilised its regional and political alliances to end the UN Special Procedures mandate that focused on human rights abuses within its territory. That country-specific mandate was political insofar as its creation and renewal were promoted by the US. But, as we have seen, there were strong reasons for Cuba receiving such attention. When the Council was created, all of the Special Procedures mandates that had been created by the Commission were reviewed. Cuba and its allies, including Russia and China, played on the idea that all country mandates are a form of imperialism.[35] They insisted that there ought to be no specific focus on individual countries because it was merely another instance of the West oppressing poor and weaker states. That tactic worked. While country-specific mandates have not been abolished, the one on Cuba ceased to exist from that time.

Cuba uses post-Marxist discourses of anti-imperialism in much the same way as other states use post-colonial language. The problem is not the underlying sentiment—some of the arguments may well make valid points. Rather the arguments are made in order to provide a smokescreen for states' own human rights records.

Conclusion

As we have seen, many countries seek to support one another's claims that they lack capacity for protecting and implementing human rights and argue that they require technical assistance and support. Yet many of those states are human rights abusers. It is good politics for them to shield one another from scrutiny, because that deflects attention from their own human rights records. The political reasons for decolonised countries and their allies to continue to utilise post-colonial discourses and emphasise anti-Western sentiment is clear. Post-colonial discourses not only unite those countries, they also shift the blame back to former colonial powers. The message is that it cannot be the fault of the abuser state that human rights are being violated within its territory—it must instead be the fault of the former colonial power. While the repercussions of colonialism cannot be underestimated, and to be sure the long-lasting damage is obvious, the claim that a state lacks capacity to prevent abuses is often a way of avoiding taking responsibility for violations. It enables a smokescreen for abuses and fails the individuals on the ground. The UN human rights bodies become fora in which political battles are waged. Meanwhile, grave violations continue with impunity.

Crucially, human rights are expensive to implement and protect. Many countries insist that human rights fall under the UN's 'development' mandate. By relying on post-colonial discourses, those states shift the human rights burden onto the international community. Of course, those countries asking for assistance include autocratic and dictatorial regimes. Wealth disparity and corruption are rife. Aid money does not always reach the people it is intended to help. Many countries that call for capacity-building have little interest in implementing international human rights laws. They may well be unwilling to use their own resources to protect human rights, perhaps because international human rights laws do not reflect their own norms, values or cultures. Or it may be because they simply do not care about human rights. Either way, those countries use post-colonial rhetoric or anti-West sentiment as a smokescreen for their abuses rather than actually asking for help.

8

HUMAN RIGHTS OF MIGRANTS

WHAT RIGHTS?

Mr Jimmy Mubenga, aged 46, was unlawfully killed[1] in October 2010 while being deported from the UK to Angola. Mr Mubenga had lived in the UK for 16 years. He was married and the father to five children. The government outsourced deportation work to private companies. Three G4S guards—Stuart Tribelnig, Terry Hughes and Colin Kaler— restrained Mr Mubenga for longer than 30 minutes. During that time a number of passengers 'said they heard him shouting that he could not breathe and that he was crying out: "They're going to kill me."'[2] His death caused public outcry over the treatment of irregular—or what is wrongly termed 'illegal'[3]—migrants and the methods used for their deportation. But that debate was held against the backdrop of increasing anti-immigration rhetoric from the media and mainstream politicians.

Increasingly, far-Right politics are on the rise within Western states, and the frontline battle seems to be on immigration. Mainstream politics is pushed further to the right when it comes to policies on migrants. In July 2012, 'Golden Dawn members rounded on a derelict factory in Patras traditionally used by immigrants for shelter. They threw petrol bombs and set fire to parts of the building' in retaliation for a Greek man's death—he was allegedly killed by three Afghani migrants.[4] Golden Dawn is a rising power in Greek politics, with many allegations surfacing that the far-Right party is supported by the police. During the summer of 2013, the UK government launched a 'Go Home' advertising campaign. Vans were driven around areas with large migrant populations, with signs on the side encouraging irregular migrants to phone a number for assistance in returning to their countries of origin.[5] In July 2013, Australian Prime Minister Kevin Rudd set out his country's new policy regarding irregular migrants who arrive by boat on Australian shores. Rudd announced that those individuals who claim asylum in that way will be sent to Papua New Guinea. The two countries signed a deal to that effect, with Papua New Guinea's Manus facility being equipped to process 3,000 asylum seekers at any one time.[6]

It is not just political rhetoric against irregular migrants that is increasing. Incidents of grave human rights violations against irregular migrants are rising steadily across many Western states. Those abuses are systematic and governments either collude with or carry out the violations. The suburb of Ponte Galeria, on the outskirts of Rome, is home to 'The Identification and Expulsion Center'. It is not an official prison, but it might just as well be:

'Tall metal fences separate rows of drab low-lying barracks into individual units that are locked down at night, when the concrete courtyards are lit bright as day. There are security cameras. Some guards wear riot gear. Detainees can move around in designated areas during the day, but they are forced to wear slippers, or shoes without laces, so as not harm themselves or others …. [S]harp objects—including pens, pencils and combs—[are] banned.'[7]

Riots have broken out at European detention centres across Italy,[8] Greece[9] and Spain,[10] as well as further afield in Australia[11] and the US. In Russia, during the summer of 2013, thousands of irregular migrants from Afghanistan, Egypt, Kyrgyzstan, Morocco, Syria, Tajikistan, Uzbekistan and Vietnam were rounded up and imprisoned, some in a tent camp.[12] Individuals held in detention facilities are not criminals—they are irregular migrants. Yet they are locked up, often for many months, and treated as though they are prisoners. They are denied fundamental rights. Little wonder, then, that they are fighting back.

Every year, tens of thousands of irregular migrants leave North Africa heading towards Europe. Many of those people do not make it alive. Bodies are found on the shores of Italy, Greece and Spain. Many more are drowned at sea. Tens of thousands of people embark upon perilous journeys from Asia, often stowed away in the holds of lorries, vans or boats. Every night, irregular migrants attempt to cross the notorious border between Mexico and the US. Many of these men, women and children die or are seriously injured. And those who do arrive face detention, discrimination and persecution. Individuals are humans, and every one of them holds fundamental rights. Yet that seems to be forgotten in the case of irregular migrants; particularly those who arrive in Western countries.

On 3 October 2013 a boat caught fire and capsized near Italy. On board were more than 500 Eritrean men, women and children. Only 155 people survived. While this disaster grabbed media attention across the world, it is only one of many such stories over recent years. The island of Lampedusa has become the landing point for thousands of migrants seeking to enter Europe. The Italian islanders stand out as compassionate and caring towards the boatloads of new arrivals.[13] They seem to understand that these people arrive on the shores seeking a better life, and this stands in stark contrast to the rhetoric across much of the Global North.

Abuses of undocumented migrants are rife: from the traffickers that bring many tens of thousands across borders and into bondage and modern-day slavery, to the employers who knowingly exploit them, to the locals who discriminate against them in shops, housing and on the streets. Legal redress, despite being a fundamental right, is denied to irregular migrants who fear that contacting the police will lead to the authorities initiating deportation processes. They largely live below the surface, undocumented and hidden from sight. Yet it is not just private parties that commit these violations. The state, the government, colludes in and sponsors abuses of migrants' fundamental rights.

State-sponsored violations occur outside of detention and deportation processes. Access to housing, healthcare, food and even sanitation is denied, despite Western states providing those fundamental, subsistence rights to all individuals within their territories. Irregular migrants' hidden existence precludes them from accessing services that meet those basic needs. Asylum seekers of whom the state is aware often do not qualify for basic services, including access to justice or subsistence rights. Even when the state does take responsibility for irregular migrants, they are still not safe from violations.

In January 2012, 'a 21-year-old man from Conakry, Guinea, died in Barcelona's immigration detention centre after complaining of chest pains or ... breathing problems'.[14] His young age, alongside allegations about the lack of medical care and more broadly at the detention centre, led to other detainees rioting. A few weeks prior to the man's death, a woman aged 41 died of meningitis 'hours after her admission to hospital from the Aluche detention centre, in the suburbs of Madrid'. A local court 'was highly critical of the "manifest overcrowding" suffered by inmates ... the lack of washing and toilet facilities or an infirmary, all of which facilitate the spread of infectious diseases'.[15] Migreurop is a network of activists and scholars who aim to document and disseminate information about the detention and treatment of irregular migrants in Europe. They are particularly critical of the lack of open access to detention facilities across Europe, with NGOs and journalists unable fully to uncover and document the raft of human rights abuses committed on a daily basis.[16] Yarl's Wood in the UK is another facility that has faced heavy criticism for human rights abuses. Irregular migrants, including thousands of children, have been dragged out of their homes in police raids and held for months at the centre.[17] Effectively, they have been imprisoned without charge.

We have seen even in this brief discussion that irregular migrants face government-sanctioned abuses of their rights to: (a) non-discrimination on the grounds of race, religion or nationality; (b) freedom of movement; (c) freedom from arbitrary detention; (d) liberty; (e) freedom from inhumane or degrading treatment; (f) basic subsistence rights; and (g) the right to life. States also routinely violate the rights of the child, to privacy, to family life, and many more.

In 2012, Europe had 473 detention sites holding 570,660 migrants.[18] Countries that have ratified the European Convention on Human Rights, as well as the international covenants and specific human rights treaties, are routinely abusing rights of migrants. The 2008 European 'Returns' directive allowed states to detain migrants for up to 18 months.[19] Effectively, state-sponsored abuses are enabled and colluded with at the regional level. It is not that governments do not know that migrants—alongside *all* individuals and by virtue of being human— hold those fundamental rights. Those governments know that they can avoid implementing and protecting those individuals' rights.

And other countries adopt similar stances. The US has approximately 250 detention centres, all of which are run by private companies. In the US 'immigration authorities are allowed to imprison any noncitizen, without bond, a process protected from judicial review'.[20] Human Rights Watch has documented the increasing criminalisation of irregular migrants within the US[21] and the human rights abuses perpetrated against them by the state.

Let us be very clear, then: it is not only countries from the Global South that try to dodge and weave their way out of protecting and implementing human rights. Western states do exactly the same. Countries from the Global North are systematically violating the rights of irregular migrants. But it goes further than that: those same countries are acting as a bloc to stop UN bodies from developing and implementing the human rights of migrants. This chapter examines how and why those states are achieving those aims, and why the UN is failing to protect migrants' rights.

In 1990, the General Assembly adopted the International Convention on the Protection of the Rights of All Migrant Workers and Members of Their Families.[22] The Convention reaffirms existing human rights instruments. Rather than creating new human rights, it is a treaty aimed specifically at this vulnerable group of individuals. There are other similar treaties that emphasise the rights of other vulnerable groups and place them within specific contexts, including on women,[23] on children[24] and on persons with disabilities.[25] The central feature of the Convention on Human Rights of Migrants is to protect all migrant workers and their families irrespective of their legal status.

A total of 46 countries have ratified[26] the Convention and a further 17 are signatories.[27] This falls far below the 120 states 'for which migration is an important feature, either as origin, transit or destination countries'.[28] None of the states from the West or from the rising global power of BRIC—Brazil, Russia, India and China—has either signed or ratified the Convention. Without those heavyweights, politically and economically, the treaty largely has failed to get off the ground. Over 20 years after its creation, the Convention is yet to have an impact upon countries from the Global North or to protect migrants who move to those states. The countries that most need to be bound to protect the rights of migrants are the ones that are studiously avoiding signing up to its provisions.

States from the Global North are the leaders in the human rights game. They control the money and resources, and therefore hold the power. Most have been instrumental in developing, promoting and protecting human rights. It seems strange, to say the least, that those same countries refuse to ratify the Convention on the Human Rights of Migrants.

FAILING TO PROTECT

The question is, why?

It appears that those countries do not want to set a precedent for protecting irregular migrants. People leave poorer countries and travel to wealthier states. Those countries, particularly Western states, do recognise the vulnerability of certain types of migrants: children, trafficked women and domestic workers. But they do not see the vulnerability of young, fit, healthy people—particularly men—who chose to cross borders illicitly in order to enter their countries. The Convention would set a precedent that those individuals are also vulnerable and in need of specific protection. Any such guarantees would cost significant money and resources, and would be politically costly for national governments.

Democratic systems are not structurally equipped to protect the human rights of irregular migrants because, crucially, those migrants do not vote. Any government that takes steps towards protecting migrants' rights will face the wrath of voters in the next election. And as irregular migrants do not have voting rights, it is not therefore in a government's political interest to ratify the Convention or to take other steps towards protecting migrants' rights. Nowhere is this clearer than under US President Barack Obama. While he made sweeping promises to protect migrants' rights when campaigning for election, in his first term President Obama deported more individuals than George W. Bush did in his entire eight years as US President.[29]

Other efforts are being expended at the UN to protect migrants' rights. The mandate of the Special Rapporteur on the Human Rights of Migrants was created in 1999[30] and continues to operate 14 years later. It covers all countries, irrespective of whether a state has ratified the Convention. The current mandate-holder—François Crépeau—has focused on violations committed by Western states. During his first year, Crépeau visited Greece,[31] Italy,[32] Tunisia[33] and Turkey.[34] He was particularly concerned to find out about and provide recommendations on the ports of departure and arrival for irregular migrants seeking to enter Europe.

Crépeau's report on Europe[35] was discussed at the Human Rights Council's 23rd Session. He offered some strong and timely recommendations. Criticising the EU's current focus on security concerns, Crépeau called for the EU and its member states to adopt a human rights-based approach to migration. But it was not just the Special Rapporteur who took the floor to remind the EU of its legal and moral obligations to uphold human rights. Country after country from across the world repeated the fundamental necessity of a human rights-based approach to migrants. Country after country, that is, other than from the European Union.

That session was well-attended by delegates from all member states. Often, the Council Chamber will be only half full during a Special Rapporteur's report and interactive dialogue. When the report is on a contentious issue, the Chamber might be three-quarters full. Discussions on crisis situations, such as Syria or Israel, provide rare occasions when the room is full. The report on the EU and migrants saw the Chamber full, with delegates sitting on their chairs rather than milling around at the back of the room. European states sent ambassadors as well as teams of legal and human rights advisers to listen to Crépeau deliver his report. It was clear that this was a significant event and one taken seriously by all Council members.

However, during the interactive dialogue, EU countries all but failed to engage with the Special Rapporteur. Portugal and Montenegro did mention his report but ignored the main thrust of his arguments. Greece and Italy sought to downplay the egregious violations that Crépeau had documented, including detention without charge and lack of access to legal services and healthcare. All other EU member states studiously avoided mentioning Crépeau's report and focused on reports delivered by other rapporteurs that day.

This was the first time that the EU had been the object of a Special Rapporteur's report. While that bloc remained almost silent during the Council's discussion, they took the matter very seriously. The EU produced a substantial written response to the report,[36] which demonstrated that it had engaged in the discussion. But engagement is not enough, particularly where states seek to justify abuses rather than address the need to protect the human rights of migrants.

Silence and justification seem to be the West's two main tactics for avoiding their human rights obligations. They claim that security issues justify human rights violations. For example, on 14 October 2013 Russian authorities rounded up and arrested more than a thousand migrant workers in Moscow following the stabbing of a Russian man, allegedly committed by a migrant.[37] Such approaches to migrants are common. Rather than viewing irregular migrants as people, state authorities across many countries focus on the unlawful actions that those individuals have committed. Frequently the unlawful action will be the crossing of a border without the required documents. Those actions are criminalised within many countries. State authorities then point to the unlawful action to justify the criminalisation of irregular migrants' existence in their territories. By securitising the issue of migration, it dehumanises the individuals involved, which makes it easier to justify or explain human rights abuses. Security concerns centre upon the law—whether regarding border entry, criminal activities or terrorism.

Whereas decolonised states use lack of capacity as an excuse—human rights are good but they lack the resources to protect them—Western countries use security as a way to 'trump' human rights. This undermines the very foundations of fundamental rights that the West was at the fore of building. Security concerns cannot be the primary basis for policies on migrants. That approach undermines the existence of basic rights for all people. Migrants are, first and foremost, human beings. Regardless of whether they are regular or irregular migrants, their status as human beings remains unchanged; therefore their rights are not and cannot be removed.

The Special Rapporteur cannot force the hands of Western countries. Nor can they be coerced into ratifying the Convention on the Human Rights of Migrants. Change will only occur through politics and diplomacy. UN reports may impact upon national political parties and might be picked up by civil society and NGOs. But direct tools and recommendations provided about changing the law at the local level are only guidance and suggestions. It is up to states to choose whether or not to change their approach to human rights and irregular migration.

So long as countries from the Global North dig their heels in, nothing will change. Meanwhile, rights continue to be violated.

'An estimated 214 million people currently live outside their country of origin …. Migrants are often to be found working in jobs that are dirty, dangerous and degrading. While for some migration is a positive and empowering experience, far too many migrants have to endure human rights violations, discrimination, and exploitation.'[38]

Ultimately, wealthy and powerful states exercise power to protect themselves. Politicisation is not just about weaker states trying to avoid obligations. Politicisation is also about stronger states manipulating the system in order to duck and weave their way out of human rights laws that they view as burdensome or having a heavy impact upon their countries.

9

THE 'GREAT' POWERS

In August 2013 videos began to be posted online of Lesbian Gay Bisexual and Transgender Russian teenagers bullied and tortured by homophobic gangs. One boy was kidnapped, tortured and died after his ordeal.[1] The Spectrum Human Rights Alliance reported that fascist gangs were luring gay teenagers on 'dates' via social media sites. When the victims arrived, they were held against their will, beaten, humiliated and tortured. Videos were then posted online in which the attackers' faces were clearly visible. 'No arrests [were] made and no charges were pressed'[2] in relation to the unnamed youngster who died.

These are not isolated incidents. Vladislav Tornovoy was killed in Volgograd in May 2013. One of his killers, who supposedly was his friend, stated that the reason for the murder was that Mr Tornovoy 'revealed he was gay'.[3] Human Rights Watch reported that 'Tornovoy's killers raped him with beer bottles and killed him by smashing his head.'[4] That same month Oleg Serdyuk was killed in Kamchatka. The Kamchatka Investigative Committee stated that Mr Serdyuk was kicked and stabbed to death 'because of his alleged "non-traditional sexual orientation"'.[5]

The summer of 2013 saw Russia moving towards state-sanctioned homophobia. Despite the country's international and regional human rights commitments, backwards steps were taken in terms of LGBT people living within that country. In June 2013, Russia introduced a federal law against gay 'propaganda'.[6] The law bans the promotion to minors of 'non-traditional' sexual relationships.

Gay Pride parades had been banned in Moscow and adoptions by same-sex couples were outlawed prior to the new legislation.[7] LGBT activists who protested against the new law were first subjected to violence from crowds supporting the Bill[8] and then detained by police.[9] A month after the legislation came into force, Russian police and migration officers detained four Dutch nationals working on a documentary about LGBT people in Murmansk.[10]

Russia's moves towards cracking down on homosexuality received significant attention from NGOs, civil society and the media. That attention in no small part centred on the Sochi Winter Olympics 2014. While the International Olympic Committee and Olympic sponsors acknowledged that the legislation 'contradicts the Olympic Charter', they declined to become involved in the mounting pressure on Russia to reverse its stance. At least they joined the debate. There was little chance of UN human rights bodies doing the same.

China's human rights abuses around the time of the Beijing Olympics 2008[11] set a precedent for UN silence and inaction regarding the Sochi Winter Olympics. Hundreds of thousands of residents were forcibly evicted from their homes, which were then demolished to make way for Olympic stadia, parks and roads. The UN Special Rapporteur on the Right to Adequate Housing failed to visit China or report on the issue despite a wealth of information being available from NGOs and civil society. Migrant construction workers who built much of the Olympic infrastructure in Beijing were subjected to human rights abuses. Journalists, human rights defenders and protesters were detained without charge in the period leading up to the Games. And that is before we even think about the ongoing, systematic violations within China such as the subjugation of ethnic and religious minorities; occupation of Tibet; media and internet censorship; and abuse of labour rights.

Many EU leaders boycotted the opening ceremony and even the Olympic Games. A raft of organisations, from Amnesty International to Médecins Sans Frontières, provided significant information on China's human rights records. Individuals protested around the world. So, why did the UN do nothing?

Former Secretary-General Boutros Boutros-Ghali once stated that exclusion from the Olympics is an expression of the international community's disapproval of a country or regime's practices.[12] That sanction was used against South Africa. But, as we have seen, it is relatively simple to secure the political will needed to take action against a pariah state. China is a powerful country—militarily, economically and politically—and the IOC was not prepared to take it on. Indeed, they even awarded China the 2008 Olympic Games. And UN bodies seemingly took the same approach.

While the General Assembly was happy to emphasise the Olympic Truce[13] regarding the Beijing Games,[14] it was not prepared to take action on China's human rights abuses. Neither was the UN human rights machinery.

The UN treaty-based bodies are the least politicised of the human rights machinery. Comprised of experts, and with jurisdiction only over states party to the relevant treaty, those bodies are far less biased or selective than the Human Rights Council or even the General Assembly and Security Council. The three main problems in terms of protecting rights are (a) that not all states are party to the relevant treaty; (b) they rely on states to engage with the bodies; and (c) enforcement.

Leaving enforcement aside for the time being, it is interesting to note that none of the treaty bodies discussed China's abuses in relation to the Beijing Olympic Games. The Committee on Civil and Political Rights cannot address abuses in China because that country is not party to the treaty that protects those rights. Other treaty bodies have considered China, but only in Concluding Observations after considering that country's periodic reports. China did not submit reports around the time of the Olympics, so those treaty bodies could not consider the human rights abuses perpetrated in the build-up to the Games.

The Human Rights Council did receive some information about China's violations from NGOs and civil society.[15] Those were altogether ignored by states during Council discussions. China was also discussed more generally in reports by Special Rapporteurs.[16] Nothing specific was raised about the human rights of migrants, housing, or other abuses committed in the run-up to the Beijing Olympics.

Let us be clear that this is nothing to do with human rights and everything to do with power-politics.

The three main powers at the United Nations are China, Russia and the US. Yes, the UK and France hold veto powers at the Security Council, but they have not used their vetoes since 1989. Those two countries are no longer the economic, military or political heavyweights that they were at the time the UN was created. Brazil and India are emerging world powers, as are Germany and Japan. But none of those countries hold permanent seats, let alone veto powers, at the Security Council. It is the economic and military might, mixed with the geopolitical power and Security Council vetoes, that make China, Russia and the US *the* countries that count.

So, when those three states commit human rights abuses—and, to be sure, they do so with regularity—the UN *might* discuss them, it *might even* provide a report or share information. But almost *invariably* it will fail to take any form of action. Why? Because any state or group of countries that presses for such action against China, Russia or the US will risk their multi-faceted relationships with those powerful nations.

Human rights are idealistic insofar as they set out what ought to occur. Indeed, lawyers and the law itself tend to be based on idealism.[17] Yet there is frequently a gap between what ought to occur and what actually happens in practice. The law in England and Wales says that we ought all to drive at or below 70 miles per hour on the motorway. Driving along any motorway at any time of day or night reveals the gap between law and practice. But just because the reality fails to live up to the standards set does not mean that there is something flawed with the idealist principles. The flaws are with how, or whether, they are implemented. The core international human rights reflect idealist values common to all states, as can be seen in the *langue* used in the Universal Declaration and key human rights treaties.[18] The problems arise not in terms of the idealist visions, but in terms of how they can be implemented in practice.

Idealists regard countries—and other actors—as being directed by shared values and norms. States are expected to behave in a way that is value-driven rather than according to what consequences may result from their actions. States' delegates at UN human rights bodies, then, ought to make decisions that reflect the ideals of human rights, rather than making choices based on other, unrelated considerations.

This clearly is not the case. As we have seen, politics is a main factor influencing state behaviour at human rights bodies. The degree to which politics is an important, or even the primary, consideration depends on the state concerned and the subject matter under discussion.

Realists view state behaviour as being driven by power-politics. They take an altogether different approach to idealists. International relations realists regard the world as centred around states. Countries are the decisive actors in international politics,[19] and they continually seek power, much as national political parties are always striving to gain and retain power.[20] The struggle for power, rather than any common ideals or values, is the focal point of all international relations.[21] International organisations are used by powerful states to implement power-politics and to pursue their own self-interest.[22]

Realist theorists see states' primary objective as asserting and ensuring their own interests. International relations becomes a game whereby states seek sufficient power to be protected from other countries.[23] Blocs of states are one way in which countries can amass and maintain power and influence at international organisations. Weaker states allied with each other can, at times, exert more influence than powerful states on their own. But the most powerful states will always exert the most influence.

There are other international relations theories[24] that are less 'black or white'. But realism is useful for understanding extreme, rather than nuanced, state behaviour. The UN's failure to take action on abuses by China, Russia or the US can be viewed through a realist lens. Those three countries are the most powerful and dominant on the world stage. They control vast resources—financial and natural—and have significant military and political might. And they hold veto powers to block the Security Council taking any enforcement action within their own territories. It is fairly obvious why weaker countries, or even groups of states, might be reluctant to take on those three powers.

That is not to say that no attention is given to China, Russia or the US. It is more that action rarely materialises.

In particular, the US has been singled out for attention by the UN human rights machinery. The US has long been a target for socialist-leaning states. Viewed as the last remaining superpower after the end of the Cold War, the US became a focal point for decolonised states seeking to end imperialism on the global stage. More recently, with the 'War on Terror', the US has faced the collective wrath of OIC states. Those countries have united within the General Assembly and the Human Rights Council, and ensured that the US human rights record was on the agenda of those political bodies. Since the election of President Barack Obama—which brought a change in US foreign policies—attention has been less pronounced than in the preceding decades.

That is not to say that the US deserves less attention under President Obama. Despite his election promises about human rights and international law, Guantanamo Bay remains open in Obama's second term as president and US troops remain stationed in Afghanistan and Iraq. Indeed, for all his rhetoric about reducing the US role as global police-man and retracting its exceptionalist and unilateralist stance towards international law, little has changed on the ground. Obama sought to intervene in the conflict in Syria—stopped only by US allies' refusal to assist[25]—and made noises about doing the same in Iran in relation to its nuclear weapons programme. The US still violates international law and human rights both at home and abroad. It still calls for other countries to adhere to their obligations while determining which rights it will implement in which situations.

Attention on the US has reduced: in part owing to Obama's greater efforts than his predecessor at diplomacy, and in part owing to the upheaval within the Arab world that has caused the spotlight on the US to shift. But attention on the US at UN human rights bodies has yielded few concrete results. Even when Cuba, Iran or Venezuela seek to refocus the Human Rights Council's attention onto the US, no significant deci-sions or resolutions are passed. When Special Rapporteurs visit the US for politicised reasons, the reports receive little attention. This happened, for example, when Arjun Sengupta examined extreme poverty in the US, despite impoverished countries pleading with him to visit their territories and provide them with much-needed support and recom-mendations.[26] The most significant fact-finding, recommendations and statements about the US are in relation to torture, arbitrary detention and other 'weapons' of the 'War on Terror'. That attention comes from not just the Council and Assembly, but also from treaty-based bodies and Special Procedures. But even then, despite the information gathered and shared, the UN takes almost no protection action regarding the US.

The UN's failure to protect individuals from abuses perpetrated by the US is similar to the failure to take action on abuses committed by China and Russia. While information exists, from NGOs, civil society and even from other countries, and while UN bodies might even discuss that information, little or no attempt is made to take any action.

All three countries have allied states, groups and political blocs. China relies upon countries from the Non-Aligned Movement, which spans four of the five regional groups. It has many natural geographic allies within the Asian Group and strong political allies in Latin America and the Middle East. Those states shield China from scrutiny, either by blocking discussions of sensitive issues on that state's violations or by voting against resolutions or decisions tabled about those abuses. The composition of the Human Rights Council, with so many of China's regional and political allies sitting as members, means that, as one European diplomat said, '"no one would dare" table a resolution on China' not least because 'the Chinese government has "managed to dissuade states from action—now people don't even raise it"'.[27]

Russia relies on similar support from the former-Soviet bloc in the Eastern European Group, and its political allies in Latin America and the Middle East. Both China and Russia have strong economic, military and political ties with some African states. China in particular uses post-colonial rhetoric that creates at least an illusion of solidarity with the African Group. Similar language was heard in countries' statements throughout the Council's creation and early years.[28] Russia uses other discourses to align itself with those allies, not least anti-US rhetoric. It also promotes issues that are of mutual interest both to Russia and to many of those countries, using its political weight and the support of its allies to pass resolutions that appeal to many countries from the African and Asian Groups and from the OIC.

In September 2012, Russia co-sponsored a Human Rights Council resolution on human rights and 'traditional values of humankind'.[29] The driving force behind that resolution was to undermine the Council's momentum with regard to protecting the rights of LGBT persons. Those discussions culminated in the Panel on LGBT Rights in March 2011—the one during which the entire OIC walked out *en masse*.[30] Although the US and some European countries objected that the rights of women and LGBT persons frequently are undermined by traditional values and religion, the resolution struck the right chord with many other countries. On that occasion 25 states voted in favour,[31] none of which were from the Western European and Others Group and only one—Ecuador—from the Group of Latin American and Caribbean states. The 15 countries that voted against[32] the resolution[33] were from the EU, joined by the US, and two moderate countries that seek to uphold the rights of LGBT persons—Mauritius and Botswana. Russia, which had recently taken steps backwards regarding human rights of LGBT persons within its territory, clearly used its political clout to further an issue that aligned it with many countries from across the world.

The US also uses power-politics to its advantage. It is not only allied with states from the Global North, which remain amongst the wealthiest and most powerful world players, but also with individual countries within other regions. Its close links with Egypt, Israel and Saudi Arabia give the US a foothold in the Middle East. Similarly, its ties with Pakistan and Sri Lanka provide the US with footholds in Asia. While the US alliances are numerically fewer than those of China or Russia, they provide a different form of protection from UN action on human rights abuses.

China and Russia can rely upon significant numbers of states' votes within the General Assembly and the Human Rights Council. That is all the more significant when it is borne in mind that the African Group and the OIC are particularly active within both of those bodies, while the EU largely remains passive other than on controversial issues. A main reason for that passivity is that those bodies' decisions and resolutions are largely hortatory and/or used for political purposes.

The US has long taken an exceptionalist and unilateralist approach to international relations and organisations. It is well-known for supporting the creation of international human rights law and mechanisms and for encouraging other states to comply with the human rights system. Once the laws or mechanisms have been created, however, the US determines whether to place itself within or outside of the system. This exceptionalist and unilateralist approach may stem from power-politics, moral high-ground or the need for autonomy, but it is striking how frequently the US has adopted a contradictory stance towards international human rights. A recent example is the US support—politically and financially—for the disbanding of the Commission on Human Rights and its replacement by the new Human Rights Council. Yet, at the last minute, the US voted against creating the Council. Moreover, it refused to stand for election to the new body and only participated as an observer during early Council sessions. Similarly, the US played a significant role in drafting and creating the Convention on the Rights of the Child. However, it has yet to ratify that treaty. One of the main reasons for the US not being party to the Convention is because it does not want to be bound by obligations about not imprisoning children for life-sentences and not imposing the death penalty on minors. This unilateralist and exceptionalist approach to international law goes beyond human rights. President Woodrow Wilson was the driving force behind the creation of the League of Nations, yet the US refused to become a member of that organisation. History repeated itself 80 years later when the US refused to ratify the Rome Statute despite being a key player in the creation of the International Criminal Court and using its influence to persuade other states to get on board.

The US approach to international law means that it is less concerned than are other countries about votes in political bodies or political attention focused on its own human rights record. However, it is concerned about human rights experts' reports and recommendations, and it takes seriously any legal attention that focuses upon US violations. The US frequently can rely on its allies' support when it comes to those matters. Its allies are powerful, and they are able to use their might within UN bodies and within its no longer smoke-filled corridors. Behind the scenes diplomatic dealings and pressures are utilised by US allies to ensure that no UN body goes too far in its criticisms.

It is not just state alliances that protect countries from scrutiny. A large proportion of the UN human rights experts come from the Global North. One reason is because the independent expert posts are unpaid, requiring individuals to retain paid employment with their institutions. Traditionally, the majority of independent experts have come from universities, and those from the Global North are more likely to be able to absorb the cost of academics undertaking this unpaid work and to recognise the prestige of the position. While that slowly is changing, with more independent experts coming from universities from other regions, and indeed from NGOs and private practice, the imbalance still remains. Similarly, individuals sitting on treaty body committees often are from Global North countries or have been educated within their universities. With the occasional exception, those individuals hold similar views on human rights to those held by the US. The legal and political infrastructure more clearly reflects Western ideologies than those of Eastern Europe or beyond. This frequently assists the US when it comes to scrutiny by those experts.

Russia and China, then, rely on greater numbers of allies while the US relies on stronger allies who are better equipped to navigate the UN infrastructure. The end result is the same. All three countries are protected from UN action despite committing serious human rights abuses. Realist power-politics win when it comes to the most powerful states. Their might on the world stage affords near-impunity when it comes to violating human rights.

Comparing the most powerful countries with the 'pariah states', such as Israel and apartheid-era South Africa,[34] demonstrates how world politics is crucial where it comes to the UN protecting and promoting human rights. The same power-politics that enable disproportionate scrutiny of some countries also allow powerful states to continue to behave as they wish. Unlike Sudan[35] and even Italy and Greece,[36] the most powerful countries do not need to provide excuses or justifications for their violations. Instead, their positions of power protect them from scrutiny and from any action being taken by UN human rights bodies. While the UN is mandated to protect rights across all member states, one might be forgiven for thinking that the most powerful countries never commit violations that require UN action.

10

OUT OF SIGHT, OUT OF MIND

HIDDEN ABUSES ACROSS THE WORLD

Do not be fooled—it is not just the powerful states that slip under the radar when it comes to UN attention or action. The same occurs at the other end of the spectrum. Other countries have found altogether different ways to avoid being held to account for systematically violating human rights within their territories. Unlike the countries in Chapter 7 which use excuses, or those in Chapter 8 which use justifications, these countries are not at all interested in engaging with the international human rights system. They do not bother to feign interest in their human rights obligations, other than on the rare occasion when one of their allies demands that they do so. This is a crucial difference.

Most states obey international law most of the time, and the same is true of international human rights laws. When most countries breach their legal obligations, they try to excuse or justify their actions because they care about the international human rights system. It does not matter whether that care is based on idealism or realism, a combination of the two, or an entirely different reason.

There are some countries, however, that simply do not give two hoots about international human rights law, the system, or their obligations. China, Russia and the US cannot be accused of that charge. Despite their self-protection mechanisms based on power-politics, those three countries have played significant roles across the UN human rights machinery. The countries that do not engage with international human rights are an entirely different kettle of fish. Largely, they are countries with autocratic, dictatorial or other repressive regimes.

The nature of democracy means that governments are held accountable by their own citizens at polling booths. Human rights abuses are not only addressed through checks and balances within democratic systems, but also by individuals exercising their right to vote. This, of course, is not true of autocratic, dictatorial and other repressive regimes. Individuals do not have the right to meaningful political participation. The regimes can, effectively, do whatever they desire. Human rights abuses go unchecked at the national level.

Regardless of whether a country has a strong or emerging democracy, it is far easier to gather information about its human rights records than about a repressive regime. Where a country systematically represses information-sharing—whether through the internet, media or free speech—and places controls on foreigners and foreign organisations entering its territory, it is extremely difficult to find out about most human rights violations and this means that they escape attention within the international arena.

Countries with closed doors to the outside world do not sit on the sidelines or even turn their backs on international human rights; they simply do not show up in the first place. How do they get away with failing to engage with the international human rights system and continuing to perpetrate abuses? Some forge alliances with one or more of the three main powers. Others create links with countries that have similar objectives. Or they use their natural resources—such as oil—or financial might to ensure protection from scrutiny. This chapter examines the gross, systemic and ongoing abuses committed by some of those states and why they largely remain hidden from the world.

Belarus

Belarus is a republic in name, but a dictatorship in reality. In September 2012, parliamentary elections failed to return any opposition party members.[1] The Organization for Security and Co-operation in Europe concluded that the elections were neither free nor fair.[2] Amnesty International reports that freedom of speech, expression and assembly

are routinely violated.[3] Belarus carries out the death penalty in conditions of 'utmost secrecy'.[4] It also systematically detains prisoners of
conscience, including opposition party members.[5] Amnesty documents
many such cases, including:

'Mykalau Statkevich, an opposition presidential candidate during the presidential election 2010, was sentenced to six years in prison on 26 May 2011 for
"organization of mass disorder" … for taking part in post-election demonstra-
tions in December 2010. Amnesty International believes that the charges
against him were unfounded, and that he has been targeted for the peaceful
exercise of his rights to freedom of assembly and expression.'[6]

'Zmitser Dashkevich, a leader of the youth opposition movement Young Front,
was sentenced to two years in a labour colony on 24 March 2011 … for alleged
assault on 18 December 2010, the day before the election. Amnesty
International believes the charges against him are unfounded and that the
charges were fabricated in order to prevent him taking part in the demonstra-
tion on 19 December 2010.'[7]

Belarus fell to 168th out of 179 in the Reporters Without Borders
World Press Freedom Index 2011–2012.[8] That index is compiled using
many criteria, ranging from legislation to violence against journalists, in
order to provide a map of governments' attitudes and intentions towards
media freedom. The UK Foreign Office continues to support sanctions
and the use of international mechanisms to apply pressure on the
Belarusian government to implement its human rights obligations.[9]

Despite some information trickling out about abuses within Belarus,
it is difficult to obtain an accurate picture. Amnesty International has
not recently conducted country visits because of the difficulty of gaining
access. Election monitoring in 2012 did enable European observers to
enter the territory but only to record any issues around the election.
National human rights defenders are regularly harassed by the government and its agents. Reporting, fact-finding and information-sharing,
then, are extremely difficult.

Since the new millennium, four of the treaty-based bodies have issued
concluding observations based on Belarus' periodic reports.[10] All of
those reports emphasise the need for national legislation to implement
human rights obligations. They also stress the need to work with civil
society and NGOs to ensure the realisation and protection of individuals' rights. Strikingly, all of those four treaty-based bodies highlighted
Belarus' failure adequately to ensure basic rights under each relevant

convention. Serious concerns about government policies, inaction and lack of work with civil society were highlighted throughout each report.

The UN Special Procedures system previously had a country-specific mandate for Belarus owing to the grave human rights abuses in that state. That mandate was scrapped during the Human Rights Council's first year but was controversially reinstated in 2012. The UN High Commissioner for Human Rights, Navi Pillay, had reported her serious concerns about violations in Belarus. Despite the significant condemnation and wealth of evidence of abuses, a long list of states including Armenia, Kazakhstan, Bahrain, Azerbaijan, Cuba, Venezuela, Uzbekistan, Iran, Sri Lanka, China, Zimbabwe, the Lao People's Democratic Republic, Tajikistan, Myanmar and Turkmenistan sought to defend Belarus' human rights record. When the EU tabled a resolution creating a new mandate on Belarus, those same countries accused the Council of being politicised.[11]

Belarus relies heavily on Russia as a political and economic ally. China and Cuba, alongside many formerly Soviet and developing states, will protect Belarus from UN attention where to do so furthers their own objectives. Those aims, of course, have nothing to do with human rights and everything to do with politics. But the by-product is that they allow Belarus to pay lip-service to international human rights obligations while systematically violating individuals' rights and avoiding their duties and responsibilities under the UN human rights machinery.

Democratic People's Republic of Korea (North Korea)

The Democratic People's Republic of Korea (DPRK) is anything but democratic. Ruled by a dynastic dictatorship, the country has one of the most oppressive regimes in the world. Political opposition barely exists, and where it does surface from underground it is altogether repressed by the state. Nor does civil society exist in any shape or form.

Government policies systematically violate almost every international human rights law. Individuals have no freedoms of speech, movement, assembly or political participation. Nor are they protected from arbitrary detention, torture or ill-treatment. The death penalty is carried out through public executions. The country continually faces severe food shortages owing to governmental agricultural and economic mismanagement as well as 'blatantly discriminatory policies that favour the military and government officials'.[12] Amnesty International reports that '[c]hronic malnutrition continues to plague most people'.[13] North Korea relies on foreign aid and food to feed many of its citizens.[14] Access to healthcare is limited, there is a shortage of adequate housing, and many children do not receive a full education.

The government retains its grip on the country through military rule, a cult of personality[15] and using forced labour camps to imprison anyone deemed a 'threat' to the state. Tens or maybe even hundreds of thousands of individuals, including the entire families of anyone accused, are detained for life in those camps:

'Information provided by escapees who have fled North Korea in the past two years has again shown that persons accused of political offenses are usually sent to brutal forced labor camps, known as *gwalliso*, operated by the National Security Agency.

The government practices collective punishment, sending to forced labor camps not only the offender but also their parents, spouse, children, and even grandchildren. These camps are notorious for horrific living conditions and abuse, including severe food shortages, little or no medical care, lack of proper housing and clothes, continuous mistreatment and torture by guards, and executions. Forced labor at the *gwalliso* often involves difficult physical labor such as mining, logging, and agricultural work, all done with rudimentary tools in dangerous and harsh conditions. Death rates in these camps are reportedly extremely high. North Korea has never acknowledged that these camps exist, but United States and South Korean officials estimate some 200,000 people may be imprisoned in them.'[16]

Detainees face ongoing violations of their fundamental rights. Torture and ill-treatment are widespread. Forced labour, lack of adequate food and denial of healthcare mean that many deaths occur within the camps.[17] Survivors gave testimony in South Korea to a UN Commission of Enquiry in August 2013.[18] 'Harrowing accounts … related how guards chopped off a man's finger, forced inmates to eat frogs and a mother to kill her own baby.'[19]

But information about DPRK comes out only in dribs and drabs, largely from the few individuals who manage to escape to South Korea or China. Few foreigners are allowed into the country, and those who do arrive are closely monitored. The government blocks its citizens from accessing foreign radio, television or internet sites, or even from making or receiving phone calls to people other than North Koreans.[20] This makes it extremely difficult to get information in or out of the country. The UN

High Commissioner for Human Rights acknowledged that 'the extreme difficulty of gaining access makes DPRK singularly problematic'.

Yet DPRK is party to four international human rights treaties. Since the turn of the millennium, the country has submitted periodic reports to the committees on the rights of the child; elimination of all forms of discrimination against women; economic, social and cultural rights; and civil and political rights. The concluding observations from all four bodies emphasise the severe and systematic nature of violations across DPRK.[21] It appears as though the country's ratification of those treaties is a method of paying lip service to human rights that they have no intention of implementing, promoting or protecting.

Interestingly, DPRK does engage with some parts of the UN human rights machinery. The Special Rapporteur specifically mandated to focus on that country has been able to enter the territory, undertake some fact-finding, write reports and deliver recommendations. Of course, little has changed as a result of the mandate-holder's work. The question, then, is why does DPRK bother to submit periodic reports to the human rights bodies or allow the Special Rapporteur to fulfil some duties?

The answer lies with politics and money. In much the same way as DPRK's government dips in and out of talks on its nuclear weapons, it does the same about human rights. And the reason for engaging at all with those issues is because the country relies on aid from the international community. In order to receive that aid—whether for food, assistance with natural disasters or any other humanitarian necessity—DPRK must engage with the international community. The problem is that its engagement is a sham.

How does the government get away with this? Not only the flagrant and thorough oppression of its own people, but also the failure to deliver on its international obligations? Once again, power-politics is crucial for understanding the protection that DPRK receives in the international arena.

North Korea received significant economic, military and political support from the Soviet Union and relied upon it as the state's biggest trading power.[22] It also has a powerful ally in China. The two so-called 'communist' states fought side-by-side in the Korean War[23] and that military alliance[24] has endured. Since the dissolution of the Soviet Union in 1991, DPRK has increasingly looked to China for protection, aid and support. The relationship has not always been smooth. Indeed, China supported the sanctions against DPRK,[25] which were passed by the Security Council in response to that country's nuclear weapons tests.[26] But then again, it seems unclear whether China adheres to those sanctions.[27]

There are other countries that ignore those sanctions and defend DPRK at UN bodies, and these include Cuba, Iran, Venezuela and at times some OIC members and some former Soviet states. Undoubtedly, the long-standing tensions between the US and DPRK contribute to continued political support for DPRK from former socialist and/or anti-American countries. The old adage 'my enemy's enemy is my friend' explains very well those alliances.

There has, however, been a chink the armour. In 2012, for the first time, the Human Rights Council[28] and the Third Committee of the General Assembly[29] unanimously passed resolutions expressing serious concerns about grave and systematic human rights violations in DPRK.[30] It may not be much, indeed it is like trying to bail out the *Titanic* with a teaspoon, but there might be some hope that the international community is shifting towards placing human rights above power-politics when it comes to the DPRK.

Equatorial Guinea

Equatorial Guinea is a former colony of Spain which achieved independence in 1968. The country's first ruler, Francisco Macias Nguema, allegedly perpetrated a genocide against the Bubi ethnic minority and repressed any political dissent. He was overthrown in a coup in 1979 and the country has since been ruled by President Teodoro Obiang Nguema Mbasogo. Transparency International places Equatorial Guinea's autocratic regime 'in the top 12 of its list of most corrupt states'.[31] A main reason for that corruption is that Equatorial Guinea is one of sub-Sahara Africa's biggest oil producers. The ruling Democratic Party of Equatorial Guinea—another ironic name—keeps a tight grip on power in order to control the oil riches.

In 2010, Equatorial Guinea built a luxury hotel complex and shopping centre in the Comandachina neighbourhood. Dozens of families were forcibly evicted from their homes in order to make way for this new development. Many more lost their homes in a nearby neighbourhood—Bata—so that the government could build a promenade on the beach. A marina and promenade development in Kogo resulted in half of the town being destroyed. Amnesty reports that '60 families were left homeless. Most of them were elderly people who owned their houses in which they had lived for decades.' The government did not consult with any of the residents prior to the evictions, and residents 'were not given monetary compensation or other assistance'. As a result, most of the evictees 'remained homeless'.[32]

Human Rights Watch estimates that Equatorial Guinea's per capita gross domestic product is approximately $30,000.[33] That is amongst the highest in the world. But corruption is rife. The World Bank reports that over 76 per cent of people in Equatorial Guinea live at or below the poverty line.[34] The vast oil riches fund the lifestyle of the ruling elite, while more than three quarters of the country are denied access to adequate housing, food, water, clothing, education or healthcare.

Meanwhile, in 2004 a US Senate investigation found that:

'[President Obiang] used the country's oil wealth to finance numerous personal transactions, including spending $3.8 million to buy two mansions in a suburb of Washington, DC.... Obiang's eldest son, Teodorin, bought a $35 million property in California in 2006. In 2004, he spent about $8.45 million for mansions and luxury cars in South Africa. His only known income was a $4,000 monthly salary as a government minister. His $43.45 million in spending on his lavish lifestyle from 2004 to 2006 was more than the $43 million the government spent on education in 2005.'[35]

The citizens of Equatorial Guinea have no means by which to hold their government to account for these corrupt activities. Political opposition is almost non-existent, and when it does occur it is repressed by the state through arbitrary arrests and detention and violence.

But it is not only subsistence rights or those of political participation that the government violates. The regime routinely abuses the rights to freedom of expression, assembly and association. Foreign journalists are harassed and detained in order to control their reporting on the country. Arbitrary arrests and detainment are common, and 'fair trial standards are disregarded'.[36] Ill-treatment and torture occur within prisons.[37] The government intimidates and harasses human rights defenders and limits the activities of foreign NGOs, meaning that there is very restricted civil society within the country.[38]

Special Procedures mandate-holders have attempted to shine some spotlight on abuses in Equatorial Guinea. The subject matters of those mandates include arbitrary detention;[39] torture and other ill-treatment;[40]

the use of mercenaries;[41] enforced and involuntary disappearances;[42] freedom of expression;[43] and independence of judges.[44] Attempts to enter the territory and undertake fact-finding missions sometimes have been ignored, and recommendations have fallen upon deaf ears. Similarly, the committees on the rights of the child, elimination of discrimination against women, economic social and cultural rights, and civil and political rights have also had their work ignored or obstructed. Equatorial Guinea has failed to submit its periodic reports on time or even at all. Ratification of human rights treaties seems redundant when examining the regime's actions against its own people and its lack of action within UN human rights bodies.

Equatorial Guinea receives significant support from its regional neighbours within the African Group. In 2012, President Obiang chaired the African Union. In order to understand how that could have occurred, we must think about how the African Group members protect and support one another. The shared history of colonialism has led to what Weiss deems a 'misplaced Southern solidarity' between developing nations. He insists that those countries protect each other through regional and political alliances.[45] Nowhere is this more obvious than within Africa. It is not just Equatorial Guinea that benefits from such support. Mugabe's regime in Zimbabwe has been deemed a 'contemporary example of misplaced Southern solidarity'.[46] Mugabe's regime commits gross and systemic human rights violations, including widespread arbitrary detention and torture of prisoners; curtailment of the right to freedom of association and assembly; attacks on human rights defenders; and violations of rights to food, sanitation, adequate housing and safe drinking water.[47] However, despite US and EU targeted sanctions and political pressure, Mugabe's retention of power reflects the strength of support from regional and political allies within the UN and particularly the African Union. Mugabe, in turn, has constantly attacked the West, particularly the UK, for imperialism and hegemony. Support for Mugabe exists 'presumably to maintain solidarity with one of the storied examples of anti-colonial and anti-imperial struggle'.[48] Those discourses prevent European states, as former colonial powers, from taking a strong and clear stance against human rights abuses within African states (with the exception of South Africa, as already discussed).

It seems that human rights abuses are not a factor that the African Union affords much weight when deciding which member states to support or whom to elect as its chair. In that capacity, President Obiang travelled across the world and created or improved links with governments of other countries. He represented the AU at the 2012 G-20 Summit in France. The US has strong links with Equatorial Guinea and is its main trading partner. US companies dominate the country's oil sector.[49] Those ties have meant that some US diplomats have defended President Obiang in press interviews and leaked cables.[50] Protection from strong allies combined with oil reserves and a refusal to engage with human rights bodies and organisations mean that Equatorial Guinea's abuses largely have flown under the radar.

The Gambia

'On 23 July 2005 a group of 50 foreign nationals ... was intercepted by Gambian security forces in the waters of Gambia on suspicion of planning to overthrow the government during Gambia's Independence Day celebrations. According to a Commonwealth Human Rights Initiative (CHRI) Report, the men were taken to the Naval Headquarters in Banjul, divided into groups of eight and taken off into a field near Siffoe in Gambia's Western Division. There they were reportedly killed by members of security forces with machetes, axes and other weapons. The bodies were indiscriminately dumped at various locations, among them the village of Brufu, near Siffoe.'[51]

Amnesty International reports that, despite international awareness of the extrajudicial killings and pressure to prosecute the perpetrators, no one has been brought to justice for those state-sanctioned murders.[52] But that is only one of countless grave atrocities committed within the Gambia. Unlike those killings, most of the very many abuses in the Gambia fly wholly under the radar of the international community.

In October 2013, the Gambia formally left the Commonwealth of Nations. It was the first country to do so since Robert Mugabe unilaterally withdrew Zimbabwe from the Commonwealth in 2003. President Yahya Jammeh, who seized power in the Gambia in 1994, called the Commonwealth a 'neo-colonial institution'. It is interesting that the country pulled out of the Commonwealth after the UK Foreign Office for the first time included the Gambia as a human rights offender in its annual Human Rights and Democracy report.[53] Around the same time, the European Union cut funding and development aid to the Gambia by 20 per cent following 'concerns' about human rights.[54] It is no coincidence that the Gambia withdrew from the Commonwealth and increased its anti-West rhetoric around the time that its human rights record was being criticised.

President Yahya Jammeh has ruled the Gambia with an iron fist since 1994. He is responsible for gross and systemic human rights violations across this tiny West African nation, whose population numbers less than 2 million people. Torture, enforced disappearances, repression of dissent, extra-judicial killings, and systematic violations of economic and social rights are rife across the country.[55] Yet even within a climate like that, stories emerge of abuses that shock even the subjugated and oppressed citizens of the Gambia.

In 2009, a 'witch-hunting campaign' was conducted around the country. So-called 'witch doctors' kidnapped up to 1,000 people and took them to 'secret detention centres' where they were 'forced to drink hallucinogenic concoctions'.

'Eyewitnesses and victims told Amnesty International that the "witch doctors", who they say are from neighbouring Guinea, are accompanied by police, army and national intelligence agents. They are also accompanied by 'green boys'— Gambian President Yahya Jammeh's personal protection guards.

According to information provided to Amnesty International by victims and their relatives, "witch doctors" have been visiting villages with armed security and taking villagers they accuse of being "witches"—many of them elderly—by force, sometimes at gunpoint. They are then taken to secret detention centres.

At the secret detentions centres, where some have been held for up to five days, they are forced to drink unknown substances that cause them to hallucinate and behave erratically. Many are then forced to confess to being a witch. In some cases, they are also severely beaten, almost to the point of death.

The liquid they are forced to drink has led many to have serious kidney problems [including death].'[56]

The *New York Times* reported that President Jammeh had become concerned about witches. The campaign led to many people fleeing their homes to live in the bush in order to avoid the witch hunts.[57] And this is not the only campaign of human rights violations that Jammeh has carried out on the basis of one of his ideas or whims.

The Gambia is party to a number of international human rights treaties: the International Covenant on Civil and Political Rights and its first Optional Protocol; the International Covenant on Economic, Social and Cultural Rights; the Convention on the Elimination of All Forms of Discrimination against Women; the Convention on the Elimination of All Forms of Racial Discrimination; the Convention Against Torture and Other Forms of Cruel, Inhuman or Degrading Treatment or Punishment; and the Convention on the Rights of the Child. However, the Gambia had ratified all of the international treaties prior to President Jammeh seizing power in 1994.[58] While those treaties are still binding upon that state, Jammeh has consistently ignored the human rights obligations contained within those instruments.

The Gambia has ratified regional human rights instruments prior to and during President Jammeh's rule.[59] While he has distanced himself from the international sphere, President Jammeh is a vocal and active leader within the African Union. To retain that position, the Gambia has to cooperate with its regional mechanisms by, for example, ratifying African treaties on human rights. It is all well and good that the Gambia has ratified regional human rights treaties, but the regime altogether fails to uphold the obligations stemming from those instruments.

The Gambia's prominent position within the African Group affords it significant protection on the international level. Relying heavily on post-colonial and anti-West rhetoric, President Jammeh has aligned himself with other leaders such as Zimbabwe's Robert Mugabe. Those two men have long histories of using post-colonial statements to blame the West for problems within their countries whilst simultaneously systematically violating their citizens' human rights. Of course, the impact of colonialism and damage caused by former colonial powers cannot be underestimated. But that does not mean that autocratic rulers ought to be allowed to hide behind post-colonial discourses as a way of deflecting attention away from state-sponsored human rights abuses.

Post-colonial discourses are also used by President Jammeh as a method for creating cross-regional ties within the Non-Aligned Movement and Like-Minded Group. Political alliances with countries such as Cuba, China, Iran and Venezuela—that old adage 'my enemy's enemy is my friend'—provide a shield against UN scrutiny of the Gambia's human rights record.

Another key reason why the Gambia flies under the radar is the lack of information available about violations within that state. Repression of dissent, of civil society actors, and of journalists and the media means that information about human rights abuses is not easily obtained. The regime refuses to cooperate or engage with almost all international monitoring bodies, investigations and human rights institutions that attempt to fact-find within that state.

Yet the Gambia is not a country with closed borders. Indeed, the opposite is true. The country has seen booming tourism under Jammeh's rule. 'Tens of thousands of winter sun-seekers flock to mainland Africa's smallest country each year, drawn by its stunning beaches, bird-watching and haunting kora music.'[60] The package holiday destination is the most popular in that region, and tourism contributes significantly to the country's GDP and employment. However, tourists and tourism boards claim to be oblivious to the dictatorial rule within the Gambia and the abuses occurring behind the scenes within their holiday paradise.

Qatar

Qatar has been ruled by the al-Thani family for nearly 150 years. Although it has financially supported the Arab Spring uprisings—leading to greater democratisation in other countries—Qatar remains an authoritarian state.[61] Although it promised to hold parliamentary elections, in June 2013 Emir Sheik Hamad bin Khalifa al-Thani announced his abdication and handed over power to his son Sheikh Tamim bin Hamad Al Thani. Sheikh Hamad issued a decree extending the term of the advisory Shura council, in effect indefinitely postponing elections.[62]

Qatar is one of the richest of the Gulf States with vast oil and gas fields. Revenue from Qatar's natural resources funds an all-encompassing welfare state. Subsistence rights—to housing, food, water and healthcare—as well as to other services such as education are widely implemented and realised by Qatar's citizens. But Qatar's autocratic regime cannot be viewed as a defender of human rights. Serious abuses are perpetrated against women, ethnic minorities, foreign nationals and migrants. Torture and ill-treatment are committed by government officials, and the death penalty is still used. Political dissent is cracked down on, with severe curbs on the freedom of expression.

Qatari poet Muhammad ibn al-Dheeb al-Ajami, a student at Cairo University, received a life sentence for writing and performing a poem that the regime said insulted the Emir. The poem, 'Tunisian Jasmine', was written as a response to the Arab Spring uprisings. While the poem centred on Tunisia, it implied that all Arab Spring uprisings ought to be supported. There was no explicit mention of Qatar or its regime within the poem. Despite this, 'Qatari officials charged Ajami with "insulting" the Gulf nation's ruler, Sheikh Hamad bin Khalifa Al Thani, and "inciting to overthrow the ruling system". The latter charge could have brought a death sentence.'[63] Mr Al-Ajami had the life sentence reduced to 15 years on appeal. Yet any sentence at all violates his freedom of expression and demonstrates Qatar's crackdown on any form of political dissent.

Qatar is by no means the most repressive regime in the Gulf region or in the Middle East. Despite its political system, NGOs are able to gain access to the country and some information is disseminated about human rights abuses within that state. Civil society plays a role, albeit a limited one, within Qatar. Despite that, the country remains a grave abuser of human rights.

Migrant workers account for approximately 94 per cent of Qatar's population of nearly 2 million people,[64] which is the highest proportion in the world.[65] Saudi Arabia, another oil-rich state, has a 30 per cent migrant population, while one quarter of Bahrain's population are non-nationals.[66] With such large numbers of migrant workers, Qatar might be expected to have laws to protect those individuals. Although some laws are in place,[67] 'inadequate monitoring and reporting mechanisms' mean that they are altogether ignored.[68] Human Rights Watch produced a report that uncovered grave failings on the part of the Qatari regime and legal system in terms of protecting migrant workers from gross and systemic violations.[69]

Migrant workers live in often cramped, unsanitary and inhumane conditions, without access to sanitation or water. Employers determine when they are allowed to leave the country, and severe penalties are imposed on any worker who absconds or on any Qatari found sheltering a worker who has absconded. Despite being a member of the International Labour Organisation, Qatar has failed to uphold its legal obligations regarding working conditions or rights of migrant workers. Employers routinely flout health and safety laws, including exposing workers to toxic chemicals.

None of this has stopped FIFA—the football world governing body—from awarding the 2022 World Cup to Qatar. The 2022 World Cup will be built using a migrant workforce, and no provisions have been put in place to prevent abuses from continuing throughout construction of football stadia, hotels or transport infrastructure. FIFA, it seems, have similar scruples and ethics as the IOC.

One year after Qatar was awarded the World Cup, the media—rather belatedly—started reporting on human rights abuses relating to migrant workers who are building the infrastructure for the football tournament. The *Guardian* newspaper, amongst others, has investigated the way Qatar treats the workers brought in to build stadia for the 2022 World Cup. Little mention has been made of the wider problems of abuses of migrant workers' rights. The UN independent expert on human rights of migrants scheduled a visit to that country for November 2013. But all of this has come too late in many respects. When Qatar bid to host the football tournament, information about such violations was available through Amnesty International, Human Rights Watch and other NGOs. Yet no one paid any heed. Sport comes *über alles*.

Qatar has not ratified the international human rights conventions on Civil and Political Rights or on Economic, Social and Cultural Rights. It does not even pay lip service to those rights. While it is party to treaties on the rights of the child, the rights of persons with disabilities, and prohibiting torture, the committees that monitor those treaties have expressed serious concerns about abuses within Qatar.[70] Special Procedures mandate-holders have been particularly concerned about human trafficking, torture and inhumane treatment, and the rights of migrants.[71] But most of these words have been ignored. Qatar largely dismissed the recommendations, unsurprisingly. Other countries have failed to ensure that there is sufficient discussion of Qatar's abuses, let alone pressure placed on it to implement fundamental human rights obligations.

Of course, oil and wealth are key to Qatar's protection from scrutiny of its human rights record. The country has close ties with the Muslim Brotherhood, leading to significant protection from many OIC states. It is a prominent player in the Arab world, with close links to the US. It has become a global political and financial power and is the world's largest exporter of liquefied natural gas. Little wonder, then, that Qatar can continue to abuse the rights of its own citizens and of non-nationals who work within its territory. Once again, power-politics, money and natural resources take priority over human rights.

Saudi Arabia

Saudi Arabia is ruled by an hereditary monarchy. The modern state— the Kingdom of Saudi Arabia—was founded in 1932 by Abdulaziz bin Abd al-Rahman Al Saud. The country's 'Basic Law of Governance'[72] decrees that the dynasty is to be passed down to the male heirs of the country's founder.[73] The government is appointed by the king. Local elections are held every six years—the first of which took place in 2005. There are no political parties in Saudi Arabia, and political dissent is cracked down upon by the government. Protesters are beaten, tortured and detained for days or weeks without charge.[74]

A broad range of human rights abuses occur in Saudi Arabia. Torture and ill-treatment are 'common, widespread and generally committed with impunity'.[75] The death penalty and corporal punishment are routinely ordered by the courts in criminal cases. Access to justice, fair trials and due process are denied, with many convictions based on confessions extracted under duress. Discrimination is rife against the Shia minority. Migrant workers face abuse, and have little government protection. Human rights defenders are harassed, detained and prevented from undertaking their work. Freedoms of expression, assembly and belief are violated by the law and by government agents.[76]

Unlike Qatar, Saudi Arabia does not provide free welfare services for its citizens. Despite Saudi Arabia's vast wealth—the country is a leading producer of oil and natural gas and holds about 17 per cent of the world's oil reserves—up to 40 per cent of its citizens live on or below the poverty line.[77] Their rights to adequate housing, food, water, healthcare and a livelihood are neither protected nor implemented by the Saudi government.[78]

On 10 October 2011, Firas Buqna and Hussam Al-Darwish uploaded onto YouTube a ten-minute documentary about poverty in Riyadh, the capital of Saudi Arabia. The film showed barefoot children in ragged clothing. Mr Buqna and Mr Al-Darwish interviewed local residents who could not afford to feed, clothe or house their families. The two young bloggers were swiftly arrested and imprisoned.[79] The government, you see, does not like the spotlight shone on the country's failings. But the online community took up the call to arms. Over a million people viewed the documentary footage. Bloggers, often anonymously, wrote about the homelessness, poverty and crises within other parts of Saudi Arabia, even places located next to oil wells. Despite keeping out international NGOs and severely restricting national civil society, information does leak out via the internet. Comparisons between poverty in Saudi Arabia and Somalia are not far off the mark, although Saudi Arabia does, of course, have ample funds and infrastructure to eradicate poverty within its territory.

Saudi Arabia also has an appalling record of discriminating against women. Using economic, political, education and health criteria, the World Economic Forum's Gender Gap Index in 2012 ranked Saudi Arabia 131 out of 135 countries. The country's governorship system effectively means that women are unable to participate in society. Women have traditionally been bound by guardianship rules in terms of their movements. Until the last couple of years, those rules were very strict. A woman required a male guardian to grant her permission before she could get married, travel, undertake paid employment or enrol in higher education. Women were prohibited from driving and from riding bicycles.

Some steps have been taken towards reforming the system in law, even if not in practice. The king has announced that women will have the right to vote in the 2015 local elections, and women have seen an expansion of employment opportunities, even if strict gender segregation is still enforced within the workplace. The Foreign and Commonwealth Office reported in 2012 that new rules on women having freedom of movement within the Gulf region were counterbalanced by a Saudi e-border system that resulted in guardians 'automatically being text-messaged whenever female dependants left the country'.[80] Saudi female athletes took part in the 2012 Olympics for the first time. The government then removed a ban on women working at supermarket checkouts, in lingerie stores and on cosmetics counters. There was even an announcement that women could ride bikes—albeit only for recreational purposes,[81] fully clothed so as not to appear immodest, accompanied by a male guardian, and in restricted areas.[82]

Of course, paying lip service to taking steps towards implementing women's rights is not the same as actually ensuring those rights are protected in practice. For all of Saudi Arabia's murmurings about moving in the right direction, their actions show that nothing much has changed:

In 2013 two Saudi women were imprisoned for ten months[83] for attempting to provide food to a woman and her three children who had been abused and locked into their home. Nathalie Morin sought to escape her spouse and flee with her children to her native Canada. She alleged that they had all been abused by her husband. Under Saudi law, however, children belong to their father.[84]

Wajeha Al-Huwaider and Fawzia Al-Oyouni are prominent human rights activists in Saudi Arabia.[85] Ms Morin contacted Ms Huwaider and

Ms Oyouni seeking their assistance. They were arrested when attempting to give food to Ms Morin and her children. The husband claimed that the two activists intended to assist his wife and children in escaping the country.

'The two activists were found not guilty of kidnapping, but the judge convicted them of "Takhbib"—inciting a woman against her husband. Apparently helping an abused wife feed her children is a crime in Saudi Arabia. Can't have that in a country where women need their male "guardian's" okay to travel, work, study or even undergo surgery, where fathers have automatic legal custody of children and the Koran, interpreted at the whim of judges, is the only legal code.'[86]

But in a country where due process rights are not often available, and where women's rights are of the lowest priority, it is little wonder that this case was prosecuted and those sentences imposed.

Perhaps somewhat perversely, Saudi Arabia is party to the Convention on the Elimination of All Forms of Discrimination against Women. The Committee that monitors states' compliance with their obligations arising under that treaty has expressed grave concerns about women's rights within Saudi Arabia.[87] Similar concerns have been raised by the Committee on the Rights of the Child, the Committee on the Elimination of All Forms of Racial Discrimination and the Committee Against Torture.[88] UN experts have spoken out against summary executions[89] by firing squad[90] and beheading.[91] Special Procedures mandate-holders have also made recommendations on torture and ill-treatment, racism and xenophobia, arbitrary detention, and freedoms of belief and of expression within Saudi Arabia.[92]

But of course most of this work falls on deaf ears when it comes to countries placing political or other pressures on Saudi Arabia to comply with international human rights laws. The country is protected by its Gulf neighbours, and by its political allies within the Organisation of Islamic Cooperation. The country's oil and wealth, its ties with the US, and its position amongst Muslim states mean that other countries pay scant attention to its abuses and care even less about holding the Saudi regime to account for its violations against its own citizens.

Turkmenistan

Turkmenistan is a Central Asian country which gained independence in 1991 following the dissolution of the Soviet Union. Its population of approximately 5 million people is ruled by President Berdymukhamedov, who took control of the country in 2006 after the death of Saparmurat Niyazov. The UN has accused his regime of systematically repressing its citizens, and grave concerns have been raised about basic human rights within Turkmenistan.

Information about Turkmenistan is difficult to obtain. Freedom of the press and freedom of expression are curtailed. Access to international media is blocked, and internet access tightly controlled by the state. Freedom House ranked Turkmenistan 196 out of 197 countries in the latest Freedom of the Press Index. Foreign NGOs and UN human rights experts face great difficulties in undertaking fact-finding or human rights work within Turkmenistan. Civil society is non-existent. Amnesty International insists that Turkmenistan is 'closed to international scrutiny' and 'that no independent international organizations have yet been granted access to carry out monitoring'.[93]

Although the country has the world's fourth-largest known natural gas reserves, the economy is underdeveloped. Recently, the country has increased its gas exports to China and started to export oil.[94] However, most people live in poverty: 30 per cent live below the poverty line, and up to 60 per cent of people are unemployed.[95] Russia remains a major player in the Turkmen economy. Corruption is rife. Transparency International ranked Turkmenistan 170 out of 176 countries in terms of corruption.[96] Money from exporting the country's vast natural resources is channelled into luxurious developments for the ruling elite.[97]

Turkmenistan does not altogether opt out of the international human rights system. It is party to many human rights treaties, including the Convention on the Elimination of All Forms of Discrimination against Women, the Convention on the Rights of the Child, the International Covenant on Civil and Political Rights, the International Covenant on Economic, Social and Cultural Rights, the Convention Against Torture, and the Convention on the Elimination of All Forms of Racial Discrimination. It has national laws that are aimed at protecting human rights. But there is 'a broad gap between the government's rhetoric on democracy and human rights and its practice'.[98]

All of the UN treaty-based committees have expressed grave concerns about the implementation, promotion and protection of rights in Turkmenistan.[99] Those concerns are echoed by other parts of the UN human rights machinery.

Ivan Šimonović, UN Assistant Secretary-General for Human Rights, who visited Turkmenistan in May 2013,[100] concluded that 'there is no independence of the judiciary' and raised issues of corruption and lack of due process rights.[101] He also discussed women's rights, 'human trafficking, juvenile justice, health, HIV/AIDS, education, human rights and counter-terrorism, enforced disappearances, as well as the situation of vulnerable groups such as persons with disabilities, refugees, asylum-seekers and stateless persons'.[102] Mr Šimonovic noted that Turkmenistan had not complied with the requests of Special Procedures mandate-holders who have attempted to visit the country.

With international bodies and organisations unable to gain access to Turkmen detention facilities, it is difficult to know the extent of torture and ill-treatment within those places. The Foreign and Commonwealth Office reports:

'Security officials are believed to use excessive force, including beating, when intent on extracting confessions from detainees .... Prison conditions are unsanitary, overcrowded and unsafe. Some facilities are located in areas of extremely harsh climate conditions, with excessive heat in the summer and freezing temperatures in the winter. The nutritional value of prison food is poor.'[103]

Amnesty International has also uncovered some facts about torture and ill-treatment in Turkmenistan:

'Amnesty International has received reports that people suspected of committing criminal offences are routinely subjected to torture and other ill-treatment in Turkmenistan. Alleged perpetrators include police, officers of the Ministry of National Security and prison personnel. Torture and other ill-treatment are used to extract confessions and other incriminating information, and to intimidate detainees. Methods of torture and other ill-treatment reported to Amnesty International include electric shocks, asphyxiation applied with a plastic bag or gas mask to which the air supply is cut, rape, forcible administration of psychotropic drugs, beating with batons, truncheons, or plastic bottles filled with water, punching, kicking, food and drink deprivation, and exposure to extreme cold combined with the removal of clothes.

Impunity for torture and other ill-treatment is the norm in Turkmenistan, with complaints by victims rarely being pursued. To Amnesty International's knowledge, none of the allegations of torture and other ill-treatment in connection with the alleged assassination attempt on the then President Saparmurad Niyazov in November in 2002 have to date been investigated. There are credible allegations that many people were tortured or ill-treated at that time, including human rights defenders, journalists, members of certain religious minorities, conscientious objectors and those labelled as "traitors to the motherland".'[104]

Turkmenistan, like the DPRK and other repressive regimes, is a closed society with a regime that curtails the flow of information into and out of the country. The lack of civil society means that most abuses remain hidden from the outside world. With Russia and China both importers of Turkmenistan's oil and gas from Turkmenistan, the country can rely on powerful allies to protect it from significant attention at UN human rights bodies. There is little global political will to address Turkmenistan's violations. Therefore, the autocratic regime can and does continue to behave as it wishes, safe in the knowledge that no one really notices, let alone cares.

Concluding remarks

These excerpts provide a few examples of the ways in which autocratic regimes can avoid attention being focused on their human rights abuses. Clearly, the less accountable a state is to its own people, the easier it is for a regime routinely to violate rights. When NGOs and civil society are banned, access to media curtailed and UN human rights experts ignored, little information can be obtained about ongoing abuses.

The very many hidden abuses undermine the credibility of the international human rights system. What is the purpose of over-scrutinising a country's human rights records while so many horrific abuses occur with impunity elsewhere? In many respects, this chapter exposes how futile and ineffectual the UN system is when it comes to protecting human rights. Politics wins every time, and nothing is sadder than politics dictating that so many countries and so very many individuals simply are not worthy of attention.

Some clear themes run through these situations. Firstly, there is a lack of available information about the human rights abuses. Non-democratic regimes are able to suppress information by restricting freedom of the press, blocking foreign NGOs from working within the country, repressing civil society actors, and blocking the flow of information into and out of the state. Secondly, where a regime represses dissent by detaining and harassing human rights defenders and undermining national human rights institutions, then violations go undocumented and unchallenged. Citizens are unable to change things on the ground. Thirdly, within all of these countries there are natural resources—whether oil, gas or other minerals—that are of use to trading partners or other countries. Those resources enable countries to have a bartering chip in terms of non-scrutiny of their human rights records. Another crucial factor is strong regional and/or political alliances. Strong relations with other states provide shields behind which countries may hide. Finally, all of the countries enjoy the backing of at least one world power, whether for political, ideological, economic or trade reasons. Such backing provides a buffer between a country and the attention of UN bodies.

It is clear that where a country is ruled by an autocratic regime, lip service may be paid to human rights but UN human rights bodies' reports and recommendations will not change anything on the ground. Repressive regimes restrict or ban civil society and media so that they can continue to violate rights with impunity, and with as little attention or reporting as possible. As long as those states have protection from strong allies, they can behave as they wish when it comes to abusing the rights of their citizens. Political blocs and regional groups have little interest in focusing on those states. UN independent experts do some-times attempt to fact-find and share information about those abuses, but their efforts frequently are ignored or rebuffed by the international com-munity acting through the UN political bodies. Alliances are key for protecting these known abusers. Those alliances may be based on ideol-ogy, oil, trade, or any other factors unrelated to human rights. Ultimately, power-politics trumps human rights. The less democratic and open a state with such alliances is, the more likely it is that their abuses will go unreported.

11

THE 'GOOD GUYS'

The previous chapter explored hidden or ignored abuses in countries where information is difficult to access or where there are geopolitical, economic or other reasons for a lack of scrutiny. This chapter looks at the flipside to that coin: abuses that are all but ignored within 'good guy' states. It also explores what happens when those countries face scrutiny from the international community. Certain states are at the fore of international human rights. They are placed on a pedestal and held out as bastions of human rights, and they take the lead in international human rights bodies. This chapter will examine two of those countries in relation to very specific rights, although any number of other states could have been chosen as case studies.

Canada Indigenous rights and shifting the spotlight

Canada is a leader and well-respected member of the international human rights system. It is at the forefront of efforts to protect and promote human rights across the world. Human Rights Watch describes Canada as 'enjoy[ing] a global reputation as a defender of human rights at home and abroad that reflects a solid record on core civil and political rights protections, and a generally progressive approach to economic and social rights'.[1] Yet its record is poor on the rights of indigenous or aboriginal populations living within Canada.

As has already been discussed, human rights abuses of indigenous populations in countries such as Australia, the US, New Zealand were not addressed by the General Assembly at the time when South Africa's apartheid regime was closely being scrutinised. Canada is another country whose founding history included the repression and subjugation of indigenous populations. Widespread discrimination has been followed by recent attempts to protect First Nations communities and to repair some of the damage done by the original settlers and colonisers. However, those efforts have been inadequate to remedy and prevent further violations. Indeed, it could be argued that the legislation merely supports Canada to claim that it is doing something to protect the rights of aboriginal people and that even those laws do not go far enough to achieve that aim. That approach, essentially, provides a smokescreen behind which the state can continue to violate the rights of First Nations individuals and communities.

In 2013 Human Rights Watch published a report entitled 'Those Who Take Us Away'.[2] That report detailed gross and systemic violations perpetrated by Canadian police against aboriginal females. It set out the physical and sexual abuse suffered by women and girls at the hands of police officers. The report caused great public outcry. Within six months of the report being published, the Enhancing Royal Canadian Mounted Police Accountability Act established a new Civilian Review and Complaints Commission. While Canada attempted to address the issues, that Act has done little to change the facts on the ground, however.[3] Abuse and violence persist,[4] and those are not the only systematic violations of the rights of indigenous populations in Canada.

During Canada's second Universal Periodic Review session in 2013, it rejected 40 recommendations made by other states, many of which related to the rights of indigenous people.[5] Canada's stance was that it refused to accept recommendations from known grave abusers such as Belarus, Cuba, Iran, North Korea and Russia.[6] The National Post reported that a government official said:

'While we look forward to talking about our human rights record, we also take the UN's review with a grain of salt …. Some of the countries "reviewing" Canada, like Iran, have abhorrent human rights records. This is a country that hangs guys and stones women.'[7]

That position might be understandable, but it essentially is throwing the baby out with the bathwater. By focusing on the countries rather than the recommendations, Canada was avoiding the substantive issues relating to the human rights of indigenous populations despite the clear evidence of grave abuses. Indeed, organisations like Amnesty International were highly critical of Canada's response to the review.[8] In particular, it highlighted Canada's

'wholesale rejection of all recommendations that Canada adopt nationwide plans or strategies to tackle serious and complicated human rights challenges such as violence against Indigenous women, poverty, racism, homelessness, food security and implementing the UN's Declaration on the Rights of Indigenous Peoples.'[9]

Canada has systemic issues in terms of the human rights of indigenous populations. Those issues must be addressed. Amnesty International, Human Rights Watch and other NGOs have highlighted the plight of aboriginal people in Canada. That information has also been shared by UN bodies. The Committee on the Elimination of Racial Discrimination[10] has called upon Canada to enact federal legislation to ensure that effective and consistent anti-racism laws and policies are implemented in practice.[11] It has called for an end to racial profiling and the socio-economic marginalisation of aboriginal people.[12] The Committee had serious concerns about access to water, education, housing, healthcare and welfare services for aboriginal communities.[13] It also emphasised land rights and environmental issues as being of ongoing concern.[14] Similar concerns have been raised by other UN bodies[15] and independent experts over recent years.[16] Yet Canada has failed to address those concerns. It has not enacted sufficient legislation to curb the human rights abuses. It has not implemented its obligations under core human rights treaties and declarations.

Canada's stance is that it generally complies well with its human rights obligations. As with almost all countries, when Canada is criticised, it becomes defensive and seeks to justify its position. That response also occurred after the UN Special Rapporteur on the right to food, Olivier de Schutter, visited and reported on the country in 2012. Rather than responding to the criticisms and concerns that he raised, the Canadian government lashed out against de Schutter. Jason Kenny, the Canadian Immigration Minister, said

'Canada is one of the wealthiest and most democratic countries in the world. We believe that the UN should focus on development … in countries where people are starving. We think it's simply a waste of resources to come to Canada to give political lectures.'

That stance is similar to Canada's reaction to criticisms about human rights violations of aboriginal people. Rather than striving to improve upon its human rights record, Canada seeks to absolve itself of responsibility by pointing, firstly, to its strong record of compliance with other obligations, and, secondly, to gross and systemic violations occurring within other countries. Attempts to shift the spotlight onto other states rather than acknowledge the need for changes within one's own country is no more acceptable when adopted by Canada than by grave human rights abusers such as those discussed in previous chapters.

Ireland: Women's reproductive rights and cultural relativism

Another country that is placed on a human rights pedestal is Ireland. That state has been and continues to be at the fore in terms of promoting human rights within the international arena. Yet Ireland's record on women's rights is poor. It is far behind its European counterparts and many other states around the world in terms of women's reproductive rights, and has 'one of the most restrictive abortion bans in the world'.[17] Pointing to its constitution, Ireland insists that abortion must comply with national laws. But its current approach is that abortion may only take place if there is a threat to the life of the mother, and even then it is difficult to access owing to doctors being able to refuse a non-emergency abortion on the grounds that s/he is a 'conscientious objector'. Abortions in any other context are criminalised, regardless of the stage of pregnancy, the viability of the foetus, the mother's health, or the circumstances in which the pregnancy occurred (including rape or incest).

There are a number of different international human rights obligations that might be violated by Ireland's restrictive laws on abortion. Article 6 of the International Covenant on Civil and Political Rights protects individuals' right to life. Abortion is criminalised under Irish law in sections 58 and 59 of the Offences against the Person Act, 1861. There is also a constitutional ban on abortion in Article 40.3.3 of the Irish Constitution. The law 'disproportionately favour[s] the interest of the foetus over the rights of pregnant women'.[18] As a result, women in Ireland are forced to procure clandestine abortions or travel abroad for the procedure, and are unlikely to seek post-abortion medical treatment owing to the possible criminal law repercussions.[19] Indeed, this is such a serious issue in terms of the right to life that the Human Rights Committee asks states party to the Convention about measures taken to enable women to prevent unwanted pregnancies and to ensure that they do not have to undergo life-threatening, clandestine abortions.[20] As a result of Ireland's restrictive abortion laws, women's health is endangered and this might violate Article 6 of the ICCPR.

The abortion laws also could violate the prohibition against torture and other cruel, inhuman or degrading treatment as set out in Article 7 of the ICCPR and in the Convention Against Torture and Other Cruel, Inhuman or Degrading Treatment or Punishment. Those provisions include mental as well as physical suffering.[21] In November 2013, Amanda Mellet became the first of three women formally to ask the UN to denounce the prohibition on abortions in cases of fatal foetal abnormalities as 'cruel and inhumane'. Those complaints are at the time of writing going through the formal processes within the UN treaty body system.

Ireland's laws also arguably violate Article 17 which protects individuals from arbitrary interference with right to privacy. The laws could be viewed as arbitrary as they are not based on national consensus, and indeed the failure to hold a constitutional referendum about liberalising the abortion laws contradicts all of the polling and other data that show a majority of Irish voters would support greater access to abortions.[22] In particular, such access would include pregnancies resulting from rape or incest, or where serious foetal abnormalities have been detected, or where the woman is at risk of permanent bodily harm as a result of the pregnancy.

Other international human rights obligations that Ireland's abortions laws might violate include provisions in the Convention on the Elimination of All Forms of Discrimination against Women and the Convention on the Rights of the Child. Ireland justifies its position by pointing to Article 40.3.3 of the Irish Constitution, which sets out:

'The State acknowledges the right to life of the unborn and, with due regard to the equal right to life of the mother, guarantees in its laws to respect, and, as far as practicable, by its laws to defend and vindicate that right.'

That provision equates the life of the woman with that of the 'unborn'. It is unclear if 'unborn' refers to a foetus from the moment of conception, from the point of viability, or includes a severely malformed foetus that cannot be born alive. The Irish Supreme Court has interpreted the law to allow abortion in cases when a woman's life is endangered by the pregnancy. But the circumstances when that might occur are ambiguous, so medical practitioners are unsure about when they may be able to perform a life-saving abortion.

In order to change those laws, a referendum is required. But Ireland has refused to hold such a referendum even in the face of pressure from the UN, the Council of Europe and its own citizens. Ireland also deploys cultural relativist arguments to insist that the vast majority of the public is Catholic and supports the current stance on abortion. Yet it refuses to hold a referendum to find out whether the public do in fact support those laws. Ireland justifies avoiding its international human rights law obligations by pointing to national laws. Regardless of how such a cultural relativist argument is presented, it is no more valid when made by a Global North state than when put forward by a country from the Global South.

Ireland's laws on abortion once again hit the headlines in 2012 when Savita Halappanavar died at University Hospital Galway after the hospital refused to terminate her pregnancy. The failures in early intervention led to septicaemia and further complications, meaning that by the time there was a real and substantial risk to Savita Halappanavar's life it was too late to save her. Allowing a 'life-saving' abortion within such restrictive limitations means that medical practitioners were unable to intervene sufficiently early to save the woman from the real and substantial risk to her life, and by the time the law permitted intervention the woman's life could not be saved. A catch-22 situation if ever there was one.

Salvita Halappanavar's husband insisted to reporters that the hospital staff told them 'Ireland is a Catholic country' in response to their repeated requests for an abortion.[23] Shortly after her death, and in response to a European Court of Human Rights ruling on a separate case,[24] Ireland began debating its legislation on abortion.[25] In July 2013, the Irish government passed a new law on abortion entitled 'Protection of Life During Pregnancy Act'. The Act only allows terminations when there is a 'real and substantial risk to the life, rather than the health, of the mother'[26] or where there is a clear suicide risk.

The new legislation was immediately criticised by Human Rights Watch as doing 'the bare minimum to comply with the European court ruling. It neither reforms nor adds grounds for legal abortion, nor does it address other rights issues women in need of abortion in Ireland face.'[27] Of course, no new grounds for abortion could be included without a constitutional referendum, and the government again refused to carry one out. Human Rights Watch emphasised that 'although the law clarifies how a pregnant woman whose life is at risk can exercise her constitutional right to an abortion, it does not otherwise reform access to abortion in Ireland'.[28] Human Rights Watch's position has been echoed by academics, practitioners and UN independent experts. The government's failure to hold a referendum to change the constitution is a failure to take seriously its human rights obligations.

At its Universal Periodic Review in 2011, Ireland rejected all of the recommendations relating to abortion.[29] Those recommendations were not onerous. Indeed, they simply stressed Ireland's human rights obligations. Norway recommended that Ireland 'bring its abortion laws in line with ICCPR', while Slovenia encouraged Ireland to '[a]llow abortion at least when pregnancy poses a risk to the health of the pregnant woman'. Spain and the Netherlands called for legislation to safeguard women's personal rights and reproductive healthcare and to provide adequate services. Yet Ireland systematically rejected those and other recommendations.

The Women's Human Rights Alliance has also strongly condemned Ireland's stance:

'Ireland's prohibitive regulation of abortion and the discriminatory nature of its application have been consistently subject to criticism by UN treaty bodies. Since 2005 the UN Human Rights Committee, the UN Committee on the Elimination of Discrimination against Women, the UN Committee Against Torture, the Council of Europe Commissioner for Human Rights and the European Court of Human Rights have all criticised Ireland's regulation of abortion as being inadequate to fulfil Ireland's internationally agreed human rights obligations and made specific and reasonable recommendations as to how this situation could be remedied. None of the recommendations of these committees ... has been addressed in any substantive way .... The WHRA is greatly concerned by the rejection of six recommendations of the UPR process on Ireland's restrictive regulation of abortion. These recommendations echo the criticisms made by three UN treaty bodies and the recent call by the UN Special Rapporteur on the Right to Health to decriminalize abortion. Ireland's rejection of these recommendations casts serious doubt on Ireland's commitment to women's reproductive health rights.'[30]

Yet such criticism has been ignored by Ireland. Its approach is based on the premise that the national constitution trumps international human rights law, and those laws cannot be changed without a constitutional referendum—something that Ireland has refused to hold. Not only does Ireland systematically violate women's human rights but it also allows medical practitioners to evade their duties by claiming that a woman's right to life conflicts with their personal religious beliefs. So the position remains that a woman in Ireland cannot access an abortion if she has been raped, or if the pregnancy results from incest, or if she requires medical treatment for anything other than a life-threatening illness. Women's rights to their bodies are superseded by their pregnancy, no matter how early a stage they are in. This European and Global North country has one of the most restrictive policies on abortion in the world. And yet nothing is done to force Ireland's hand or to protect women, such as Savita Halappanavar, from gross and systemic violations of their fundamental rights.

Where Have All the Good Guys Gone?

There are no countries with perfect human rights records, as we well know. All states could and should improve upon their compliance with their obligations. But it is important to understand that even the so-called bastions of human rights deploy the same tactics as other states when seeking to avoid scrutiny of their abuses. Sweden resists criticisms of its register of Roma people within the country, Norway avoids scrutiny of systemic racism, and the Netherlands fails to respond to attention being focused on religious intolerance. These are the so-called 'good guys'. They are held out, and indeed hold themselves out, as role models in human rights. And they are well justified in doing so. Those states, alongside Canada, Ireland and others, lead the efforts to protect and promote human rights. They provide resources (financial and otherwise), peer support, capacity-building, training, expertise and assistance to countries that have fundamental problems with human rights compliance. But what we must not forget is that those same states have problems, and that they too are reluctant for those issues to be scrutinised or to be told that they must effect changes within their own territories. And when attention turns to those states, the same shifting of the spotlight and deployment of cultural relativist or other discourses takes place.

12

IT IS NOT ALL DOOM AND GLOOM

The preceding chapters in this book have shown that the United Nations fails adequately to protect human rights. Political concerns prevail over human rights in many of the gravest human rights situations. But it is not all doom and gloom. The United Nations does very many things to ensure that human rights are implemented across the world. We must not lose sight of what the UN does and what it does well.

The United Nations is a collection of countries. For it to achieve its aims of international peace and security, development and human rights, it is of critical importance that states engage with the UN and cooperate with its mechanisms as well as with one another. When states do not engage and cooperate, they place themselves outside the system of international relations and diplomacy. Given that most of the enforcement mechanisms for international law rely on international relations and diplomacy, it is crucial that countries remain within the system. There will always be some states on the edges of the UN—such as Democratic People's Republic of Korea, Iran, Israel, apartheid-era South Africa or Zimbabwe—but even those countries engage and cooperate to some extent.

The weaknesses that occur in terms of protecting rights—lack of enforcement mechanisms; political objectives of states, regional groups and blocs; requirements for states to consent to human rights treaties and monitoring bodies; inclusivity and engagement—are fundamental components of the UN. And those weaknesses become strengths where it comes to promoting rights. Because of the way international law works, with states creating the laws that govern them, it is absolutely necessary that countries engage with the UN bodies and cooperate with its mechanisms for developing and monitoring those laws. Engagement and cooperation also occur both between states and with one another, as well as between countries and non-state actors and UN staff. This takes the form of dialogue, discussion and negotiation, as well as information-sharing, peer support, capacity-building and technical assistance. Those processes take place formally within bodies, regional groups and political blocs, and informally through diplomatic channels, side events and informal meetings at the UN. State engagement and cooperation in these ways lead to the creation, development and promotion of international law.

To understand the impact of these processes and why state engagement and cooperation are crucial, we must first look at international human rights law treaties. Treaties are a main source of international law. They bind the states that are party to them and develop and enshrine broader provisions or statements found in declarations, resolutions or customary international law. The obvious weakness is that states choose which treaties to ratify and the extent to which they are willing to be bound by all provisions contained therein. If states do not engage with the UN human rights machinery, then they will not write treaties, and if they are not part of that drafting process, then they are less likely to ratify the instruments.

First and foremost, the UN enables human rights to be created and developed in the form of treaties. It provides a forum for countries to meet, discuss and engage with one another. States use UN bodies to facilitate dialogue on human rights. Those debates lead to new treaties, frameworks and normative guidelines on human rights. Discussing human rights gives countries the opportunity to hone and shape their views through the process of engaging with other countries and with UN human rights experts. The power of these processes should not be underestimated. Not only does it lead to new human rights law and greater specificity of what those laws mean, it also allows all countries to become part of the human rights discussion. By engaging with the process, countries are able to put forward their views—based on their own norms, cultures and values—and help to determine the final product.

To understand the central importance of those processes, we must explore the outcomes that arise as a result of human rights discussions. The starting point is to look at the international treaties that states have created at the UN. The arena provided by the organisation allows countries from across the world to work together to codify and enshrine international human rights law.

The process of creating the Universal Declaration of Human Rights (UDHR) began in 1946, with the first draft proposed in September 1948. More than 50 member states were involved in the final drafting. The Declaration was adopted by the General Assembly on 10 December 1948.[1] The UDHR is the grandmother of modern international human rights law. The Declaration sets out the fundamental rights held by *all* individuals. It is a universal text to which all countries agree as part of their UN membership, although as a Declaration it is not binding on states.

Two core human rights treaties codify—enshrine in law—the UDHR. The initial intention was to create one treaty containing laws based on the whole Declaration. Cold War politics not only delayed the process of enshrining those rights but also resulted in two separate instruments that divide human rights into two categories: the International Covenant on Civil and Political Rights[2] and the International Covenant on Economic, Social and Cultural Rights.[3] The former represents Western ideologies during the Cold War; the latter represents ideologies from the former Soviet bloc. At this point it is crucial to remember that states can choose the treaties to which they become a party and, therefore, by which human rights obligations they are bound. The need for two treaties arose because countries from opposing ends of the spectrum could not sufficiently bridge the ideological divide in such a way as to create one, single treaty. Despite those difficulties, the treaties turned the UDHR into binding international law. The two Conventions resulted from negotiations and discussions at UN bodies, including the Commission on Human Rights and the General Assembly. Much of the work occurred in meeting rooms at the UN compounds in Geneva and New York. Those compounds are equipped with rooms of varying sizes, long corridors, cafes and restaurants. Indeed, most of the hard work and negotiating occurs within the wider compound but away from the formal setting of the official bodies.

Since then, other core international human rights treaties have been created at UN bodies: the conventions on the rights of the child; elimination of discrimination against women; the rights of persons with disabilities; elimination of all forms of racial discrimination; the protection of all migrant workers; the protection of all persons from enforced disappearance; and the Convention Against Torture. All of those treaties either develop specific rights or protect vulnerable groups of people. They move beyond the core texts found in the Universal Declaration and the two codifying covenants, providing more concrete and specific obligations.[4]

There are two main types of treaties created at the United Nations: firstly, the treaties on specific human rights obligations; secondly, treaties created to protect particular vulnerable groups of individuals. Both are crucial for expanding upon and enshrining fundamental human rights.

International law prohibits torture as a rule that is binding upon all countries.[5] The prohibition against torture is one from which states cannot derogate even in times of public emergency[6] and which they cannot modify by treaty.[7] The starting point is Article 5 of the UDHR, which says: 'No-one shall be subjected to torture or to cruel, inhuman or degrading treatment or punishment.' That right was enshrined in the International Covenant on Civil and Political Rights[8] and the principal regional human rights treaties.[9] It is a law of such importance that it has been recognised to bind all states regardless of whether they are party to those treaties. One key problem, however, is that the definition of torture was drafted broadly so as to avoid an overly technical or narrow approach. As such, much of what constituted torture was left to courts or individual states to determine. Whilst this was fine in Europe, for example, because the European Court of Human Rights was willing to define torture and break it down into component parts, the same was not true for other regions.

Amnesty International's campaign for the abolition of torture began in 1972. Throughout the 1970s, it reported on torture across the world[10] and in 1973 published a report on torture to help launch its campaign.[11] That same year, Amnesty International convened the first International Convention for the Abolition of Torture to raise awareness of torture and to emphasise the need for further and more specific international laws prohibiting these practices. Although Amnesty International focused mainly on torture in Latin America, it named 60 countries worldwide,[12] noting that torture was being used as a mode of governance, political control or manipulation.[13] As a result, it became clear that there was a need to develop and enshrine specific laws and regulations about torture.

IT IS NOT ALL DOOM AND GLOOM

By 1975, the UN General Assembly had adopted a non-binding Declaration on Torture.[14] Article 1 sets out a more detailed definition of torture than that contained within the UDHR or ICCPR:

1. For the purpose of this Declaration, torture means any act by which severe pain or suffering, whether physical or mental, is intentionally inflicted by or at the instigation of a public official on a person for such purposes as obtaining from him or a third person information or confession, punishing him for an act he has committed or is suspected of having committed, or intimidating him or other persons. It does not include pain or suffering arising only from, inherent in or incidental to, lawful sanctions to the extent consistent with the Standard Minimum Rules for the Treatment of Prisoners.

2. Torture constitutes an aggravated and deliberate form of cruel, inhuman or degrading treatment or punishment.

The Declaration then set out states' obligations to take effective measures to protect individuals from torture[15] and to criminalise and prosecute any acts of torture.[16] Two years later, the General Assembly called upon its members to make—non-binding—unilateral statements of their intent to comply with the Declaration on Torture. These soft law instruments were crucial components of the growing trend towards codifying and enshrining in international law the prohibition against torture.

The UN facilitated discussions between states and involving non-state actors—such as Amnesty International and the International Commission of Jurists[17]—that led to the creation[18] of the Convention Against Torture and Other Cruel, Inhuman or Degrading Treatment or Punishment.[19] The treaty was a product of more than a decade of discussions, fact-finding, information-sharing and negotiating. It goes beyond the fundamental right not to be tortured, and sets out specific obligations that expand upon the underlying norm. One key example is found in Article 3 (1) of the Convention:

'No State Party shall expel, return (*refouler*) or extradite a person to another State where there are substantial grounds for believing that he would be in danger of being subjected to torture.'

The principle of *non-refoulement* is crucial: states cannot claim that their agents did not torture an individual, but must also ensure that they do not send a person to a country where s/he is exposed to the risk of torture. That was the issue that arose when the UK considered deporting Abu Hamza to the US to face charges of terrorism. His defence team relied upon evidence from the UN Special Rapporteur on torture and other cruel, inhuman or degrading treatment or punishment in relation to whether 'supermax' prisons amount to torture. The argument centred around the way supermax prisons are designed to ensure minimal social interaction for inmates in solitary confinement. The *Guardian* reported that:

'The regime is designed to prevent all physical contact between an inmate and others and to minimise social interaction with staff. For those in solitary confinement, contact with staff could be as little as one minute a day.

On the basic regime inmates have only 10 hours a week of recreation time outside their cells. Indoor recreations were little more than cages with a single pull-up bar for exercise. All they can do in the outdoor cages is pace up and down. Even these "privileges" can be terminated. One inmate was denied outdoor exercise for 60 days for trying to feed crumbs to birds.'[20]

Although the European Court of Human Rights eventually dismissed those claims on the basis that the solitary confinement did not amount to torture, the principle of *non-refoulement* was at the heart of the legal decision as to whether Abu Hamza could be extradited. Had those practices been found to have violated international laws on torture or other cruel, inhuman or degrading treatment or punishment, then Abu Hamza could not have been extradited to the US.

Three decades after its creation, the Convention Against Torture has been widely ratified.[21] Although torture still exists, the Convention can be viewed as a success insofar as it has shaped the legal principles that most states have adopted and to which they adhere most of the time. The Convention created a monitoring body[22]—the Committee Against Torture—that has widely been used to promote and protect that right. Such a treaty can only be viewed as positive and the UN's role is promoting the right can only be applauded.

The other category of core human rights treaty is designed to protect vulnerable groups of individuals. While all treaty obligations apply to all individuals, further protection is needed where it comes to members of vulnerable groups. Those treaties often do not create additional human rights obligations but rather provide specific obligations and normative guidelines for states in their treatment of vulnerable groups. Identifying the need for protecting a specific group of people, let alone securing widespread agreement to do so, requires considerable state cooperation and engagement. The UN has been successful in creating treaties such as the Convention on the Elimination of All Forms of Discrimination against Women, and it has garnered considerable support from states despite their differing national, regional and cultural laws regarding gender. However, such treaties require extensive negotiations and discussions before they are brought to the table. There are currently two movements towards protecting two different vulnerable groups, both of which are facing significant opposition from groups of states.

The Convention on the Protection of the Rights of All Migrant Workers and Members of their Families has developed as a result of sustained discussions and negotiations at the UN. It was signed in 1990 and entered into force in 2003, by which time 20 states had ratified the treaty. As of 2013, only 47 states are party to the Convention.[23] Despite ongoing information-sharing, discussions, reports, declarations and resolutions, the Convention is not widely being ratified owing to opposition from countries from the Global North. Those states resist the treaty because they have political objectives unrelated to human rights. The political impact of migrants within democratic states is clear when looking at party politics across Europe, North America and Australia. Governments in democratic countries require re-election at the end of each term of office, and immigration is a political hot topic within those states, particularly during times of economic recession. Since migrants have no vote, their rights are unlikely to be high on the political agenda of governments.

As previously discussed, another vulnerable group that requires protection are LGBT persons. Steps towards creating international law specifically designed to protect that group have been hampered from the outset by countries from the African Group and from the Organisation of Islamic Cooperation and by some states from the former Soviet bloc. Attempts to use UN human rights bodies to advance LGBT rights have stalled during the past two years. In 2011, the Human Rights Council held its first ever panel on LGBT rights. The OIC bloc walked out of the chamber *en masse*. In September 2012, Russia sponsored a resolution on 'traditional values' that the Council passed by 25 votes to 15 with 7 abstentions. Discussions and dialogue are not currently leading anywhere in terms of developing, enshrining or promoting LGBT rights at the UN level. Political objectives are clear, not least from states that criminalise homosexuality under their own national laws.

Those two examples might be depressing, but one must remember that it took two decades to create the treaties that codify the Universal

Declaration of Human Rights. Processes of engagement and cooperation do lead to changes, evolution and development of international
human rights law. Ongoing efforts to share information, enter into
dialogue with all countries, engage a wide range of actors, and to keep
migrants and LGBT persons on the agenda do result in promotion of
their rights. The problem is that these changes take time and require
great patience and efforts; meanwhile rights continue to be abused. But
once the treaties are negotiated, created and ratified, significant changes
can occur worldwide.

There are, then, severe problems with states deciding which treaties to
ratify and by which to be bound. There are also problems with enforcing
those obligations against rogue states or those which only pay lip service
to human rights. But we must not lose sight of the fact that most countries obey most of their obligations most of the time. If it was not for the
United Nations, many of the specific obligations—developed from the
fundamental rights—would not exist as part of international law.
Treaties would not have been created at the international level, leaving
some states bound by the very different regional treaties—in Europe,
Africa and the Americas—and others not bound by any such instruments at all. Some countries would be bound by very specific provisions,
others less so, and many countries would not have any codified obligations. Not only would this lead to a lack of uniformity in state practice,
it would also result in uncertainty for individuals in terms of what their
rights actually mean.

State engagement and cooperation do not end with the ratification of
treaties. Each of the core international human rights law treaties have
their own monitoring bodies—human rights committees—that provide
a corpus of law stemming from provisions found within the main instruments. The committees are composed of independent experts who monitor compliance with the obligations contained within the treaties.[24] They
receive periodic reports from states that are party to the treaty, and then
issue Concluding Observations that contain specific recommendations
for the country concerned. Those observations also inform other states
about the nature of their own obligations and how they ought to be
implemented. Committees also issue General Comments[25] which further
develop specific obligations found within the treaties. Some treaty bodies
are able to receive individual complaints or communications about violations.[26] Decisions made by the committees, as with their Concluding

Observations, are relevant to all parties to the treaty in terms of developing and explaining specific human rights obligations.

Again, it is crucial that states engage with these bodies. Countries can opt out: either tacitly by choosing not to be subject to the committees or aspects of their work such as complaints procedures; or passively by not submitting reports or adopting recommendations. By consenting to the committees' work, states demonstrate a commitment to the corpus of law created. The weaknesses, such as lack of enforcement mechanisms and dependence on state cooperation, are counterbalanced by the fact that those states that do engage are likely to take on board the committees' decisions and recommendations.

The Committee on Economic, Social and Cultural Rights produced General Comment No. 15 in 2002.[27] That General Comment set out the human right to water, a right not recognised *per se* in either the Universal Declaration of Human Rights or the International Covenant on Economic, Social and Cultural Rights. Paragraphs 1 and 2 of the General Comment emphasise the integral nature that the right to water has for the realisation of other human rights and for dignity. Paragraph 3 then places the right within Article 11 of the Covenant, which sets out the right to an adequate standard of living 'including adequate food, clothing, and housing'. The Committee determined that Article 11 provides a non-exhaustive list and that the right to water fits naturally into that list. Not all states agreed with the Committee's approach. Canada opposed the introduction of a right to water, insisting on a narrow interpretation of Article 11 and arguing that the creation of a new right went beyond the Committee's competence.

General Comment No. 15 started the process of creating, codifying and promoting the right to water. It built on the Commission on Human Rights' 2001 resolution that mandated the independent expert on the right to food to address issues relating to the right to water.[28] A separate mandate for an independent expert solely on the right to water was created by the Human Rights Council in 2008.[29] Although countries such as the UK opposed this backdoor method of creating a new human right—arguing that rights ought to be created by treaty or customary international law—it is now enshrined within the system. The right to water binds states and non-state actors, and UN promotion activities on drinking water, sanitation and agricultural uses of water have been widespread since it was created. More than 780 million people worldwide lack access to safe drinking water, and 3.4 million people die each year from a water-related disease. More people have a mobile phone than a toilet.[30] It is obvious, then, that developing and promoting the right to water represents a major UN achievement.

The body of law created is relevant to all states party to the treaty but, perhaps more importantly in terms of its wide-reaching effect, it is utilised by other bodies, courts and tribunals, which may refer to general comments and concluding observations within their own work. In this way we can see why this work is so crucial. It promotes and develops rights not only by informing the international and regional human rights systems, but also through its relationship with states that are party to the treaties.

It is not only treaty bodies that contribute to the growing corpus of law referred to by other institutions. The UN also provides a forum, facilities and expertise for states to create 'soft law' in the form of decisions, resolutions and declarations on human rights. While not binding, they provide significant indication of the development of this area of law. Soft law demonstrates states' evolving understandings of human rights and indicates the direction in which that area of law is moving. Soft law is created through countries engaging with one another, negotiating and discussing texts of resolutions, decisions and declarations, and producing a final output that is accepted by at least a majority of UN member states. Cooperation and dialogue are key to this process. Most of the work occurs during sessions of UN bodies, when state delegates are in the same vicinity. The UN provides meeting places for those delegates, as well as expertise from UN staff, to assist with these processes. Soft law stemming from the General Assembly, the one truly universal body, is most frequently cited. Yet the resolutions, decisions and documents from the Assembly often have developed from texts adopted within more specialised UN bodies.

UN human rights bodies therefore play significant roles in creating soft law. They bring to the fore human rights issues, whether thematic or country-specific, and enable states and non-state actors to interact with one another when discussing those situations. NGOs, whether large ones like Amnesty International and Human Rights Watch or specialised niche organisations, provide expertise, facts and information that have been gathered on the ground. NGOs also bring in speakers, such as the refugee from Darfur who spoke to the Human Rights Council in 2008, to give first-hand testimony that government delegates would likely never otherwise hear.[31] UN bodies, particularly the Human Rights Council where NGOs have their own speakers list during the body's sessions, act as a forum for civil society actors to interact with government delegates. Those non-state actors provide expertise and information that countries may not be able to access. NGOs also run side-events during Human Rights Council sessions, bringing experts, activists and delegates together in meeting rooms next to the Council's chamber. Information-sharing and discussion lead to greater awareness of issues and greater understanding of how to develop, promote and implement human rights. That encourages states and UN independent experts then to take up the reins and move forward with creating soft law.

Information-sharing, along with fact-finding and monitoring, are important methods for promoting human rights. All of those roles require states to engage and cooperate with the UN. While the Council and the committees undertake all three roles, those are only aspects of their mandates. The UN human rights mechanism that focuses mainly on fact-finding, monitoring and information-sharing is the Special Procedures system. Countries must consent to visits from UN independent experts. That consent is two-legged: there must be a formal acceptance of a visit request and tacit acceptance in terms of the conditions of the visit. Countries can and do block visits by refusing the independent experts' terms.

When a Council-appointed mission of independent experts sought to enter Darfur, for example, Sudan banned one individual from entering the country. It alleged that Bertrand Ramcharan was a political appointment and that he had previously exhibited bias against Sudan. Despite the government offering to allow all other members to enter Sudan, the mission decided to abandon the visit and to write its report from Chad—a neighbour country on the border of the Darfur region. A similar incident occurred when a group of independent experts went to visit Guantanamo Bay. The US refused to accept the condition that the experts have access to inmates without the presence of any prison, military or other officials. This resulted in the experts deciding not to carry out the visit. Having recently visited Russia and China, which had accepted those conditions, the experts determined that the US refusal was unacceptable.

Once a state has consented to a visit, the independent expert enters the country and undertakes fact-finding and dialogue with local actors.

This again requires state cooperation, not least where local actors provide information about systematic human rights violations. The independent experts gather information from all parties, including the government, in order to compile a report and provide recommendations to the state concerned. Those reports are discussed at the Human Rights Council and other human rights bodies. Other countries may use them when determining best practice for implementing human rights or to understand the nature of their own obligations.

Countries cooperate with Special Procedures for a variety of reasons. Some states request visits where they appreciate that they need assistance and support in implementing human rights. The independent experts on extreme poverty, on adequate housing and on food are regularly asked to visit states who seek guidance, recommendations and support in implementing those rights. Others can see broader benefits, such as yielding evidence of a demonstrable willingness to engage with human rights, which can then assist with applications for aid or other funding from international or regional bodies. Some countries cooperate with independent experts but do not then implement the recommendations. Others cherry-pick which measures to take on board. But once the reports are published, they form part of the broader corpus of human rights.

There has been a recent trend of Global North states resisting reports of independent experts. The EU (especially Greece and Italy), Canada and the UK have all recently received visits, from experts on the rights of migrants, food and adequate housing respectively. The argument from those countries has been that graver human rights abuses occur elsewhere and that experts would better use their time by visiting those countries. However, the reports and recommendations are useful for many states as they provide guidelines that may be implemented elsewhere. The visits also demonstrate the universality of Special Procedures which are not aimed solely at the Global South. That universality is fundamental for the system's legitimacy and credibility. It is only by recognising that all countries have human rights abuses that promotion activities will continue to be accepted by all states.

Special Procedures is a key mechanism that works. Its universal nature, coupled with the independent expertise, is vital to its success. Another universal mechanism that monitors, reports and provides recommendations is Universal Periodic Review. This is relatively new and was created as part of the Human Rights Council. All UN member states are reviewed, through UPR, during a four-year cycle. Each review is carried out by a troika of states, with those three countries chosen randomly. The UPR brings together the country concerned, which submits a report in advance of the review; civil society actors, who also submit reports; and any other state that chooses to attend the review. Information-sharing is crucial, with countries' human rights records, such as the treaties they have and have not ratified together with information about violations, being central to the process. Questions may be asked by other countries, either in advance or from the floor. Cooperation is key; states submit their own reports, choose whether to answer questions, and decide whether or not to act on the UPR recommendations. As with Special Procedures, UPR focuses on guidance and recommendations about human rights implementation and promotion. It centres around state cooperation and capacity-building, and brings the additional weight of peer-support into the arena. UPR has some similarities to the monitoring roles undertaken by treaty bodies, but it goes further because it is universal[32] and focuses on peer-to-peer monitoring and recommendations.

As we can see, the UN human rights machinery consists of interconnected bodies and mechanisms that bring together a range of actors. Treaty bodies are made up of independent experts who have particular experience of human rights. Staff members from the Office of the High Commissioner for Human Rights also provide expertise and support in the creation and development of human rights. The Human Rights Council, on the other hand, is composed of government delegates representing member states that have been elected to that body. Those delegates frequently have no prior experience of or expertise on human rights. The expertise provided by the OHCHR assists states in their work at the Council when developing and creating international human rights. The interactions of those three parts of the UN human rights machinery—treaty bodies, the OHCHR and the Human Rights Council—ensure that international human rights law is a living, organic system that shapes and changes according to societal need in such a way as to engage states from around the world and is supported by individuals with human rights expertise.

The United Nations, then, creates and develops international human rights, and also successfully promotes those rights within member states. Promotion activities are aimed at ensuring that states understand their obligations and are able to implement human rights. Each part of the UN human rights machinery undertakes a broad range of promotion activities. Although the UN might protect rights only ineffectually, it has achieved considerable success in promoting such rights.

Conclusion

It takes longer to promote and implement rights than to protect them. Promotion requires working with countries to improve their understandings of rights and their capacity to implement those rights. This involves fact-finding, information-sharing, technical assistance, dialogue, recommendations, and peer and expert support. All of those things require resources and, crucially, time. Promoting rights results in long-term implementation through changing national interests and capabilities. The changes are fundamental and systemic, lasting beyond the facts of an individual case and with far-reaching effects. Whilst not as swift and decisive as protection mechanisms, and whilst unable adequately to respond to crisis situations, promotion activities represent one of the crucial roles played by the UN in the field of international human rights.

But there is a paradox here. Promotion activities rely on politics and diplomacy, on cooperation and engagement, on discussion and dialogue. Those same strengths that are needed for promoting rights are weaknesses when it comes to protecting rights. The very nature of international law, in general, and the UN human rights machinery facilitate effective promotion activities and undermine effective protection activities. Protection only takes place either where a country asks for those activities to occur or where the Security Council steps in and enforces protection through the powers and measures at its disposal. Rather than criticising the UN human rights machinery for failing to undertake activities for which it has not been designed nor afforded the requisite powers, we ought to focus upon how to enable the UN to fulfil those duties. One such way is a rather radical proposal that has been developed since the turn of the Millennium—the establishment of a World Court of Human Rights. It is to that and other proposals that we must now turn our attention.

13

ALTERNATIVES

A RADICAL PROPOSAL

The previous 12 chapters have set out the problems encountered in protecting human rights. These final chapters explore alternatives to the current system. Firstly, we will turn to a radical proposal created and developed by a handful of leading scholars and practitioners of international law and human rights. Chapter 14 then looks at regional mechanisms as a proposed method for universally protecting rights. These two alternatives are examined in order to explore whether the UN human rights machinery is the most viable vehicle for universal protection of human rights. Finally, I consider potential reforms to the UN human rights machinery as well as the pragmatic option of using 'linkage' to coerce states to comply with their human rights obligations. None of these is the perfect or even particularly strong solution, but they are all attempts to move forwards rather than accepting the stagnant and suboptimal *status quo*. First, we shall examine the radical proposal for a World Court of Human Rights.

In September 2000, Professor Manfred Nowak and Professor Martin Scheinin found themselves travelling together after the constituent meeting of the Association of Human Rights Institute in Iceland. Scheinin reports that they 'spent the whole flight and afterwards an hour or two more at Copenhagen airport discussing the feasibility and modalities of a future World Court of Human Rights'. It was that discussion—presumably conducted without putting pen to the back of a cigarette packet—that provided the springboard for a rather radical proposal. The two academics, joined by some of their colleagues, set out their aim to create a World Court of Human Rights.

Eight years later, after countless discussions and after-dinner speeches, the Swiss government gave Scheinin a platform to propose this idea more fully.[1] At the same time, Nowak was working on a parallel project drafting a statute for the proposed court. Those two projects can be viewed as constituting the foundations for what might become an effective international mechanism for protecting human rights. I shall explore the proposal, examining where more work needs to be done if there is to be a chance of turning the dream into a reality.

The arguments in favour of creating a World Court of Human Rights centre around the lack of available judicial and enforcement mechanisms to protect individuals from violations and to provide effective remedies where abuse has occurred. As discussed in Chapter 3, despite the overlap between different areas of international law, there is little room for violations of international human rights law to be brought before any of the existing international courts or tribunals. There may be some overlap between human rights abuses and breaches of international criminal law or humanitarian law, but the vast majority of human rights violations are not covered by those areas. As such, neither the International Criminal Court nor the International Court of Justice (which only hears cases between two states) is able to hear cases from individuals alleging human rights violations. The proposed World Court of Human Rights would fill a void in the international human rights system. But the question is whether it is realistic or viable.

Nowak and Scheinin both focus on the gap between regional human rights courts—in Europe, the Americas and Africa[2]—and UN committees that monitor the core treaties at the international level. The committees are hampered in their work by a lack of judicial authority and enforcement mechanisms, which lead to insufficient weight afforded to their decisions by all parties to the treaties. Moreover, many countries do not consent to the committees hearing individual complaints about alleged abuses. Those failings can be contrasted with the regional courts, which have protected human rights, albeit to varying degrees. It is proposed that the World Court of Human Rights would take over from the treaty bodies both in terms of delivering binding interpretations of treaties and deciding about individual complaints of violations.[3]

The proposed World Court of Human Rights would play a very different role in international human rights law from the role that the International Criminal Court fulfils in international criminal law. While the International Criminal Court focuses only on the gravest international crimes, the World Court of Human Rights would streamline all international human rights laws. In many ways that is a far more ambitious undertaking, although it does underline the fact that human rights are interdependent, interrelated and indivisible. Unlike the International Criminal Court, which hears cases against individual perpetrators, the World Court of Human Rights would only hear cases about alleged violations committed by states or non-state actors. While individuals would be able to bring cases to the World Court of Human Rights, they would not appear as defendants before the Court. The World Court seems to be based more upon a regional court of human rights than any of the international criminal courts or tribunals.[4]

Nowak and Scheinin are European academics and both have been heavily influenced by national and regional understandings of human rights. The European Court of Human Rights is the most highly developed and respected of all the regional courts. The European Convention on Human Rights was the first international human rights treaty. The Court's jurisprudence has widely been accepted, not just as binding by states that are party to the treaty but also as persuasive by other courts and tribunals across the world. The success of the European system is at least partly due to the homogeneity of democratic states within that region, the fact that they respect human rights, and the political and diplomatic pressures to comply with the European human rights mechanisms. Moreover, the European Court has so far effectively managed the tension between interpreting and applying the Convention and ensuring that it remains legitimate and relevant to the states party to that treaty.[5] As such, state compliance rates are high. But the European system represents only one region. Nowak and Scheinin's emphasis on that system fails to acknowledge that this is not the experience elsewhere in the world.

As idealists, these two eminent scholars may well expect that by reproducing the European system they will be able to emulate its success. That does not, however, address the lack of homogeneity across the world; the need for stronger enforcement mechanisms when dealing with non-democratic states; and crucially how to encourage countries that are less concerned with human rights to become party to the court.

However, this well-intentioned proposal has not been accepted as realistic—or even 'desirable'[6]—by all human rights commentators. Two fundamental concerns have been raised: whether countries would accept the Court's jurisdiction; and the extent to which any of its judgements would or even could be enforced. The draft World Court of Human Rights statute,[7] produced in 2010, has done little to allay those fears. While it focuses on the technical details of how the court will operate, it fails to address the fundamental issues of state consent and enforcement that have plagued the UN human rights machinery. The World Court of Human Rights in its current form will not be mandatory but will rely on states consenting to its jurisdiction to hear cases of alleged violations. Secondly, it will not have the types of enforcement powers that are available to the UN Security Council, nor will it have the political clout that the Council of Europe uses to encourage—or coerce—states to comply with the European Court of Human Rights. As will now be explored in detail, it seems that Nowak and Scheinin have done little to address the very same consent and enforcement issues that have led them to create this draft statute.

The idea is that the World Court will be able to receive complaints regarding states that have consented to the Court doing so by becoming party to its treaty. So the World Court requires states to consent to be bound, which of course raises the same problems that we have already encountered regarding human rights treaties. If countries need to consent to becoming party to a treaty, then it only operates vis-à-vis those states that choose to be bound by its obligations. Countries can and do simply choose not to opt into the system. Indeed, we have seen that countries most likely to opt out are those known for their disregard for human rights.

The proposal seeks to address this deficiency by stating that any country that is not a party to the World Court treaty will be able to give *ad hoc* consent to cases being heard by the Court. This, they insist, will enable the Court to hear specific complaints. Of course, the Court will not be able to hear cases about countries that have not expressly given their consent and that are not parties to the treaty. And in reality, it seems unlikely that grave abusers will any more consent to the Court hearing cases on an *ad hoc* basis than they will to ratify the World Court's treaty.

Again, the drafters of the proposal for the World Court have done little to address the systemic problems within the international human rights system. As long as states have the option to become party to a treaty, there will be countries which choose to remain outside the system. We might hope that the World Court will bind all countries, but we know that in reality many of the states that most need to be brought to the Court will be the ones which do not consent to cases being heard.

But the drafters seem to believe that there is a way to deal with the problem of states that altogether withhold their consent. They envisage that the United Nations High Commissioner for Human Rights could refer complaints about states that have not consented to the Court hearing cases about alleged violations. The Court could then 'issue an Opinion representing its interpretation of the issues of international human rights law raised by the complaint'.[8] The extent to which such an Opinion would be binding or enforceable is somewhat glossed over. If such Opinions were to carry the same weight as judgements, then it would render obsolete the need for state consent. But if they were to carry lesser weight than judgements, then we are back to a system that may be universal in theory but never will be in practice.

This is unsatisfactory, to say the least. The basic premise seems to be an idealistic hope that most countries will consent to jurisdiction either by ratifying the treaty or on an *ad hoc* case-by-case basis. But there is nothing to indicate that countries would sign up to the Court having jurisdiction. Indeed, recent history shows us that the contrary is true, and not just in relation to human rights treaties. The experience of the International Criminal Court demonstrates the difficulties that such courts have in convincing states to consent to the court's jurisdiction. Fifteen years after the Rome Statute was written, creating the International Criminal Court, 122 countries have ratified that treaty, with 72 states outside the Court's jurisdiction.[9] The International Criminal Court only deals with the gravest international crimes and has an inbuilt complementarity system whereby a contracting state can choose to prosecute an individual rather than the International Criminal Court hearing the case. Despite those inbuilt safeguards to state sovereignty in terms of giving countries the option to prosecute their own citizens rather than send them to the International Criminal Court, many countries have chosen to remain outside the system. No doubt, a World Court of Human Rights—dealing with many more legal obligations than the International Criminal Court and without a complementarity principle because it is not hearing cases about individual perpetrators—would face even greater resistance from states in terms of consenting to the court's jurisdiction.

Scheinin sets out four reasons why he thinks states ought to ratify the World Court of Human Rights statute:

(1) 'to demonstrate their unwavering commitment to human rights';
(2) to 'enhance the coherence and consistency in the application of human rights treaties';
(3) 'to improve foreseeability and legal certainty'; and
(4) to expand 'the binding force of human rights norms beyond States'.[10]

All four reasons are worthy. But none is likely to persuade countries that are not (a) absolutely committed to advancing human rights and (b) absolutely certain that they are not going to be hauled before the court any time soon. That knocks out a large majority of countries from across the world. The likelihood is that many states, particularly known abusers, would remain outside this system. It is all well and good stream-lining international human rights obligations and having a World Court capable of hearing cases about violations, but if states are not subject to its jurisdiction then the whole thing falls apart.

It might make better sense for the proponents of a World Court to find a way of making ratification mandatory for all UN members. In much the same way that European Union states are required to have ratified the European Convention on Human Rights, this might be considered as a condition upon which continued UN membership is based. Whether this is possible in practice is yet to be explored. But the principle of requiring states to commit, in principle, to human rights could well be coupled with a requirement that they submit to jurisdiction of a World Court when allegations of violations surface. At that point, the World Court of Human Rights would become mandatory for any state seeking to be included in the international arena in much the same way as the European Court of Human Rights is for any country seeking to be included in the Council of Europe.

Another fundamental problem concerns the question of enforcement. The current problem of enforcing human rights judgements is one that has been widely addressed, not least by the proponents of the World Court.[11] The solution, according to the drafters of the Statute, is for the UN Human Rights Council to 'oversee the effective implementation of the judgements by the Court'.[12] Article 48 entrusts the Council with that task. This, remember, is the same Human Rights Council which is a political body and which itself does not hold binding powers and is unable to enforce its own resolutions and decisions.

But even if the idea of the Human Rights Council overseeing effective implementation of judgements worked in theory, which is very doubtful, in practice the Council barely fulfils its own mandate to protect human rights. The Council has been so biased, selective and shackled by politicisation since its creation in 2006 that it lacks credibility even within the UN system, let alone in the wider world. Expecting the Human Rights Council to oversee implementation of a Court's rulings is taking an idealist vision too far. Nowak and Scheinin place great emphasis on the political processes that take place at the Council. But that is not a realistic understanding of how political bodies operate. In reality, those same political processes are the ones that have undermined the Human Rights Council and are exactly the reason why such a body ought not to be tasked with implementing Court judgements.

To understand why the World Court of Human Rights would not work in practice, we only need to think back to some the examples set out throughout this book and explore whether those rights could have been protected through such a court.

As has already been seen, approximately 70 UN member states criminalise sexual orientation and gender minorities. The question of whether LGBT rights would be protected through a World Court of Human Rights, then, is likely to be a resounding 'no'. Countries that imprison, torture or even kill individuals on the basis of their sexual orientation or gender identity are unlikely to sign up to a World Court statute that enables judicial protection of those rights. And even if they did, and did so without placing a reservation regarding LGBT rights, the likelihood of compliance with a World Court ruling is low. Indeed, as we have seen with the Human Rights Committee, some states carry out the death penalty while the Committee is considering the merits of a case.

LGBT individuals are not the only vulnerable group that the World Court would struggle to protect. Migrants are unlikely to utilise such a court. Not only have Global North states refused to ratify the Convention on the Protection of the Rights of All Migrant Workers and Members of their Families, but those countries have taken backwards steps regarding migrants' rights. And even if they did accept the Court's jurisdiction to hear such cases, irregular migrants remain in the shadows for fear of being found and removed by state authorities—so why would such individuals risk the ensuing attention that would come by bringing a case to a World Court?

These are not the only examples that one could cite to demonstrate that the World Court would do little in practice to protect human rights. The most powerful states and the world's pariah states are not party to the International Criminal Court. It is unrealistic, then, to expect that the US, China and Russia, or Iran, Israel and Zimbabwe—to choose a few examples—would accept the jurisdiction of a World Court of Human Rights. And even if they did, the lack of enforcement powers and reliance on political processes mean that those states would simply be as selective about the judgements as they are about their obligations in the first place.

Another crucial issue that would arise if the World Court was enacted is the problem of hidden abuses and closed states. If UN independent experts are unable to enter those territories, and if local NGOs and civil society actors cannot access information, then how would individuals in such repressive regimes be able to bring a case to the World Court? And even if such a case were to be brought, how would evidence be secured and placed in front of the judges? These are practical questions that have an important bearing on the reality of such a court. In essence, the World Court would not be able to protect the rights of the individuals who are most in need of such a mechanism. Abuses in Norway might be adjudicated upon, but those in North Korea would continue to be ignored altogether. We would be back to the same problem that the countries which most require attention are the ones least likely to receive it from international bodies.

When looking at the practical realities, it becomes clear that the World Court will probably remain only an idealistic vision. But we ought not to forget that Nowak and Scheinin are great human rights scholars who have both devoted their careers to international human rights law, both as academics and also as unpaid UN independent experts. So why is it that they retain an idealist belief in the World Court and in a political body such as the Human Rights Council? At least part of the answer is that they are European academics and their experiences are closely tied to the European human rights system. As Scheinin points out:

'The proposal draws inspiration from the monitoring of the European Convention of Human Rights where the unconditional and nonselective duty of the main political body of Council of Europe, the Committee of Ministers, is to supervise the implementation of the judgments by the European Court of Human Rights.'[13]

The argument is that if the system works in Europe, then why not map it across onto the world? The World Court might be a great dream, but in my view it simply would not work in reality or at least not in its present state.[14] But that argument does lead to a different and less radical proposal: why not utilise the existing regional mechanisms, including from the European system, and enable the development of strong human rights bodies within every region across the world? We shall now consider that proposal.

14

ALTERNATIVES

A LESS RADICAL ALTERNATIVE

If UN bodies are not providing adequate protection for all individuals and if it is unlikely that a World Court of Human Rights will ever be created, then other proposals must be tabled. It is simply unacceptable to do nothing and allow the *status quo* to continue. In this chapter I explore how we might be able to utilise regional human rights mechanisms to protect individuals across the world. While what I propose is an imperfect solution, I shall argue that it is more practicable than a World Court of Human Rights and that it will at least represent a step in the right direction towards protecting individuals from violations.

Currently, there are human rights mechanisms in three of the world's regions: Europe, the Americas and Africa. That leaves people in Asia, parts of Eastern Europe and Australasia without any access to regional human rights systems. Each of the existing mechanisms is based on regional rather than universal understandings of human rights. They emphasise different rights from one another. Having been created at different times, each system is at a different stage in its development, and the level of protection afforded, therefore, is markedly different within each. And yet, despite these differences, there are strong reasons in favour of those mechanisms for protecting individuals from grave abuses. While the proposal will not result in universality in its purest sense, it addresses some of the key weaknesses in the current approach to protecting human rights at the international level.

Before discussing how to strengthen those systems and how to utilise their experiences in other regions, we must first understand how the mechanisms work. Each system has developed in ways that can be traced to the local politics, history and culture. The extent to which they protect human rights varies, as will be shown by reference to some of the examples of violations set out in previous chapters.

Europe

The European human rights system is the oldest and most developed of the three existing regional mechanisms. The European Convention on Human Rights[1] was drafted in 1950 and came into force in 1953.[2] Any country wishing to join the Council of Europe must ratify the Convention. One of its central aims is to ensure that there is an independent judicial process available when a state allegedly violates a Convention right. The lesson learned from this is that making ratification of a human rights treaty mandatory does not stop countries from joining a regional system if—and only if—that system is sufficiently attractive. Europe has used 'linkage' to ensure that all members of the Council of Europe are bound by the European Convention on Human Rights and have accepted the Court's jurisdiction to hear cases about alleged violations. But what is that 'linkage'? It is to trade, to politics, to the Eurozone, and to the many other benefits that come with being a member of the Council of Europe. The same could have been done at the United Nations, as it is clear that all countries wish to be members of that organisation. But that opportunity is long gone; it is infinitely more difficult to apply such mandatory rules retroactively.

Initially, the European system was concerned almost exclusively with Civil and Political Rights. Although Economic, Social and Cultural Rights have now been protected at the theoretical level through newer European human rights treaties, the Court remains focused on violations of Civil and Political Rights. That reflects the liberal ideology prevalent in Western Europe. The main focus is on protecting individuals from state interference. Protecting those rights is much easier in practice than protecting Economic, Social and Cultural Rights let alone Collective or Third Generation Rights. That does not mean that the other two categories of rights cannot be brought before a court. It is just easier for courts to reach a judgement on Civil and Political Rights because those cases require the Court to look solely at legal issues rather than also including budgetary and other policy matters.

There is some tension between contracting states and the Court. The UK has recently threatened to pull out of the ECHR and some UK politicians and judges have criticised the Court's increasingly wide-reaching judgements, arguing that the Court has taken on an interpretive role that extends far beyond what was originally intended. One example of a contentious ruling concerns prisoners' voting rights. The 2005 ruling against the blanket ban on prisoners voting has led to an increasingly polarised national debate about the role of the European Court of Human Rights. In 2013 Thorbjørn Jagland, the secretary-general of the Council of Europe, warned the UK that its failure to implement the judgement weakened the regional system. The Justice Secretary, Chris Grayling, responded by insisting that 'there's a real debate about who governs Britain and that the remit of the court has gone far too far with the unlimited jurisprudence that it has and that that is no longer acceptable'.[3] But on the whole, the Court has found a way to balance the competing need of keeping states within the system while also interpreting questions of law and protecting individuals from violations.[4] The Court's decisions are highly regarded and referred to not only by member states but also other international, regional and national courts and tribunals.

Of course there are problems, not least with the backlog of tens of thousands of cases and the Court's lack of enforcement powers. But by and large states view judgements as binding and implement them as such. Indeed, a system that focuses almost exclusively on adjudicatory mechanisms only works because the Council of Europe was created by liberal democracies with long-established judicial systems. National respect for law being implemented through courts combines well with the pressure that can be exerted on countries through regional, political, economic and other ties.

But how has the European system addressed key issues that plague the international human rights mechanisms?

Cultural relativism has been less of an issue regarding the relatively homogenous states in Europe than it is within the international arena. But there still remain differences between states in terms of cultures, norms and values; while it can be seen, for example in terms of religious symbols (France) and women's reproductive rights (Ireland), the arguments those states present are based on national laws rather than on cultures. This stands in contrast with the emphasis on religion, culture and values presented by many members of the Organisation of Islamic Cooperation political bloc, the African Group and the Asian Group. The European emphasis on law and legal infrastructure once again enables more effective protection of rights, as the European system can more easily seek to challenge national laws than the international system can do in relation to cultures.

Political capture and instrumentalism, too, have been less of a problem at the European level. Relative homogeneity between the founding states, combined with the political desire of newer members to join the system, has resulted in a less politicised system than the United Nations. That is not to say that there have not been issues of politicisation, particularly in relation to how the founding states have sought to use the system to influence and change countries seeking to join or newly joined members of the Council of Europe. And of course judges' nationalities can affect the rulings given by the Court. But those issues have less of an impact on the system than occurs within the international arena.

The European human rights mechanism does less well where it comes to marginalised groups. Some vulnerable groups have received significant support and attention within the regional system. Others have fared less well. In particular, irregular migrants and the Roma remain inadequately protected by the European human rights system. And, as in any system, the more powerful an actor the more easily it can avoid complying with rulings, as has been the case recently with the UK and France. But, ultimately, the European system works well because there is a common aim of protecting and promoting human rights, and because that aim is bound tightly with all the other regional ties. Former Justice Minister Crispin Blunt puts the matter succinctly when he defends the need for the compliance with the European Court of Human Rights:

'what is happening in the rest of Europe, where there is language being used by the president of Russia in speeches to the Duma, around the rights of minorities, that frankly would do credit to some speeches being made in the 1930s in Germany, don't you have a duty to other nationalities not to upset the only transnational human rights system within Europe?'[5]

As is clear from the earlier discussion about the World Court of Human Rights, a proposal which is based loosely on the European experience, the system cannot easily be mapped onto other regions. Each state has its own common history, experiences, ideologies and human rights values. The lessons that can be drawn from the European system can only be mapped across to other regions where there are cross-regional similarities on particular issues. What can broadly be seen, however, is that where a group of states is generally in agreement, then that system can advance effectively the protection of human rights.

The Inter-Americas

The Inter-Americas human rights system began in 1969 with the American Convention on Human Rights.[6] The Inter-American Court was established in 1979, but hears far fewer cases than the European Court of Human Rights. Instead, the Inter-American Commission takes the primary role in overseeing state parties' compliance with their human rights obligations. All complaints begin before the Commission and may be made by states, individuals, groups of persons, or a non-governmental entity legally recognised in a member state. The Commission undertakes fact-finding and non-contentious activities to encourage the parties to reach a friendly settlement. If that does not occur, the Commission recommends measures to remedy the violation. These are all aimed at state engagement, cooperation, inclusivity and promoting human rights compliance. Where that does not work, the Court may be brought into play.

The Court hears cases that cannot be dealt with through the Commission's mechanisms. Where an alleged violation reaches the Court, it must be brought by the Commission or a state. Unlike in Europe, individuals do not have the right to petition the Court. The Inter-American system is far less focused than the European mechanisms on adversarial processes. This difference between Europe and the Americas reflects the different cultures and norms within those regions. The Inter-American system focuses more on engagement, dialogue and cooperation, leaving adversarial adjudication as a last resort.

Exploring some of the cases heard by the Court gives an insight into the types of rights in most need of protection in Latin America. Unlike Europe, where a broad range of rights is ruled upon by the Court, the Inter-American Court only hears cases about those rights that states are unwilling to implement through cooperation with the Commission.

The first case the Inter-American Court heard was on enforced disappearances,[7] a problem rife across Latin America in the 1960s, 1970s and

1980s. Latin America has a recent history of military dictatorships or weak and often corrupt governments. Those regimes refused to consent to Commission activities aimed at protecting individuals from state-sanctioned disappearances. It was not surprising, then, that the first case the Commission successfully referred to the Court was on one such disappearance. The case concerned a Honduran student, Manfredo Velásquez, who was 'involved in activities the authorities considered "dangerous" to national security'.[8] He was kidnapped on 12 September 1981[9] and remained disappeared seven years later when the case was heard by the Inter-American Court of Human Rights. The Court heard evidence that people 'connected with the Armed Forces or under its direction carried out that kidnapping'. His disappearance was similar to 'the systematic practice of disappearances' in Honduras at that time. The Court ruled in this case that Honduras had violated the rights to life, liberty and humane treatment by failing to protect Mr Velásquez, to investigate his disappearance or punish those responsible. That judgement opened the door for the Court to protect individuals from similar violations by adjudicating on a string of similar cases.[10]

The protection of individuals from enforced disappearances occurred throughout the region and is one of the great successes of the Inter-Americas human rights system. Both the Commission and the Court have played significant roles in that regard. The Court has also been particularly concerned with defending the rights of indigenous people,[11] which is another issue that is endemic across the Americas.[12]

It is clear that the regional human rights mechanism is designed mainly with Latin American states in mind. The homogeneity amongst those countries is far greater than the similarities with the US and Canada. Those two states place greater emphasis on adversarial judicial systems aimed at protecting rights and less on cooperative, inclusive promotion mechanisms. What is interesting, then, is that neither the US nor Canada has accepted the jurisdiction of the Inter-American Court. Unlike in Europe, members of the Organisation of American States are not required to ratify the human rights treaties or consent to the Court hearing cases about alleged violations. In much the same way as occurs in the international arena, the two most powerful states within the Inter-American system are able to opt out of the human rights mechanisms knowing that there will be little political fall-out. In Europe no state is so much more powerful—economically, geographically, militarily and politically—than the other regional members. In a system where such power discrepancies exist, it is much more difficult to encourage—or coerce—countries to cooperate with the human rights mechanisms.

Powerful countries adopting an exceptionalist or unilateralist approach also undermine the UN system. Leaving that to one side, it is important to explore how the Commission and Court have dealt with some of the other problems that beset the UN human rights machinery.

Latin American states are less politically and economically homogenous than European countries. However, there is a common history of military dictatorships and socialist revolutions as well as common problems such as high levels of extreme poverty, illiteracy and marginalisation of indigenous populations. Promotion activities, then, are aimed at working with states to ensure implementation and realisation of rights. While some countries might claim that they require capacity-building and technical assistance, if they do not cooperate with the assistance offered by the Commission, then they may be referred to the Court. At the regional level, countries are less likely to get away with the types of hollow claims heard at the UN in relation to supposedly wanting to comply with human rights obligations but lacking the necessary resources to do so. However, the Inter-American system is underfunded and therefore cannot assist all countries with implementing all rights. Greater levels of funding would significantly improve human rights compliance across the region.

As with Europe and the UN, some vulnerable groups receive greater attention than others within the Inter-American system. Whilst the rights of indigenous populations in many Global North states remain a key human rights issue, the Inter-American system has devoted significant time and resources to those groups. However, that focus has only impacted upon Latin America because the US and Canada do not accept the Court's jurisdiction to hear cases alleging violations of indigenous rights within their territories. Focus on indigenous peoples, however, does not mean that there are no marginalised groups within Latin America. As with the other human rights systems, some groups receive significant attentions whilst others—invariably including irregular migrants—fall through the cracks.

The Court's role and powers are similar to the protection activities carried out by the European system. Unlike Europe, which has a backlog of tens of thousands of cases, the Inter-American Court hears only the gravest or the most contentious allegations. Much of the regional system's human rights work takes place through the Commission, which focuses on cooperation, engagement and dialogue. This represents a hybrid approach towards human rights, with emphasis placed on both promotion and protection of rights. The Inter-American system in many ways achieves what the UN fails to do, mainly because the regional system has the mechanisms necessary to achieve both aims. But the greater level of problems faced by countries, owing not least to underdevelopment and poverty, means that human rights compliance and implementation are far less advanced than within Europe.

Africa

The African human rights system is the newest of the three regional mechanisms. While the European system focuses mainly on adjudicatory processes, the African system is mainly concerned with fact-finding, cooperation and state engagement when addressing human rights violations. The African Charter on Human and Peoples Rights was adopted in 1981 and came into force in 1986. The Charter is more duty-oriented than any other international human rights treaty. Emphasis on duties reflects the view that the 'African conception of man is not that of an isolated and abstract individual but rather an integral member of a group animated by a spirit of solidarity'.[13] This conception is radically different from the liberal concept of the individual holding rights against the state's duties. As such, the African system focuses less on criticising state violations and far more on protecting rights through promotion, capacity-building and technical assistance activities.

As with the Inter-American mechanisms, the African system primarily relies on its Commission rather than the Court. Indeed the Court was only created in 2004. The Charter includes Civil and Political Rights, Economic, Social and Cultural Rights and Collective Rights, with the Commission responsible for protecting all categories. Individuals and states may bring complaints to the Commission. Since its establishment in 1987, the Commission has handed down over 150 decisions.[14] It is used more for monitoring, fact-finding, recommendations and resolutions than for adjudicatory proceedings. This fits with the ideology prevalent across the African Union, with a focus on engagement and cooperation rather than on adversarial processes. The Commission will take a case to the Court if it has handed down a decision and a state does not comply with that ruling. Such cases are likely to be few and far between.

Until now the African human rights mechanism has functioned almost exclusively through the Commission's activities. The Commission undertakes promotion work, looking at mid- and long-term implementation of rights. Much has been done to promote human rights in Africa. The Commission's special rapporteurs have played a significant role in fact-finding and providing recommendations to states. Most notably they have radically improved prison conditions across Africa. States are required to submit reports to the Commission about human rights within their territories. While those are not published publicly, the human rights body uses them to provide targeted recommendations to the state concerned. The Commission's main aim is to facilitate greater awareness of, and compliance with human rights obligations. The African system has the tools and the African Union has demonstrated a willingness to ensure that human rights are implemented.

But protecting rights remains an issue, not least because of the African Union's reluctance to interfere in states' internal affairs and the very many violations occurring across the region at any given time. The focus on cooperation and inclusivity allows states to claim, as they do at UN bodies, that they lack capacity for human rights. The use of post-colonial discourses as a smokescreen for violations occurs within the African system in much the same way as it does in the international arena. While not all states use those discourses for cynical reasons, the reality is that the countries that most require scrutiny are able to deflect attention by reverting to post-colonial language and statements. Those claims are not followed by protection activities, leaving states able to avoid their obligations with impunity. Yet African Union members do listen to one another, as was seen with Sudan and the intervention of African Union peacekeepers to end the atrocities in Darfur. African countries are prepared to engage with the regional human rights system. That partly is because of a shared history, heritage and experiences, and partly owing to political, economic and other ties.

Grave human rights problems exist across Africa. Marginalised groups include LGBT persons, migrants, religious minorities and indigenous populations. Torture and extra-judicial killings remain serious problems across many African countries, and many fundamental rights are systematically violated. Africa faces far greater human rights issues than either

Europe or the Americas. The regional system's reluctance to criticise states through an adversarial judicial system means that protection activities are inadequate. While an increase in state capacity, assistance and development will enable better protection, that will require resources and time—both of which must be provided by the international community as well as by the African Union.

Conclusions

The key differences between the three systems stem from the different ideologies, norms, cultures and practices within each region. But one common thread running through all three is that states do comply with the mechanisms. That compliance occurs with judicial or overseeing processes or both, and demonstrates that states can and do respect the systems despite a lack of enforcement mechanisms. The crucial question is: What makes countries engage, respect and comply with regional mechanisms so much more readily than UN bodies?

There are two main reasons:

Firstly, regional mechanisms are aimed at a group of heterogeneous states or at least ones with many similarities in terms of governance, cultures and legal norms. Therefore, the methods used for fact-finding and adjudicating on human rights issues go hand-in-hand with local practices. Countries are more likely to understand, agree and engage with those processes. At the international level, states are often faced with processes that do not reflect their own practices, thus making compliance less likely than with regional mechanisms. Regional mechanisms are also able to handle the cultural sensitivities around human rights because many of those issues will be shared by neighbouring countries. The European Court of Human Rights has had to address cultural and religious issues, such as abortion and the ban on religious dress, but these tend to be exceptions rather than the norm. The local understanding of cultures means that judges are more aware of those issues. Protection processes are then more palatable for countries concerned.

Secondly, regional mechanisms deal with countries that are tied to one another through geography, politics and economics. Countries wishing to engage with the broader regional system face overt or tacit pressure to cooperate and comply with the human rights mechanisms. The pressure placed on states from regional neighbours has a strong impact on compliance rates. At the UN, countries are less likely to feel swayed by pressure from states with which they have few other dealings or with which they may have negative political interactions. At the regional level, countries are acutely aware of the diplomatic, trade or other ramifications of ignoring the pressure placed on them by other states. That linkage is significant for ensuring human rights compliance.

The second factor is crucial and something that can be mapped onto UN human rights bodies. Linkage, through economics, politics and other ties, can be strong leverage for human rights compliance. We shall return to this point in the next chapter when discussing reforms to the UN human rights machinery.

Of course it is not as simple as saying 'let us hand over protection activities to the regional systems and be done with it'. In order for those mechanisms to fulfil the role of providing protection for all individuals, every country must belong to a regional human rights system. The starting point would be to create human rights mechanisms in Asia and Eastern Europe, and for pressure—through law or diplomacy—on all countries to join one of those systems. This in itself would be no small feat. But the UN could place a requirement on all states to join a regional system, or countries could place trade or economic pressure on others to do so.

If that were achieved, then sufficient resources, in terms of money and technical assistance, would need to be devoted to all regional mechanisms to ensure that they were capable of protecting human rights. Again, this would be a significant undertaking. But considering the amount of financial aid and capacity-building that occurs at the national level, it is surely achievable in practice. Indeed, it seems a far more viable alternative than creating a World Court of Human Rights to which few states will become parties, let alone comply with its rulings. However, until such regional mechanisms exist around the world, and until no country falls through the cracks in those systems, we must ensure that the UN is functioning to the best of its capacity in order to ensure that there is universal protection of human rights.

15

ALTERNATIVES

REFORM

As has been repeatedly seen in earlier chapters, the UN is failing to protect individuals from grave human rights abuses. We have seen that the very weaknesses that undermine the UN bodies' protection capabilities are their strengths in terms of developing and promoting rights. So any radical reforms of those bodies might well tip the scales from inadequate protection to inadequate development and promotion. While alternative methods for protecting rights have been proposed, in practice they will not result in universal protection as traditionally understood. The World Court of Human Rights is unlikely to be implemented or to work in practice. Strengthening and utilising regional human rights mechanisms will result in different levels and forms of protection. It is clear that the UN provides the best possible mechanism for universal protection. However, there are significant weaknesses that must be addressed if the UN is to fulfil its duties adequately. Having explored the protection deficiencies throughout this book, the final matter to consider is how to address those issues in a way that does not undermine other UN human rights activities. In this final chapter I examine whether there are practicable ways of strengthening the UN human rights machinery.

The path of least resistance would be to do nothing. The UN bodies would continue developing and promoting human rights effectively whilst simultaneously failing adequately to protect those rights. That path seems to be the one on which we are now travelling. Less than 15 years after the great reforms to the UN human rights machinery, it is unlikely that the UN will be in any rush to implement new changes. Firstly, that would involve acknowledging the deficiencies of the very recent reforms. Secondly, the costs involved are vast, not only the money and resources but also the time that is diverted from human rights work in order to create and implement reforms. It took six years from the first official reform proposals until the Human Rights Council was created. The final year of the Commission was largely devoted to discussions about the new body. The Council's first year saw the suspension of all human rights mandates—and of almost all substantive human rights discussions—so that adequate time could be devoted to setting up new mechanisms and writing the Council's 'Institution Building Package'.[1] Of course, during that time, countless abuses against countless victims were simply not addressed by the Council. Any radical proposals for reforming UN human rights bodies must take these considerations into account.

It seems improbable, then, that any great changes will take place in the foreseeable future. Yet simply ignoring the UN's deficiencies in human rights protection has serious implications for the many victims of abuses, for states, and for the UN's credibility. For those who advocate maintaining the *status quo*, some minor changes would make the individual bodies operate more efficiently. While that might have some merit, it will not address the systemic and inherent protection problems.

But what else can be done at the UN?

Linkage is crucial. Countries apply to the UN, to the WTO, and to the IMF, for money, for resources, for capacity-building regarding a whole range of areas. States also apply to the EU for aid, and to other international organisations. That money, those resources, support for development, alongside economic and trade ties, might well be used to place pressure on countries to comply with human rights obligations. This works at the regional level. Political, economic and other pressures encourage—or coerce—many states to comply with regional human rights mechanisms. So, why not use this type of linkage between human rights and other areas such as economic aid and trade?

'But that is neo-imperialism', some will cry. 'Human rights ought not to be used as a neo-colonial tool of oppression.' Perhaps that is true on many human rights issues, but not on the protection of fundamental rights. Can anyone truly claim that it would be neo-imperialist to use linkage to protect individuals from torture, or from state-sponsored slavery, or from arbitrary extra-judicial killing? Can anyone really claim that those rights are Global North ideologies to which other countries do not subscribe? Are the most fundamental rights only applicable in some states or regions? Or ought we, the international community, to use every tool available to ensure that every person around the world has their most basic rights protected? If states are prepared to politicise the international human rights system, then at some point fire might be fought with fire— political linkage might be the best tool available with which to force states to implement the most fundamental rights and freedoms.

But that is a radical suggestion. There are others that would be easier to implement and less contentious.

One possible reform would be to make better use of the full range of bodies under the umbrella of the human rights machinery. The Human Rights Council in its current form as a political body is ill-equipped to undertake protection activities. However, the committees that monitor the core human rights treaties are designed for exactly that purpose. Composed of independent experts, they are able to fulfil adjudicatory functions. The major obstacle here is that the bodies only have jurisdiction over states party to the relevant human rights treaty.

One method for utilising treaty bodies for universal protection is to require all UN member states to ratify the core codifying treaties—the International Covenant on Civil and Political Rights and the International Covenant on Economic, Social and Cultural Rights. The treaty bodies would then be able to adjudicate on alleged violations that fall under those two broad treaties. The question is how practicable such an idea might be.

On the one hand, the new Universal Periodic Review demonstrates that it is possible to require all UN member states to comply with a human rights mechanism. Diplomatic pressures have ensured that all countries—even Israel, which between 2012 and 2013 was the only country to withdraw from the mechanism—attend and engage with their review sessions. While the reviews are not adjudicatory or adversarial, it is a peer-led process that states view as intrusive and embarrassing owing to the information-sharing and criticisms that occur within sessions. Yet all countries feel sufficiently pressured to attend. Surely, those experiences and lessons can be mapped across in order to ensure universal engagement with the human rights treaty bodies that are tasked with protecting rights?

But it is not quite as simple as that.

As has already been argued, international law relies on state consent to be bound. States would be likely to withdraw from a system that eroded their sovereignty by undermining the consent principle. Mandating that countries ratify a treaty directly contradicts the central tenet of state sovereignty. It is one thing to require states to ratify a treaty before becoming a member of an international organisation, but quite another to make that demand *ex post facto*. And from a political perspective, powerful countries—not least the US and China, with their exceptionalist approach to international law and ideological issues with certain categories of rights—would strongly oppose such a requirement.

Another method for better protecting human rights would be to rely more heavily upon the Security Council when dealing with gross and systemic human rights violations. That body has enforcement powers and is equipped to act swiftly and decisively. Enforcement powers are what make the Security Council so attractive for protecting human rights. Giving such powers to the Human Rights Council is not a realistic possibility within the current geopolitical climate, however. The most powerful members of the UN—China, Russia and the US—would not consider a proposal that empowered other countries to use enforcement mechanisms over which those three states did not hold a veto power. The only UN body likely ever to have such powers is the Security Council.

Human rights form part of international peace and security, and therefore fall squarely within the Security Council's mandate. Indeed, as we have seen, the Security Council increasingly has taken on the role of protecting human rights within the context of international peace and security. But so many abuses do not occur within that context. Violations of rights do not always, or even usually, have a link to peace and security. So the Council cannot always use its powers to act to protect them.

Even if the Security Council's mandate was extended, there is only so much work that any one body can do. The Security Council's focus is maintaining international peace and security—it simply would not have the time or resources to devote to broader human rights protection. And while security, development and human rights are inextricably linked, there must be apparatus and mechanisms for each separate area in order to ensure that adequate expertise, resources and time are devoted to each one.

Lastly, it must not be forgotten that the Security Council is not itself immune from politicisation. It is hampered by international politics, and its work is directed by the permanent members' threat or use of the veto power. Action on peace and security is politicised, as is the Security Council's protection of human rights. It does fail to take any action regarding its permanent members' allies—for example Israel or Syria—despite gross and systemic violations within the context of threats to international peace and security. Holding up the Security Council as the great hope for depoliticised protection of human rights is, then, naïve to say the least.

Concluding observations

So, should we just give up on protecting individuals from gross and systemic abuses? Ought we to focus only on protecting rights within states that engage with and are affected by international relations? Clearly not. Yet it is equally clear that the current system is not fit for purpose when it comes to the gravest human rights situations. Political bodies have little influence on countries that do not care or need to worry about politics. So, if we want change, other approaches must be followed. But, let me re-emphasise that these approaches need only focus on protection activities. The UN system for developing and promoting rights ain't broke; so why fix it?

Global North states each contribute tens or even hundreds of millions of dollars to human rights every year. The United Nations achieves great successes in developing and promoting those rights. But it is failing to protect individuals from grave abuses. We need to understand the problem before we can find solutions. NGOs, the media, policy-makers and voters all need to engage with the subject in order to propose and implement changes that will actually make a difference on the ground. This book has sought to start that conversation—to detail some of the things that are not working with a view to finding a way in which they can be fixed. The proposed solutions are only a start. What we need is a conversation to take place not just at the UN or diplomatic level or amongst the human rights elite, but also amongst the wider public. Where we go next is not simply for the diplomats and government delegates to decide. It is our money; it is our world; it is our problem.

NOTES

PROLOGUE

1. On the situation in Darfur, generally, see S. Totten, *Genocide in Darfur: Investigating the Atrocities in the Sudan* (London: Routledge), 2006; and contributions in A. F. Grzyb (ed.), *The World and Darfur: International Response to Crimes against Humanity in Western Sudan* (Quebec: McGill-Queen's University Press, 2009).

2. 'Mass Rape Atrocity in West Sudan', 19 March 2004, *BBC News Online*, available at http://news.bbc.co.uk/1/hi/world/africa/3549325.stm (reporting on an interview given to BBC Radio 4).

3. Ibid.

4. Kofi Annan, address to the UN Commission on Human Rights, Geneva, 7 April 2004, UN News Service, http://www.un.org/apps/news/printnewsAr.asp?nid=10377

5. For example, Security Council, 'Security Council Resolution 1547 (2004) on the situation in Sudan', 11 June 2004, UN Doc. S/RES/1547; Security Council, 'Security Council Resolution 1588 (2005) on the United Nations Advance Mission in Sudan (UNAMIS)', 17 March 2005, UN Doc. S/RES/1588; Security Council, 'Security Council Resolution 1590 (2005) [on establishment of the UN Mission in Sudan (UNMIS)]', 24 March 2005, UN Doc. S/RES/1590; Security Council, 'Security Council Resolution 1651 (2005) Reports of the Secretary-General on the Sudan', 21 December 2005, UN Doc. S/RES/1651; and Security Council, 'Security Council Resolution 1665 (2006) Reports of the Secretary-General on the Sudan', 29 March 2006, UN Doc. S/RES/1665.

6. For example, Security Council, 'Security Council Resolution 1574 (2004) on Sudan', 19 November 2004, UN Doc. S/RES/1574; and Security Council, 'Security Council Resolution 1627 (2005) Reports of the Secretary-General on the Sudan', 23 September 2005, UN Doc. S/RES/1627.

7. For example, Security Council, 'Security Council Resolution 1556 (2004) on measures to prevent the sale or supply of arms and related material', 30 July 2004, UN Doc. S/RES/1556.

8. For example, Security Council, 'Security Council Resolution 1564 (2004) on Darfur, Sudan', 18 September 2004, UN Doc. S/RES/1564.

9. For example, Security Council, 'Security Council Resolution 1591 (2005) on Sudan', 29 March 2005, UN Doc. S/RES/1591.

10. For example, Security Council, 'Security Council Resolution 1593 (2005) on Violations of International Humanitarian Law and Human Rights Law in Darfur', Sudan, 31 March 2005, UN Doc. S/RES/1593.

11. See, for example, Opheera McDoom, 'China Urges Dialogue Not Sanctions on Darfur', *Reuters*, 2 September 2007, available at http://www.reuters.com/article/africaCrisis/idUSMCD230720; United Nations Panel of Experts on Sudan, *Final Report from the Panel of Experts* (New York: United Nations, 2006), UN Doc. S/2006/65, available at http://www.un.org/sc/committees/1591/reports.shtml; and Andrei Chang, 'Analysis: China Sells Arms to Sudan', *United Press International*, 15 February 2008, available at http://www.upi.com/International_Security/Industry/Analysis/2008/02/15/analysis_china_sells_arms_to_sudan/7530/

12. See, for example, Amnesty International Report, 'Darfur: New weapons from China and Russia fuelling conflict', *Amnesty International*, 8 February 2012, available at http://www.amnesty.org/en/news/
darfur-new-weapons-china-and-russia-fuelling-conflict-2012-02-08

13. R. Freedman, *The United Nations Human Rights Council: A Critique and Early Assessment* (Abingdon: Routledge, 2013), ch. 8.

14. For example, Pakistan and Algeria both abstained from Security Council resolutions criticising Sudan's government.

1. INTERNATIONAL LAW: WHAT LAW?

1. Richard Norton-Taylor, Peter Walker and Robert Booth, 'Binyam Mohamed returns to Britain after Guantanamo ordeal', *The Guardian*, 23 February 2009, available at http://www.theguardian.com/uk/2009/feb/23/binyam-mohamed-guantanamo-plane-lands

2. Ibid.

3. '"Human Cargo": Binyam Mohamed and the Rendition Frequent Flier Programme', *Reprieve*, 10 June 2008, available at http://www.reprieve.org.uk/static/downloads/Microsoft_Word_-_2008_06_10_Mohamed_-_Human_Cargo_Final.pdf

4. Ibid.

5. Clare Algar, 'It's time to come clean about a shameful chapter in our history', *Reprieve*, 23 February 2009, available at http://www.reprieve.org.uk/blog/2009_02_23binyammmohamedreturn/

6. Clive Stafford Smith, 'A statement from Binyam Mohamed', *Reprieve*, 23 February 2009, available at http://www.reprieve.org.uk/articles/statementofbinyammohamed/

7. Open Society Justice Initiative, *Globalizing Torture: CIA Secret Detention and Extraordinary Detention* (New York: Open Society Foundations, 2013), available at http://www.opensocietyfoundations.org/sites/default/files/globalizing-torture-20120205.pdf

8. See, for example, Dana Priest, 'Wrongful Imprisonment: Anatomy of a CIA Mistake—German Citizen Released After Months in "Rendition"', *Washington Post*, 4 December 2005, available at http://www.washingtonpost.com/wp-dyn/content/article/2005/12/03/AR2005120301476_pf.html

9. See, for example, William J. Kole, 'Austria probes CIA's alleged use of flight space: Joins widening European inquiry', *Associated Press*, 24 November 2005; and Andrew Higgins and Christopher Cooper, 'CIA-Backed Team Used Brutal Means To Break Up Terrorist Cell in Albania', *Wall Street Journal*, 20 November 2001.

10. W. Kaleck, K. Majchrzak, G. Sotiriadis and C. Peterson, 'CIA Extraordinary Rendition Flights, Torture and Accountability—A European Approach', *European Center for Constitutional and Human Rights*, March 2008, pp. 95–101 (The Case of Bensayah Belkacem, Hadj Boudellaa, Lakmar Boumediene, Sabir Mahfouz Lahmar, Mustafa Ait Idr, and Mohammad Nechle).

11. Ibid., pp. 75–80 (The Case of Maher Arar).

12. 'Statement on U.S. Secret Detention Facilities in Europe', *Human Rights Watch*, 7 November 2005, available at http://www.hrw.org/en/news/2005/11/06/human-rights-watch-statement-us-secret-detention-facilities-europe

13. Kaleck, Majchrzak, Sotiriadis and Peterson, *supra* note 10, pp. 140–44 (The Governmental Inquiry in Denmark).

14. Ibid., pp. 115–18 (The Criminal Complaint against Arbitrary Detention and Torture).

15. Human Rights Watch, *supra* note 12.

16. Ibid.

17. Kaleck, Majchrzak, Sotiriadis and Peterson, *supra* note 10, pp. 80–86 (The Case of Osama Mustafa Hassan Nasr 'Abu Omar').

18. Amnesty International, 'Further Information on UA 22/05 (MDE 24/005/2005, 26 January 2005)—Fear of torture/incommunicado detention', 18 April 2005, AI Index MDe 24/019/2005.

19. Kaleck, Majchrzak, Sotiriadis and Peterson, *supra* note 10, pp. 122–7 (The Criminal Investigation into the Existence of Black Sites in Poland).

20. Human Rights Watch, *supra* note 12.

21. Kaleck, Majchrzak, Sotiriadis and Peterson, *supra* note 10, pp. 68–75 (The Case of Ahmed Agiza and Mohammed Al Zery); HRW, 'Swedish TV4 Kalla Fakta Program: 'The Broken Promise', Part IV', *Human Rights Watch*, 22 November 2004, available at http://www.hrw.org/en/news/2004/11/21/swedish-tv4-kalla-fakta-program-broken-promise-part-iv

22. Kaleck, Majchrzak, Sotiriadis and Peterson, *supra* note 10, pp. 87–95 (The Cases of Binyam Mohamed, Bisher al-Rawi and Jamil el-Banna).

23. Open Society Justice Initiative, *supra* note 7; and Jessica Elgot, 'Extraordinary Rendition: Israel, Russia and France 'Surprisingly' Not On List', *Huffington Post UK*, 5 February 2013, available at http://www.huffingtonpost.co.uk/2013/02/05/extraordinary-rendition_n_2622079.html

24. See M. L. Satterthwaite, 'Rendered Meaningless: Extraordinary Rendition and the Rule of Law', 75 *George Washington Law Review* (2007, pp. 1333–420); Association of the Bar of the City of New York and Center for Human Rights and Global Justice, *Torture by Proxy: International and Domestic Law Applicable to 'Extraordinary Renditions'* (New York: ABCNY and NYU School of Law, 2004); L. N. Sadat, 'Ghost Prisoners and Black Sites: Extraordinary Rendition Under International Law', 37 *Case Western Reserve University Journal of International Law* (2005), pp. 309–42.

25. The prohibition against torture is one of *jus cogens*; see, for example, *Ex parte Pinochet (No. 3)* [2000] 1 AC 147; and the *Furundzija* case, 121 ILR, pp. 213, 260–2. Rules of *jus cogens* are 'substantive rules recognised to be of a higher status as such …. The concept of *jus cogens* is based upon an acceptance of fundamental and superior values within the system.' M. N. Shaw, *International Law* (6th edn, Cambridge: Cambridge University Press, 2008), pp. 124–5.

26. Human rights are applicable in times of war and peace (HR Cttee General Comment No. 31 (2004), para 11; ICJ, *Legality of the Threat or Use of Nuclear Weapons* [1996] ICJ Rep 226; ICJ, *Legal Consequences of the Construction of a Wall in the Occupied Palestinian Territory* [2004] ICJ Rep 136). However, in times of genuine emergency, derogations—temporary repeal of particular guarantees—may be permitted when states are not in a position fully to comply with their obligations. Derogation clauses are found in, for example, International Covenant on Civil and Political Rights, Article 4(1); European Convention on Human Rights, Article 15; American Convention on Human Rights, Article 27; European Social Charter Article 30. Not all human rights treaties include derogation clauses, although state parties may be able to invoke necessity as grounds for breaching its obligations if (a) it is the only way for a state to safeguard an essential interest against an imminent threat, and (b) it does not seriously impair an essential interest of the right-holder (Article 25(1), International Law Commission Draft Articles on State Responsibility).

27. *Supra* note 25.

28. E.g. General Assembly Resolution 39/46, *Convention Against Torture and Other Cruel, Inhuman or Degrading Treatment or Punishment*, 10 December 1984, UN Doc. A/RES/39/46; GA Res. 2200A (XXI), 'International Covenant on Civil and Political Rights', 16 December 1966, UN Doc. A/6316 (1966), Article 7. For example, torture is prohibited by Article 3 common to the four Geneva Conventions, Article 12 of the First and Second Geneva Conventions, Articles 17 and 87 of the Third Geneva Convention, Article 32 of the Fourth Geneva Convention, Article 75 (2 a & e) of Additional Protocol I and Article 4 (2 a & h) of Additional Protocol II. In international armed conflict, torture constitutes a grave breach under Articles 50, 51, 130 and 147 respectively of these Conventions. Under Article 85 of Additional Protocol I, these breaches constitute war crimes. Article 75 (2 b & e) of Additional Protocol I and Article 4 (2 a & h) of Additional Protocol II prohibit 'outrages upon personal dignity, in particular humiliating and degrading treatment'. In international armed conflict, these acts constitute grave breaches; in non-international armed conflict, they constitute serious violations.

29. See, for example, General Assembly Resolution 39/46, *Convention against Torture and Other Cruel, Inhuman or Degrading Treatment or Punishment*, 10 December 1984, UN Doc. A/RES/39/46, Article 3.

30. For a thorough and comprehensive analysis of all the international instruments of a universal character violated by the practice of extraordinary rendition, see D. Weissbrodt and A. Bergquist, 'Extraordinary Rendition: A Human Rights Analysis', 19 *Harvard Human Rights Journal* (2006), pp. 123–60.

31. On international law and the 'War on Terror', see for example H. Duffy, *The 'War on Terror' and the Framework of International Law* (Cambridge: Cambridge University Press, 2005). For an international relations perspective, see M. Evangelista, *Law, Ethics, and the War on Terror* (Cambridge: Polity Press, 2013).

32. For detailed analyses of enforcement in international law, cf. E. Katselli Proukaki, *The Problem of Enforcement in International Law: Countermeasures, the Non-injured State and the Idea of International Community* (Abingdon: Routledge, 2010); and C. J. Tams, *Enforcing Obligations Erga Omnes in International Law* (Cambridge: Cambridge University Press, 2005).

33. The concept of state sovereignty emerged in the sixteenth century. Jean Bodin provided the first systematic analysis of the concept; cf. A. Gardot, 'Jean Bodin—Sa Place Parmi les Fondateurs du Droit International', 50 *HR* (1934). For a brief history of the development of the concept of state sovereignty (and, more broadly, international law), see M. N. Shaw, *International Law* (6th edn, Cambridge: Cambridge University Press, 2008), pp. 13–42.

34. *Supra* note 25.

35. See M. Cherif Bassiouni, 'International Crimes: *Jus cogens* and *obligatio erga omnes*', 59 *Law and Contemporary Problems* (1996), pp. 63–74.

36. *Yearbook of the International Law Commission* (1966), vol. II, p. 238.

37. The US has signed but not ratified the UN Convention on the Rights of the Child. For an analysis, cf. S. Kilbourne, 'U.S. Failure to Ratify the U.N. Convention on the Rights of the Child: Playing Politics with Children's Rights', 6 *Transnational Law and Contemporary Problems* (1996), pp. 437–62.

38. See J. Hovi, D. F. Sprinz and G. Bang, 'Why the United States did not become a party to the Kyoto Protocol: German, Norwegian, and US perspectives', 18 *European Journal of International Relations* (2012), pp. 129–50.

39. See, for example, N. T. Saito, *Meeting the Enemy: American Exceptionalism and International Law* (New York: New York University Press, 2010). On American exceptionalism and international human rights, cf. M. Ignatieff (ed.), *American Exceptionalism and Human Rights* (Princeton, NJ: Princeton University Press, 2005).

40. General Assembly Resolution 34/180, 'Convention to Eliminate all forms of Discrimination Against Women', 18 December 1979, UN Doc. A/RES/34/180.

41. See, for example, N. Parpworth, 'Succession to the Crown Act 2013: Modernising the Monarchy', 76 *Modern Law Review* (2013), pp. 1070–93.

42. For a general discussion on reservations to international human rights treaties, see

E. Lijnzaad, *Reservations to Un-Human Rights Treaties: Ratify and Ruin?* (Brill: Martinus Nijhoff, 1995).

43. For example, the US was at the fore in the processes developing the Rome Statute (creating the International Criminal Court) and yet is not party to that treaty.

44. For a more detailed exploration of treaties as a source of international law, see E. Cannizarro (ed.), *The Law of Treaties Beyond the Vienna Convention* (Oxford: Oxford University Press, 2011).

45. *Nicaragua v. United States*, ICJ Reports (1986), p. 14; 76 ILR, p. 349.

46. The US used its veto against a Security Council Draft Resolution proposed by Congo, Ghana, Madagascar, Trinidad and Tobago, and United Arab Emirates (28 October 1986, UN Doc. S/18428) that was proposed in response to 'Letter dated 17 October 1986 from Nicaragua to the President of the Security Council'.

2. THE UN: A BRIEF EXPLANATION

1. The splintered leg of the monumental chair reminds us of the fractured limbs of the injuries caused by landmines, and yet the chair stands firmly in place, much the same as victims of landmines do, that is, if they survive the horrific accident. Initially the installation weighing 5.5 tons and measuring 12 metres (39 ft) in height was planned to stay at the Place des Nations for only three months, until the Mine Ban Treaty, also known as the Ottawa Treaty, would be signed in December 1997. But then not every country signed the treaty, and it was decided to keep the chair in place as long as it was needed as a reminder. Although more and more countries sign both treaties, some still have not, amongst them the USA and Israel, who used landmines in the Iraq War and in the bombing of Lebanon respectively.

2. The origins of international law are widely accepted as beginning with the Peace of Westphalia. That term refers to a series of peace treaties signed between May and October 1648, which ended the Thirty Years' War (1618–1648) in the Holy Roman Empire and the Eighty Years' War (1568–1648) between Spain and the Dutch Republic. For a detailed exploration of the origins of international law, see for example R. Lesaffer, 'The Classical Law of Nations (1500–1800)', in A. Orakhelashvili (ed.), *Research Handbook on the Theory and History of International Law* (Cheltenham: Edward Elgar, 2011), pp. 408–40.

3. United Nations Charter (1945), Article 2.

4. Thomas Weiss gives a short but important account of how state sovereignty and the continuation of 'Westphalia' undermine the UN's activities: T. G. Weiss, *What's Wrong with the United Nations and How to Fix It* (Cambridge: Polity Press, 2009), pp. 37–48.

5. Preamble to the United Nations Charter (1945).

6. United Nations Charter (1945). For a detailed analysis of the Charter, see B. Simma (ed.), *The Charter of the United Nations: A Commentary* (Oxford: Oxford University Press, 1995).

7. United Nations Charter (1945), Article 4.

8. United Nations Charter (1945), Article 2(6): 'The Organization shall ensure that states which are not Members of the United Nations act in accordance with these Principles so far as may be necessary for the maintenance of international peace and security.'

9. China, France, Russia (USSR and now Russian Federation), United Kingdom and United States.

10. A. P. Dobson and S. Marsh, *US Foreign Policy since 1945* (2nd edn, Abingdon: Routledge, 2007).

11. Russia, together with China, used its veto power to block Security Council Draft Resolutions on Syria on 4 October 2011 (UN Doc. S/S/2011/612), 4 February 2012 (UN Doc. S/2012/77) and 19 July 2012 (UN Doc. S/2012/538).

12. See, for example, Alexei Anishchuk, 'Russia could boost Iran arms sales if U.S. strikes Syria: Putin ally', *Reuters*, 11 September 2013, available at http://www.reuters.com/article/2013/09/11/us-syria-crisis-russia-idUSBRE98A0Q120130911

13. See, for example, Michael Martina, 'China replaces Britain in world's top five arms exporters: report', *Reuters*, 18 March 2013.

14. See, for example, Hilary Andersson, 'China "is fuelling war in Darfur"', *BBC News Online*, 13 July 2008, available at http://news.bbc.co.uk/1/hi/world/africa/7503428.stm

15. For a more detailed background on the history and operation of the Security Council, see D. M. Malone, 'Security Council', in T. G. Weiss and S. Daws (eds), *The Oxford Handbook on the United Nations* (Oxford: Oxford University Press, 2007), pp. 117–35.

16. George Orwell, *Animal Farm* (London: Penguin Modern Classics, 2004).

17. Throughout the UN's existence, proposals have continued to be made to create such an army. For a recent example see R. C. Johansen (ed.), *A United Nations Emergency Peace Service: To Prevent Genocide and Crimes Against Humanity* (New York: World Federalist Movement Institute for Global Policy, 2006).

18. United Nations Charter (1945), Articles 41, 42 and 43.

19. United Nations Charter (1945), Articles 40 and 41.

20. See D. Cortright and G. A. Lopez, *The Sanctions Decade: Assessing UN Strategies in the 1990s* (Colorado: Lynne Rienner, 2002). For explanations of the limitations of sanctions in theory and in practice, see S. W. Drezner, *The Sanctions Paradox: Economic Statecraft and International Relations* (Cambridge: Cambridge University Press, 1999).

21. These are a form of targeted sanctions, often used in conjunction with other sanctions. They have been used as a stand-alone measure, for example in relation to Rwanda, Somalia and Yugoslavia. For a detailed discussion on arms embargoes, see A. Knight, *The United Nations and Arms Embargoes Verification* (New York: Edwin Mellen Press, 1998).

22. See, for example, Security Council Resolution 1441, 'Resolution 1441 (2002)', 8 November 2002, UN Doc. S/RES/1441, which authorised a weapons inspection regime on Iraq.

23. See, for example, Security Council Resolution 1973, 'Resolution 1973 (2011)', 17 March 2011, UN Doc. S/RES/1973, which authorised no-fly zones over Libya.

24. See, generally, M. Lyons, D. A. Baldwin and D. W. McNemar, 'The 'Politicization' Issue in the UN Specialized Agencies', 32 *Proceedings of the Academy of Political Science* (1977), pp. 81–92.

25. For a more detailed exploration of the history and practices of this body, see M. J. Peterson, 'General Assembly', in T. G. Weiss and S. Daws (eds), *The Oxford Handbook on the United Nations* (Oxford: Oxford University Press, 2007), pp. 97–116.

26. 'Diplomacy' is a board game based on real-life practices. For an engaging and thoughtful discussion about the game, see R. Sharp, *The Game of Diplomacy* (London: Arthur Baker, 1978).

27. R. Freedman, *supra* Prologue note 13, p. 135.

28. J. Mertus notes that each year approximately 20 per cent of GA resolutions relate to human rights, which underlines the disproportionate attention given to Southern Africa. J. Mertus, *The United Nations and Human Rights: A Guide for a New Era* (Abingdon: Taylor and Francis, 2009), p. 40.

29. E. Heinze, 'Truth and Myth in Critical Race Theory and Lat Crit: Human Rights and the Ethnocentrism of Anti-Ethnocentrism', 20(2) *National Black Law Journal* (2007), p. 23.

30. Indeed, the majority of those focusing on the financing of the UN peacekeeping mission within that country.

31. R. Freedman, 'The United Nations Human Rights Council: More of the Same?' 31 *Wisconsin Journal of International Law* (2013), pp. 208–251.

32. The five regional groups were established in 1963 and are used by the UN to ensure proportionate geographic representation when apportioning seats or membership to UN bodies. See, for example, R. Thakur, *What is Equitable Geographical Distribution in the 21st Century?* (New York: United Nations University, 1999).

33. See, generally, B. Andemicael (ed.), *Regionalism and the United Nations* (New York: Oceana Publications Ltd, 1979).

34. Particularly Iraq and Saudi Arabia.

35. M. Dennis, 'Human Rights in 2002: The Annual Sessions of the UN Commission on Human Rights and the Economic and Social Council', 97 *American Journal of International Law* (2003), p. 384.

36. D. Nicol, 'Interregional Co-ordination Within the United Nations: The Role of the Commonwealth', in B. Andemicael (ed.), *Regionalism and the United Nations* (New York: Oceana Publications Ltd, 1979), p. 102.

37. See, for example, G. Lundestad, *East, West, North, South: Major Developments on International Politics Since 1945* (Oxford: Oxford University Press, 1999); P. Worsley, *The Third World* (London: Weidenfeld and Nicolson, 1964); M. T. Berger, 'After the Third World? History, Destiny and the Fate of Third Worldism', 25 *Third World Quarterly* (2004), p. 13; and T. G. Weiss, *supra* note 4, pp. 51–2.

38. See, generally, J. S. Nye, 'UNCTAD: Poor Nations' Pressure Group', in R. W. Cox and H. K. Jacobson (eds), *The Anatomy of Influence: Decision Making in International Organization* (New Haven: Yale University Press, 1973), pp. 334–70.

39. The Treaty of Lisbon (European Union, 'Treaty of Lisbon Amending the Treaty on European Union and the Treaty Establishing the European Community', 13 December 2007, 2007/C 306/01) requires EU member states to seek and advance common foreign policies (European Union, 'Consolidation Version of the Treaty on European Union', reproduced 30 March 2012, 2010/C83/01. Title V, in particular Articles 24–35). Article 34(1) TEU (ex. Article 19 (1)) provides that EU members 'shall coordinate their action in international organisations and [...] shall uphold the common positions in such forums'. EU member states were, from 1993, required to speak with one voice on foreign policy matters, which occurs by negotiating and compromising to find common ground between member states (the common position requirement was first adopted in European Union, 'Treaty on European Union [Consolidated Version], Treaty of Maastricht', 7 February 1992, *Official Journal of the European Communities* C 325/5, entered into force 1 November 1993). This requirement is particularly difficult regarding foreign policy as member states have different interests, allegiances, priorities and preferences. U. Khaliq comments that the process is rarely straightforward, in *Ethical Dimensions of the Foreign Policy of the European Union: A Legal Appraisal* (Cambridge: Cambridge University Press, 2008), p. 88.

40. 21 Sub-Saharan African, 12 Asian, 18 Middle Eastern and North African States, 3 Eastern European and Caucasian, 2 South American, and 1 Permanent Observer Mission. See 'Organisation of the Islamic Conference; Permanent Missions of OIC Member States to the United Nations in New York', http://www.oic-oci.org/oicv2/

41. For a detailed exploration of the OIC, see E. Hisanoglu, *The Islamic World in the New Century: The Organisation of the Islamic Conference, 1969–2009* (London: Hurst & Co., 2010).

3. INTERNATIONAL HUMANITARIAN LAW, CRIMINAL LAW, HUMAN RIGHTS LAW

1. For more detailed analysis and exploration of international humanitarian law, see D. Fleck (ed.), *The Handbook of International Humanitarian Law* (2nd edn, Oxford: Oxford University Press, 2009).

2. On the history and origins of the Red Cross, see, for example, D. P. Forsythe, *The Humanitarians: The International Committee of the Red Cross* (Cambridge: Cambridge University Press, 2005).

3. 'Geneva Convention for the Amelioration of the Condition of the Wounded and Sick in Armed Forces in the Field', signed in Geneva 22 August 1864. The Convention was replaced by Geneva Conventions on the same subject in 1906, 1929 and 1949.

4. 'Geneva Convention for the Amelioration of the Condition of the Wounded and

Sick in Armed Forces in the Field', 12 August 1949, 75 United Nations Treaty Series, p. 31.

5. For example, 'Geneva Convention Relative to the Treatment of Prisoners of War', 12 August 1949, 75 United Nations Treaty Series, p. 175, Article 7; and 'Geneva Convention relative to the Protection of Civilian Persons in Time of War', 12 August 1949, 75 United Nations Treaty Series, p. 287, Article 8.

6. F. Kalshoven, 'The Undertaking to Respect and Ensure Respect in All Circumstances from Tiny Seed to Ripening Fruit', (1999) 2 *Yearbook of International Humanitarian Law* 60; ICJ, *Legal Consequences of the Construction of a Wall in the Occupied Palestinian Territory* (Advisory Opinion), ICJ Reports 2004, Separate Opinion of Judge Higgins, para.14.

7. The second category is split into those in the power of a party to an international armed conflict and those in the power of a party to a non-international armed conflict. Different legal obligations apply to the sub-categories. See, for example, W. Kalin and J. Kunzli, *The Law of International Human Rights Protection* (Oxford: Oxford University Press, 2009), pp. 171–2, 175.

8. M. N. Shaw, *International Law* (6th edn, Cambridge: Cambridge University Press, 2008), pp. 1200–3.

9. T. Meron, *Human Rights in Internal Strife: Their International Protection* (Cambridge: Cambridge University Press, 1987), p. 28.

10. See Kalin and Kunzli, *supra* note 7, p. 179.

11. G. Lawrence, 'The Nuremberg Trial', 23(2) *International Affairs* (1947), pp. 151–9, at pp. 152–3.

12. The Extraordinary Chambers in the Courts of Cambodia (ECCC) is a hybrid court established in 2003 by the Cambodian government and the United Nations and consists of Cambodian and international judges. It prosecutes senior members of the Khmer Rouge for international crimes that took place between 1975 and 1979.

13. The International Criminal Tribunal for Yugoslavia was established in 1993 to prosecute individuals most responsible for international crimes in the former Yugoslavia during the 1990s. It is a UN *ad hoc* court. The ICTY was the first UN war crimes court and the first international war crimes tribunal since the Nuremberg and Tokyo tribunals. It was established by the Security Council in accordance with Chapter VII of the UN Charter.

14. The International Criminal Tribunal for Rwanda was created in 1994 to prosecute individuals most responsible for international crimes and violations of international humanitarian law in Rwanda and neighbouring areas between 1 January 1994 and 31 December 1994. It is a UN *ad hoc* court and was established by the Security Council in accordance with Chapter VII of the UN Charter.

15. The Special Court for Sierra Leone was set up jointly by the Government of Sierra Leone and the United Nations in 2002. It prosecutes individuals who bear the greatest responsibility for violations of international humanitarian law and Sierra Leonean law committed in the territory of Sierra Leone since 30 November 1996. It is funded entirely by voluntary contributions from the international community.

16. See, for example, D. McGoldrick, P. Rowe and E. Donnelly (eds), *The Permanent International Criminal Court* (Oxford: Hart Publishing, 2004).

17. See, for example, Amnesty International, 'UN: Demand al-Bashir's surrender to the International Criminal Court', *Amnesty International News*, 20 September 2013, available at http://www.amnesty.org/en/news/un-demand-al-bashir-s-surrender-international-criminal-court-2013–09–20

18. General Assembly Resolution 217A (III), 'Universal Declaration of Human Rights', 1948, UN Doc. A/810, 71.

19. Council of Europe, 'European Convention for the Protection of Human Rights and Fundamental Freedoms', 4 November 1950, European Treaties Series no. 5; 213 United Nations Treaties Series, p. 221.

20. General Assembly Resolution 2200A (XXI), 'International Covenant on Civil and Political Rights', 16 December 1966, UN Doc. A/6316.

21. General Assembly Resolution 2200A (XXI), 'International Covenant on Economic, Social and Cultural Rights', 16 December 1966, UN Doc. A/6316.

22. International Covenant on Civil and Political Rights, *supra* note 20, Article 2(1) and ICESCR, *id.*, Article 2(2) both contain the same provisions on non-discrimination in terms of the substantive rights within the treaties. Common Article 3 sets out a similar provision regarding gender quality. ICCPR Article 26 also sets out an autonomous right to equality.

23. Article 1 in both treaties contains identical provisions on the right to self-determination.

24. See, for example, 'Third Generation of Solidarity Rights: Progressive Development or Obfuscation of International Human Rights Law?' (1982) 29 *Netherlands International Law Review* 307; G. Triggs, 'The Rights of "Peoples" and Individual Rights: Conflict or Harmony?' in J. Crawford (ed.), *The Rights Of Peoples* (1988), p. 141.

25. See, for example, B. H. Weston, 'Human Rights', 6(3) *Human Rights Quarterly* (1984), p. 257.

26. See, for example, Freedman, '"Third Generation" Rights: Is There Room for Hybrid Constructs within International Human Rights Law?', 2(4) *Cambridge Journal of International and Comparative Law* (2013), pp. 935–59.

27. See, for example, P. Alston and G. Quinn, 'The Nature and Scope of States Parties' Obligations under the International Covenant on Economic, Social and Cultural Rights', 9(2) *Human Rights Quarterly* (1987).

28. For example, *Olga Tellis v. Bombay Municipal Corporation*, Supreme Court of India (1985), AIR 1986 Supreme Court 18; *People's Union for Civil Liberties v. Union of India & Others*, Supreme Court of India (2001) Writ Petition (Civil) No. 196/2001; *State of Karnataka v. Appa Balu Ingale*, 1993, AIR 1993 SC 1126.

29. For example, *Soobramoney v. Minister of Health (Kwazulu-Natal)*, Constitutional Court of South Africa, Case CCT 32/97, 27 November 1997; *Government of South Africa v. Grootboom*, Constitutional Court of South Africa, Case CCT 11/00,

4 October 2000; *Minister of Health and Others v. Treatment Action Campaign*, 2002 5 SA 721 (CC).

30. H. Hamilton, 'Mori v. Japan: The Nagoya High Court Recognises the Right to Live in Peace', 19(3) *Pacific Rim Law and Policy Journal* (2010), p. 549.

31. See, J. E. Pim, *Non-Killing, Security and the State* (Omaha: Creighton University, 2013), pp. 188–90, concerning the three Costa Rica cases: Ruling 9992–040; Executive Order 33240-S (2006); and Ruling 14193–08.

32. International Covenant on Economic, Social and Cultural Rights, *supra* note 21, Article 2(1). See also Committee of Economic, Social and Cultural Rights, 'General Comment No. 3, The Nature of States Parties' Obligations', 14 December 1990, UN Doc. E/1991/23, paras. 2 and 3.

33. Ibid.

34. Ibid. at para 13.

35. Ibid. at para 10.

36. Louis Henkin, *How Nations Behave: Law and Foreign Policy* (2nd edn, New York: Columbia University Press, 1979), p. 47.

4. UNIVERSAL RIGHTS OR CULTURAL RELATIVISM?

1. Excerpt from 'The Waris Dirie Story', *Readers Digest*, June 1999, available at http://www.fgmnetwork.org/articles/Waris.html

2. Ibid.

3. For an overview of the law and practice of FGM, see A. Rahman and N. Toubia, *Female Genital Mutilation: A Guide to Laws and Politics Worldwide* (London: Zed Books, 2000).

4. General Assembly Resolution 44/25, 'United Nations Convention on the Rights of the Child', 20 November 1989, UN Doc. A/RES/44/25, Article 2 (gender equality); Article 19(1) (prohibition of all forms of mental and physical violence and maltreatment); Article 24(1) (right to the highest attainable standard of health); and Article 37(1) (States must take effective and appropriate measures to abolish traditional practices prejudicial to the health of children).

5. Human Rights Council, 'Report of the Special Rapporteur on torture and other cruel, inhuman or degrading treatment or punishment, Manfred Nowak', 15 January 2008, UN Doc. A/HRC/7/3, paras. 50–55.

6. For a brief overview, see World Health Organisation, *Eliminating Female Genital Mutilation: An Interagency Statement, OHCHR, UNAIDS, UNDP, UNECA, UNESCO, UNFPA, UNHCR, UNICEF, UNIFEM, WHO* (New York: WHO, 2008).

7. See, for example, J. K. Cowan, M. B. Dembour and R. A. Wilson (eds), *Culture and Rights: Anthropological Perspectives* (Cambridge: Cambridge University Press, 2001). From a legal perspective, see, generally, S. Long, 'Multiculturalism and Female Genital Mutilation', *UCL Jurisprudence Review* (2004).

8. On FGM, see S. Harris-Short, 'International Human Rights Law—Imperialist, Inept

and Ineffective? Cultural Relativism and the United Nations Convention on the Rights of the Child', 25 *Human Rights Quarterly* (2003), p. 130.

9. See, for example, N. El Saadawi, *The Hidden Face of Eve: Women in the Arab World* (2nd edn, London: Zed Books 2007); see also D. Royer, *A Critical Study of the Works of Nawal El Saadawi, Egyptian Writer and Activist* (New York: Edwin Mellen Press, 2001).

10. CEDAW, *supra* Ch. 1 note 40.

11. On the issue of Western imperialism and international law, generally, see A. Anghie, *Imperialism, Sovereignty and the Making of International Law* (Cambridge: Cambridge University Press, 2005).

12. Although, of course, they are discussed at the theoretical level. See, for example, J. Donnelly, 'The Relative Universality of Human Rights' (2007), 29(2) *Human Rights Quarterly*, p. 315; D. Kennedy, 'The International Human Rights Movement: Part of the Problem?' (2002), 15 *Harvard Human Rights Journal*, p. 101; and A. Pollis and P. Schwab, 'Human Rights: A Western Construct with Limited Applicability in Human Rights: Cultural and Ideological Perspectives', in A. Pollis and P. Schwab (eds) (Westport, CT: Praeger Publishers, 1979), pp. 1–14.

13. See, for example, A. An-Na'im, 'Toward a Cross-Cultural Approach to Defining International Standards of Human Rights' and 'Conclusion' in A. An-Na'im (ed.), *Human Rights in Cross-Cultural Perspectives—A Quest for Consensus* (University of Pennsylvania Press, 1995).

14. I. Bantekas and L. Oette, *International Human Rights Law and Practice* (Cambridge: Cambridge University Press, 2013), p. 38.

15. 'African [Banjul] Charter on Human and Peoples' Rights', 27 June 1981, OAU Doc. CAB/LEG/67/3 rev. 5, 21 I.L.M. 58 (1982).

16. See, for example, U. O. Umozurike, 'The African Charter on Human and People's Rights', 78 *American Journal of International Law* (1983), p. 902. For an exploration of the differences between the regional treaties on human rights, see B. Obinna Okere, 'The Protection of Human Rights and the African Charter on Human and People's Rights: A Comparative Analysis with the European and American Systems', 6(2) *Human Rights Quarterly*.

17. There is a wealth of literature on hate speech, including, for example, M. Herz and P. Molnar (eds), *The Content and Context of Hate Speech: Rethinking Regulation and Responses* (Cambridge: Cambridge University Press, 2012); and E. Heinze, 'Wild-West Cowboys versus Cheese-Eating Surrender Monkeys: Some Problems in Comparative Approaches to Extreme Speech', in J. Weinstein and I. Hare (eds), *Extreme Speech and Democracy* (Oxford: Oxford University Press, 2009), pp. 182–203.

18. See, for example, R. Falk, 'Foreword' in R. Normand and S. Zaidi (eds), *Human Rights at the UN: the Political History of Universal Justice* (Bloomington and Indianapolis: Indiana University Press, 2008), p.xv.

19. See, for example, R. E. Robertson, 'Measuring State Compliance with the Obligation

to Devote the Maximum Available Resources to Realizing Economic, Social, and Cultural Rights', 6 *Human Rights Quarterly* (1994), p. 693.

20. See Chapter 3, Section 3.3.
21. For detailed analysis of this argument, see E. Heinze, 'Sexual Orientation and International Law: A study in the Manufacture of Cross-Cultural Sensitivity', 22 *Michigan Journal of International Law* (2001), pp. 283–309.
22. See, for example, G. Mapondera and D. Smith, 'Human Rights campaigners attack Malawi gay couple conviction', *The Guardian*, 19 May 2010; X. Rice, 'Gay activists attack Ugandan preacher's porn slideshow', *The Guardian*, 19 February 2010; Editorial, 'The Church must not be complicit in gay persecution in Africa', *The Observer*, 23 May 2010.
23. This will be explored in depth in Chapter 7.
24. World Health Organisation, 'Female Genital Mutilation Fact Sheet', WHO Fact Sheet N 241, available at http://www.who.int/mediacentre/factsheets/fs241/en/
25. Ibid.
26. Convention on the Rights of the Child, *supra* note 4, Article 19(1).
27. Ibid., Article 24(1.)

5. UN HUMAN RIGHTS MACHINERY

1. Steven Gray, '"Milestone" LGBT discussion at UN Human Rights Council welcomed despite walkout', *Pink News*, 8 March 2012, available at http://www.pinknews.co.uk/2012/03/08/milestone-lgbt-discussion-at-un-human-rights-council-welcomed-despite-walkout/
2. Human Rights Council Resolution 17/19, 'Human rights, sexual orientation and gender identity', 14 July 2011, UN Doc. A/HRC/RES/17/19.
3. Rosa Freedman, 'The United Nations Human Rights Council's Backwards Step on LGBT Rights', *IntLawGrrls*, 7 June 2013, available at http://ilg2.org/2013/06/07/the-united-nations-human-rights-councils-backwards-step-on-lgbt-rights/
4. International Lesbian, Gay, Bisexual, Transgender and Intersex Association, *State-sponsored Homophobia: A World Survey of Laws Criminalising Same-sex Sexual Acts Between Consenting Adults* (Brussels: ILGA, 2011), p. 9.
5. See, for example, E. Heinze, *Sexual Orientation: A Human Right—An Essay on International Human Rights Law* (Leiden: Brill, 1995).
6. Steven Gray, *supra* note 1.
7. Rosa Freedman, *supra* note 3.
8. For detailed analysis of the Human Rights Council, cf. R. Freedman, *supra* Prologue note 13.
9. Including the treaty-based committees, the Special Procedures system, the Office of the High Commissioner for Human Rights, as well as UN specialised agencies and the Charter-based bodies.

10. For an explanation of the differences between protection and promotion of human rights, see R. Freedman, *supra* Prologue note 13, pp. 70–74.

11. See Chapter 2, Section 2.2.

12. L. Henkin, *How Nations Behave: Law and Foreign Policy* (2nd edn, New York: Columbia University Press, 1979), p. 47.

13. General Assembly Resolution 60/251, 'Human Rights Council', 15 March 2006, UN Doc. A/RES/60/251. On the failure of the Commission, see R. Freedman, *supra* Prologue note 13, pp. 17–37. On the creation of the Council see P. Alston, 'Reconceiving the UN Human Rights Regime: Challenges Confronting the New UN Human Rights Council', 7 *Melbourne Journal of International Law* (2006), pp. 185–224; N. Ghanea, 'From UN Commission on Human Rights to UN Human Rights Council: One Step Forwards or Two Steps Sideways?', 55 *International and Comparative Law Quarterly* (2006), pp. 704–5; and P. Maurer, 'About the Negotiation Process in New York (from 2005 until 2006): Of Ants, Caterpillars and Butterflies', in L. Müller (ed.), *The First 365 Days of the United Nations Human Rights Council* (Switzerland: Baden, 2007), pp. 33–6.

14. Meaning that states elected as members send government delegates to represent them at the Council, rather than the body being comprised of independent experts on human rights.

15. Resolution 60/251, *supra* note 13, para. 7.

16. Resolution 60/251, *supra* note 13, para. 10.

17. International Labour Organisation.

18. World Health Organisation.

19. United Nations High Commissioner for Refugees.

20. R. Freedman, *supra* Prologue note 13, pp. 39–54.

21. Resolution 60/251, supra note 13, para. 8.

22. Ambassador Dr Remigiusz Achilles Henczel serves as Poland's delegate and is President of the Human Rights Council during the body's 7th cycle. See 'UN Human Rights Council: new President will help promote human rights equitably', *UN News Centre*, 10 December 2012, available at http://www.un.org/apps/news/story.asp?NewsID=43731&Cr=&Cr1#.UqNda-K0MrA

23. Amnesty International, *Amnesty International Report 2013: The State of the World's Human Rights* (London: Amnesty International, 2013), pp. 175–7.

24. See, for example, Monica Mark, 'Slavery still shackles Mauritania, 31 years after its abolition', *The Guardian*, 14 August 2012, available at http://www.theguardian.com/world/2012/aug/14/slavery-still-shackles-mauritania

25. Freedom House, 'Freedom in the World 2013—Mauritania', available at http://www.freedomhouse.org/report/freedom-world/2013/mauritania

26. Stephanie Oertel, 'Mauritania: Promise and Challenge', *World Economic Forum*, available at http://www.weforum.org/pdf/Global_Competitiveness_Reports/Profiles/Mauritania.pdf

27. Amnesty International, *supra* note 23, pp. 171–2.

28. See, for example, H. Keller and G. Ulfstein (eds), *UN Human Rights Treaty Bodies: Law and Legitimacy* (Cambridge: Cambridge University Press, 2012).

29. See, for example, I. Nifosi, *The UN Special Procedures in the Field of Human Rights* (Antwerp: Intersentia, 2005).

6. LOOK! WE DID SOMETHING: SOUTH AFRICA AND ISRAEL

1. Human Rights Centre 'Memorial', 'The Situation in the Chechen Republic and Republic Ingushetia: May 2004', available at http://www.chechnyaadvocacy.org/local%20bulletins/Memorial%20Bulleting%20May04.pdf

2. Mark Oliver, '"No end" to Chechnya rights abuses, says Amnesty', 30 September 2005, *The Guardian*, available at http://www.guardian.co.uk/world/2005/sep/30/russia.chechnya

3. Rachel Denber, '"Glad to be Deceived": the International Community and Chechnya', in *Human Rights Watch World Report 2004* (New York: Human Rights Watch, 2004), pp. 121–39.

4. Amnesty International, '2004 UN Commission on Human Rights. Mission: to promote and protect human rights Addendum', AI Index: IOR 41/001/2004, available at http://impact22.amnesty.org/en/library/asset/IOR41/010/2004/en/6d2fbe6a-d60c-11dd-bb24-1fb85fe8fa05/ior410102004en.html

5. See Chapter 5.

6. Although, note Lebovic and Voeten's study suggesting that politicisation of the Commission's country-specific actions was not as systemic as others have claimed: J. H. Lebovic and E. Voeten, 'The Politics of Shame: The Condemnation of Country Human Rights Practices in UNCHR', 50 *International Studies Quarterly* (2006), pp. 861–88.

7. See, for example, M. Dennis, 'Human Rights in 2002: The Annual Sessions of the UN Commission on Human Rights and the Economic and Social Council', 97 *American Journal of International Law* (2003), pp. 384–6; and T. Franck, 'Of Gnats and Camels: Is there a Double Standard at the United Nations?' 78 *American Journal of International Law* (1984), pp. 819–25. More generally, see J. Donnelly, 'Human Rights at the United Nations 1955–85: The Question of Bias', 32 *International Studies Quarterly* (1988), pp. 275–303.

8. See, for example, M. Dennis, ibid., p. 384.

9. Commission on Human Rights 60th Session Draft Resolution, 'Situation of Human Rights in the Republic of Chechnya of the Russian Federation', 8 April 2004, UN Doc. E/CN.4/2004/L.29.

10. Armenia, Brazil, China, Congo, Cuba, Egypt, Eritrea, Ethiopia, Gabon, India, Indonesia, Nepal, Nigeria, Russian Federation, Sierra Leone, South Africa, Sri Lanka, Sudan, Swaziland, Togo, Uganda, Ukraine and Zimbabwe.

11. Australia, Austria, Croatia, France, Germany, Hungary, Ireland, Italy, Netherlands, Sweden, United Kingdom and the United States.

12. Argentina, Bahrain, Bhutan, Burkina Faso, Chile, Costa Rica, Dominican Republic, Guatemala, Honduras, Japan, Mauritania, Mexico, Pakistan, Paraguay, Peru, Qatar, Republic of Korea and Saudi Arabia.

13. See, for example, S. Akbarzadeh and K. Connor, 'The Organization of the Islamic Conference: Sharing an Illusion', 12 *Middle East Policy* (2005), pp. 79–92.

14. Jean-Claude Buhrer, 'UN Commission on Human Rights Loses All Credibility: Wheeling and Dealing, Incompetence and "Non-Action"', *Reporters Without Borders*, July 2003, p. 8 available at http://www.rsf.org/IMG/pdf/Report_ONU_gb.pdf

15. See, for example, P. Okowa, 'Congo's War: The Legal Dimension of a Protracted Conflict', 77 *British Yearbook of International Law* (2006), pp. 203–55.

16. Amnesty International, *supra* Ch. 5 note 23, pp. 68–70.

17. R. Freedman, *supra* Prologue note 13, pp. 133–8.

18. E. Heinze, 'Truth and Myth in Critical Race Theory and Lat Crit: Human Rights and the Ethnocentrism of Anti-Ethnocentrism', 20 *National Black Law Journal* (2007), p. 122.

19. Ibid., p. 123.

20. D. Matas, *No More: The Battle Against Human Rights Violations* (Toronto: Dundurn Press, 1994), p. 211.

21. M. Moskowitz, *The Roots and Reaches of United Nations Actions and Decisions* (Leiden: Brill, 1980), p. 49.

22. See D. Birmingham, *The De-colonization of Africa* (Abingdon: Routledge, 1995), pp. 28–39, 51–61; R. H. Shultz, *The Soviet Union and Revolutionary Warfare: Principles, Practice and Regional Comparisons* (Stanford: Hoover Institution Press, 1988.)

23. Ibid.

24. Ibid.

25. For example, 18 Resolutions on South Africa were passed at the 33rd Session, with 15 of those focusing specifically on aspects or effects of apartheid policies.

26. General Assembly Resolution 1353, 'Question of Tibet', 21 October 1959, 14th Session, UN Doc. A/RES/1353 (XIV); General Assembly Resolution 1723, 'Question of Tibet', 20 December 1961, 16th Session, UN Doc. A/RES/1723 (XVI); General Assembly Resolution 2079, 'Question of Tibet', 18 December 1965, 20th Session, UN Doc. A/RES/2079 (XX).

27. General Assembly Resolution 717, 'Complaint by the Union of Burma regarding aggression against it by the Government of the Republic of China', 8 December 1953, 8th Session, UN Doc. A/RES/717 (VIII); General Assembly Resolution 815, 'Complaint by the Union of Burma regarding aggression against it by the Government of the Republic of China', 29 October 1954, 9th Session, UN Doc. A/RES/815 (IX).

28. General Assembly Resolution 285, 'Violation by the Union of Soviet Socialist Republics of fundamental human rights, traditional diplomatic practices and other principles of the Charter', 25 April 1949, 4th Session, UN Doc. A/RES/285 (III).

29. General Assembly Resolution 1312, 'The situation in Hungary', 12 December 1958, 13th Session, UN Doc. A/RES/1312 (XIII); General Assembly Resolution 1454,

'Question of Hungary', 9 December 1959, 14th Session, UN Doc. A/RES/1454 (XIV); General Assembly Resolution 1741, 'Question of Hungary', 20 December 1961, 16th Session, UN Doc. A/RES/1741 (XVI).

30. See M. Moskowitz, *supra* note 21, pp. 65–8.

31. Commission on Human Rights 60th Session, 'Grave situation in the Occupied Palestinian Territory', 23 March 2004, UN Doc. E/CN.4/RES/2004/1; Commission on Human Rights 60th Session, 'Israeli settlements in the occupied Arab territories', 23 March 2004, UN Doc. E/CN.4/RES/2004/9; Commission on Human Rights 60th Session, 'Situation in occupied Palestine', 8 April 2004, UN Doc. E/CN.4/RES/2004/3; Commission on Human Rights 60th Session, 'Human rights in the occupied Syrian Golan', 15 April 2004, UN Doc. E/CN.4/RES/2004/8; Commission on Human Rights 60th Session, 'Question of the violation of human rights in the occupied Arab territories, including Palestine', 15 April 2004, UN Doc. E/CN.4/RES/2004/10.

32. Amnesty International, 'Conflict, Occupation and Patriarchy: Women Carry the Burden', March 2005, AI Index MDE 15/016/2005, available at http://www.amnesty.org/en/library/asset/MDE15/016/2005/en/623916bd-f791–11dd-8fd7-f57af21896e1/mde150162005en.pdf

33. General Assembly Resolution 3379 (XXX), 'Elimination of All Forms of Racial Discrimination', 10 November 1975, UN Doc. A/RES/3379 (XXX).

34. M. M. Bosch, *Votes in the UN General Assembly* (The Hague: Kluwer Law International, 1998), pp. 41–2.

35. Ibid., p. 41.

36. General Assembly Resolution 46/86, 'Elimination of Racism and Racial Discrimination', 16 December 1991, UN Doc. A/RES/46/86.

37. By 1991, when Resolution 3379 was repealed, international opinion on Israel's treatment of Palestinians had not changed fundamentally. However, there was widespread agreement that the resolution had been aimed not at the occupation but at delegitimising the State of Israel. The shifting global political climate allowed regional groups and political blocs to advance more of their own interests rather than participating in the ideological warfare between the US and the USSR. The only states to continue to support the original resolution were OIC members. In 1991 only 25 states, out of the UN's then 166 members, voted against repealing Resolution 3379. All of those countries were either OIC members, or closely allied with that bloc. Of the 71 countries that had supported the resolution in 1975, 13 absented themselves in 1991, 5 abstained, 2 had merged with other states, 29 did a complete about-face, and only 22 opposed its repeal (the other 3 opponents of the repeal were not member states when Resolution 3379 was passed).

38. For example, Myanmar (Burma), or DPRK (North Korea).

39. Human Rights Council Resolution 5/1, 'Institution Building of the United Nations Human Rights Council', 18 June 2007, UN Doc. A/HRC/RES/5/1, Chapter IIV, Part C, Item 7.

40. Diane Taylor, 'Aged 1 to 90, the victims of hidden war against women', *The Guardian*, Friday 5 December 2008, available at http://www.theguardian.com/world/2008/dec/05/congo-rape-testimonies-walungu

41. Gethin Chamberlain, 'Sri Lanka death toll "unacceptably high", says UN', *The Guardian*, 29 May 2009, available at http://www.theguardian.com/world/2009/may/29/sri-lanka-casualties-united-nations

42. B'Tselem, 'Statistics—Fatalities Before Operation Cast Lead', *B'Tselem—The Israeli Information Center for Human Rights in the Occupied Territories*, available at http://www.btselem.org/statistics/fatalities/before-cast-lead/by-date-of-event

43. Frances Harrison, 'One Hundred Thousand Tamils Missing After Sri Lanka War', *Huffington Post*, 16 December 2012, available at http://www.huffingtonpost.co.uk/frances-harrison/one-hundred-thousand-peop_b_2306136.html

44. Ibid.

45. Ibid.

46. Ibid.

47. See, for example, Xan Rice, 'ICC accuses six Kenyans of crimes against humanity during 2007 violence', *The Guardian*, 15 December 2010, available at http://www.theguardian.com/world/2010/dec/15/kenya-election-violence-suspects-named

48. See, for example, UN Press Release, 'Secretary General in Message to Human Rights Council Cautions against Focusing on Middle East at expense of Darfur, Other Grave Crises', 29 November 2006, UN Doc. SG/SM/10769-HR/4907. See also speech by Kofi Annan, 8 December 2006, in which he stated 'we must realize the promise of the Human Rights Council which so far has clearly not justified the hopes that so many of us placed in it'.

49. See, for example, R. Freedman, *supra* Ch. 2 note 31.

7. STOP SHOUTING, START HELPING: POST-COLONIALISM, HUMAN RIGHTS AND DEVELOPMENT

1. 'Survivor of Darfur horrors rejects calls for her silence', *Victoria Times Colonist*, 21 September 2008, available at http://www.canada.com/victoriatimescolonist/news/arts/story.html?id=2cfbc95d-d7ce-47aa-ab5b-4490bb85793d

2. See, for example, Nic Robertson, 'Rape is a way of life for Darfur's women', *CNN Online*, 19 June 2008, available at http://edition.cnn.com/2008/WORLD/africa/06/19/darfur.rape/

3. UNAMID is a hybrid African Union–United Nations peacekeeping mission in Darfur. It was formally established by the Security Council adoption of Resolution 1769, 31 July 2007 (UN Doc. S/RES/1769). It formally started its operations on 31 December 2007.

4. Dr Sima Samar (Afghanistan) is a medical doctor, former Deputy President and Minister for Women's Affairs under Hamid Karzai in Afghanistan's interim govern-

ment, and currently serves as Chairperson of the Afghanistan Independent Human Rights Commission.

5. Human Rights Commission, 'The situation of human rights in Sudan', 21 April 2005, UN Doc. E/CN.4/RES/2005/82. This mandate was subsequently extended by the Human Rights Council, 'Mandate of the Special Rapporteur on the situation of human rights in the Sudan', 14 December 2007, UN Doc. A/HRC/RES/6/34.

6. For a critical appraisal of Security Council action see, generally, A. F. Grzyb, *supra* Prologue note 1.

7. Amnesty International, *Annual Report 2006* (London: Amnesty International, 2007), pp. 242–3.

8. S. Totten, *supra* Prologue note 1.

9. S. M. Hassan and C. E. Ray, *Darfur and the Crisis on Governance in Sudan* (Ithaca, NY: Cornell University Press), 2009.

10. For example, 'The policy of the Sudanese government is to offer unlimited cooperation with institutions of the international community and with human rights institutions.' Sudanese delegate, 2nd Session, 27 September 2006, in response to Samar, Special Rapporteur on Sudan.

11. Sudanese delegate, 2nd Session, 18 September 2006, in response to UNHCHR, Louise Arbour.

12. Algerian delegate, 2nd Session, 27 September 2006, in response to Samar, Special Rapporteur on Sudan.

13. Ibid.

14. All comments made by the Algerian delegate, 4th Special Session, 12 December 2006.

15. In 2005, the Security Council-appointed Commission of Inquiry on Darfur emphasised that its conclusion that genocide was not occurring in the region 'should not be taken in any way as detracting from the gravity of the crimes perpetrated in that region. International offences such as the crimes against humanity and war crimes that have been committed in Darfur may be no less serious and heinous than genocide.' 'Report of the International Commission of Inquiry on Darfur to the United Nations Secretary-General', 25 January 2005, Part II, p. 4, available at http://www.un.org/News/dh/sudan/com_inq_darfur.pdf

16. All of which also received Council attention through various mechanisms, including agenda items, resolutions, fact-finding missions and special sessions.

17. E. Sanders, 'Is the Darfur bloodshed genocide? Opinions differ', *LA Times*, 4 May 2009.

18. International Criminal Court Second Warrant of Arrest for Omar Hassan Ahmad Al Bashir, in the case of *The Prosecutor v. Omar Hassan Ahmad Al Bashir ('Omar Al Bashir')*, 12 July 2010, ICC-02/05–01/09.

19. Philip Alston, 'Reconceiving the UN Human Rights Regime: Challenges Confronting the New UN Human Rights Council', 7 *Melbourne Journal of International Law* (2006), pp. 205–6.

20. For an explanation of Cuba's 'Black Spring' crackdown on journalists and freedom of expression see, for example, Carlos Lauria, Monica Campbell and María Salazar, 'Cuba's Long Black Spring', *Committee to Protect Journalists*, 18 March 2008, available at http://cpj.org/reports/2008/03/cuba-press-crackdown.php

21. See, for example, Amnesty International, 'Cuba: Submission to the UN Universal Periodic Review, Fourth session of the UPR Working Group of the Human Rights Council, February 2009', 8 September 2008, p. 5 available at http://www.amnesty.org/en/library/asset/AMR25/002/2008/en/40acb931–0148–486d-b2c0–6d67976ab049/amr250022008en.pdf

22. Amnesty International, 'Cuba: Submission to the UN Universal Periodic Review, Fourth session of the UPR Working Group of the Human Rights Council, February 2009', 8 September 2008, pp. 4–5 available at http://www.amnesty.org/en/library/asset/AMR25/002/2008/en/40acb931–0148–486d-b2c0–6d67976ab049/amr250022008en.pdf

23. Rory Carroll, 'Dissident dies on hunger strike in Cuban jail', *The Guardian*, 24 February 2010, available at http://www.theguardian.com/world/2010/feb/24/cuba-political-hungerstriker-zapata-dies

24. Ibid.

25. Ibid.

26. See, for example, 'World Report 2012: Cuba', *Human Rights Watch*, January 2012, available at http://www.hrw.org/world-report-2012/world-report-2012-cuba; and Foreign and Commonwealth Office, *Human Rights and Democracy: The 2012 Foreign and Commonwealth Office Report* (London: Foreign and Commonwealth Office, 2013), pp. 152–7 available at http://www.hrdreport.fco.gov.uk/wp-content/uploads/2011/01/2012-Human-Rights-and-Democracy.pdf

27. R. Freedman, *supra* Prologue note 13, pp. 182–7.

28. Cuban delegate, 4th Session, 27 March 2007, in response to Special Rappoteur (SR) on Torture, Manfred Nowak.

29. Cuban delegate, 6th Session, 17 September 2007, during discussion on Agenda Item 3 'Protection and Promotion of All Rights'.

30. Syrian delegate, 5th Session, 12 June 2007, in response to SR on Cuba, Christine Chanet.

31. Venezuelan delegate, 7th Session, 6 March 2008, during general discussions.

32. DPRK delegate, 23 March 2007, 4th Session, in response to SR on DPRK, Vitit Muntarbhorn.

33. DPRK delegate, 7th Session, 6 March 2008, during general discussions.

34. See, for example, Human Rights Watch, 'Cuba: Fidel Castro's Abusive Machinery Remains Intact', 19 February 2008, available at http://www.hrw.org/news/2008/02/18/cuba-fidel-castro-s-abusive-machinery-remains-intact

35. R. Freedman, *supra* Ch. 2 note 31.

8. HUMAN RIGHTS OF MIGRANTS: WHAT RIGHTS?

1. Matthew Taylor, Paul Lewis and Guy Grandjean, 'Jimmy Mubenga was unlawfully killed, inquest jury finds', *The Guardian*, 9 July 2013, available at http://www.theguardian.com/uk-news/2013/jul/09/jimmy-mubenga-unlawfully-killed-inquest-jury
3. Individuals cannot be 'illegal'. A person may have migrated in an irregular way, and s/he may have broken national laws in terms of how s/he migrate, but that does not make the individual 'illegal'. The use of the term 'irregular migrants' seeks to shift the focus back to the unlawful nature of the act rather than the individual.
4. Mark Lowen, 'Journey across crisis-hit Greece', *BBC News Online*, 9 June 2012, available at http://www.bbc.co.uk/news/world-europe-18371800
5. See, for example, Patrick Wintour, '"Go home" vans to be scrapped after experiment deemed a failure', *The Guardian*, 22 October 2013, available at http://www.theguardian.com/uk-news/2013/oct/22/go-home-vans-scrapped-failure
6. Angelo Young, 'Australia Takes Hard Stance Against People Arriving By Boat, Says "Genuine Refugees" Will Be Sent To Papua New Guinea', *International Business Times*, 19 July 2013, available at http://www.ibtimes.com/australia-takes-hard-stance-against-people-arriving-boat-says-genuine-refugees-will-be-sent-papua
7. Elisabetta Povoledo, 'Italy's Migrant Detention Centers Are Cruel, Rights Groups Say', *New York Times; International Herald Tribune*, 5 June 2013, available at http://www.nytimes.com/2013/06/05/world/europe/italys-migrant-detention-centers-are-cruel-rights-groups-say.html?pagewanted=all&_r=2&
8. Ibid.
9. 'Greek police end riot at migrant detention camp', *BBC News Online*, 10 August 2013, available at http://www.bbc.co.uk/news/world-europe-23653493
10. IRR European News Team, 'Two deaths in three weeks in Spain's notorious detention centres', *Institute of Race Relations*, 18 January 2012, available at http://www.irr.org.uk/news/two-deaths-in-three-weeks-in-spains-notorious-detention-centres/
11. Associated Press in Canberra, 'Nauru riot: 125 asylum seekers arrested', *The Guardian*, 21 July 2013, available at http://www.theguardian.com/world/2013/jul/21/nauru-riot-asylum-seekers-arrested
12. Jim Kouri, 'Russian detention of illegal aliens blasted by human rights groups', *The Examiner*, 10 August 2013, available at http://www.examiner.com/article/russian-detention-of-illegal-aliens-blasted-by-human-rights-groups
13. Lizzy Davies, 'Why Lampedusa remains an island of hope for migrants', *The Guardian*, 16 October 2013, available at http://www.theguardian.com/world/2013/oct/16/lampedusa-island-of-hope
14. IRR European News Team, 'Two deaths in three weeks in Spain's notorious detention centres', *Institute for Race Relations*, 18 January 2012, available at http://www.irr.org.uk/news/two-deaths-in-three-weeks-in-spains-notorious-detention-centres/

15. Ibid.
16. Press Release, 'Civil Society is Kept Outside; Infringements on Human Rights Continue', *Migreurop*, 9 July 2013, available at http://www.migreurop.org/article2268.html?lang=fr; and Brief, 'Detention of migrants: The favourite means of migration "management"', *Migreurop*, April 2013, available at http://www.migreurop.org/IMG/pdf/Note_de_MIGREUROP_detention_EN_Web.pdf
17. Phil Shiner and Daniel Carey, 'Yarl's Wood: a disgrace', *The Guardian*, 23 February 2010, available at http://www.theguardian.com/commentisfree/libertycentral/2010/feb/23/yarls-wood-detention
18. Migreurop Brief, *supra* note 16, p. 2.
19. Ibid.
20. C. G. T. Ho, 'U.S. Immigration Detention: An Inhumane System Violating Human Rights', *Society for Applied Anthropology*, 1 February 2013, available at http://sfaanews.sfaa.net/2013/02/01/u-s-immigration-detention-an-inhumane-system-violating-human-rights/
21. 'Turning Migrants Into Criminals: The harmful impact of US Border Prosecutions', *Human Rights Watch*, May 2013, available at http://www.hrw.org/sites/default/files/reports/us0513_ForUpload_2.pdf
22. General Assembly Resolution 45/158, 'International Convention on the Protection of the Rights of All Migrant Workers and Members of Their Families', 18 December 1990, UN Doc. A/RES/45/158.
23. Convention to Eliminate all forms of Discrimination Against Women, *supra* Ch. 1 note 40.
24. Convention on the Rights of the Child, *supra* Ch. 4 note 4.
25. General Assembly Resolution 61/106, 'Convention on the Rights of Persons with Disabilities', 13 December 2006, UN Doc. A/RES/61/106.
26. Albania, Algeria, Argentina, Azerbaijan, Bangladesh, Belize, Bolivia, Bosnia and Herzegovina, Burkino Faso, Cape Verde, Chile, Colombia, Ecuador, Egypt, El Salvador, Ghana, Guatemala, Guinea, Guyana, Honduras, Indonesia, Jamaica, Kyrgyzstan, Lesotho, Libya, Mali, Mauritania, Mexico, Morocco, Nicaragua, Niger, Nigeria, Paraguay, Peru, Philippines, Rwanda, Senegal, Seychelles, Sri Lanka, St Vincent and the Grenadines, Syrian Arab Republic, Tajikistan, Timor-Leste, Turkey, Uganda, Uruguay.
27. Benin, Cambodia, Cameroon, Chad, Comoros, Congo, Gabon, Guinea-Bissau, Liberia, Montenegro, Mozambique, Palau, São Tomé and Príncipe, Serbia, Sierra Leone, Togo, Venezuela.
28. OHCHR, 'A new Guide on strengthening legal protection of migrants' rights is now available', April 2009, available at http://www.ohchr.org/EN/NewsEvents/Pages/GuideonStrengtheningofMigrantsrights.aspx
29. C. G. T. Ho, *supra* note 20.
30. Commission on Human Rights Resolution 1999/44, 'Human Rights of Migrants', 27 April 1999, UN Doc. E/CN.4/RES/1999/44.

31. Human Rights Council, 'Report of the Special Rapporteur on the human rights of migrants, François Crépeau: Addendum, Mission to Greece', 17 April 2013, UN Doc. A/HRC/23/46/Add.4.

32. Human Rights Council, 'Report of the Special Rapporteur on the human rights of migrants, François Crépeau: Addendum, Mission to Italy (29 September–8 October 2012), 30 April 2013, UN Doc. A/HRC/23/46/Add.3.

33. Human Rights Council, 'Report of the Special Rapporteur on the human rights of migrants, François Crépeau: Addendum, Mission to Tunisia', 3 May 2013, UN Doc. A/HRC/23/46/Add.1.

34. Human Rights Council, 'Report of the Special Rapporteur on the human rights of migrants, François Crépeau: Addendum, Mission to Turkey (25–29 June 2012)', 17 April 2013, UN Doc. A/HRC/23/46/Add.2.

35. Human Rights Council, 'Report of the Special Rapporteur on the human rights of migrants, François Crépeau: Regional study: management of the external borders of the European Union and its impact on the human rights of migrants', 24 April 2013, UN Doc. A/HRC/23/46.

36. Human Rights Council, 'Note verbale dated 21 May 2013 from the Permanent Delegation of the European Union to the United Nations Office and other international organizations in Geneva addressed to the Office of the United Nations High Commissioner for Human Rights', 24 May 2013, UN Doc. A/HRC/23/G/2.

37. Tom Balmforth, 'Moscow police arrest 1,200 migrants after riots', *The Guardian*, 14 October 2013, available at http://www.theguardian.com/world/2013/oct/14/moscow-police-arrest-migrants-riots

38. OHCHR, 'Migration and Human Rights', available at http://www.ohchr.org/EN/Issues/Migration/Pages/MigrationAndHumanRightsIndex.aspx

9. THE 'GREAT' POWERS

1. 'Gay teen dies after being kidnapped, tortured in Russia', *GayStarNews*, 8 August 2013, available at www.gaystarnews.com/article'gay-teen-dies-after-being-kidnapped-tortured-russia060813

2. Ibid.

3. 'Russia: Drop Homophobic Law: Investigate Murders, Stop Prosecuting LGBT Groups', *Human Rights Watch*, 11 June 2013, available at http://www.hrw.org/news/2013/06/10/russia-drop-homophobic-law

4. Ibid.

5. Ibid.

6. 'Russia: Putin signs anti-'gay propaganda' bill into law', *Pink News*, 30 June 2013, available at http://www.pinknews.co.uk/2013/06/30/russia-putin-signs-anti-gay-propaganda-bill-into-law/

7. Owen Gibson and Alec Luhn, 'Stephen Fry calls for ban on Winter Olympics in

Russia over anti-gay laws', The Guardian, 7 August 2013, available at www.theguard-ian.com/world/2013/aug/07/stephen-fry-russia-winter-olympics-ban

8. Katie Halper, 'Russia Anti-Gay Bill: Russia Passes Radical Family Values Bill While President Announces Divorce on TV', *PolicyMic*, June 2013, available at www.pol-icymic.com/articles/48411/russia-anti-gay-bill-russia-passes-radical-family-values=bill-while-president-announces-divorce-on-tv

9. Human Rights Watch, *supra* note 3.

10. Andrew Katz, 'Russia's Anti-Gay Laws: How a Dutch Activist Got Caught in the Crosshairs', *TIME*, 5 August 2013, available at world.time.com/2013/08/05/russia-faults-in-first-test-of-anti-gay-propaganda-law-but-future-remains-bleak/

11. For discussion of the human rights abuses leading up to the Beijing Olympics, see M. Worden, *China's Great Leap: The Beijing Games and Olympian Human Rights Challenges* (Seven Stories Press, 2011).

12. M. Kauless and D. Starck, 'Peace Through Sanctions?', Policy Paper 7 of the Development and Peace Foundation (Bonn, Germany), 15 January 1998, available at http://www.globalpolicy.org/security/sanction/kulessa.htm

13. 'Beginning in 1994, the President of the General Assembly began making a Solemn Appeal for the observance of a truce during the Olympics. Since 2006, the appeal was also made for the subsequent Paralympic Games. The appeal is made every two years, right before the start of either the Summer or Winter Olympics and Paralympics.' See, http://www.un.org/events/olympictruce/appeal.shtml

14. General Assembly 62nd Session, 'Solemn appeal made by the President of the General Assembly on 28 July 2008 in connection with the observance of the Olympic Truce', 24 July 2008, UN Doc. A/62/912.

15. For example, Human Rights Council 5th Session, 'Written statement submitted by the International Federation of Human Rights Leagues (FIDH), a non-governmen-tal organization in special consultative status', 7 June 2007, UN Doc. A/HRC/5/NGO/14.

16. For example, Human Rights Council 7th Session, 'Report of the Special Rapporteur on torture and other cruel, inhuman or degrading treatment or punishment, Manfred Nowak', 18 February 2008, UN Doc. A/HRC/7/3/Add.2; and Human Rights Council 7th Session, 'Opinions adopted by the Working Group on Arbitrary Detention', 16 January 2008, UN Doc. A/HRC/7/4/Add.1.

17. R. Freedman, *supra* Prologue note 13, pp. 91–4.

18. Idealism and human rights present their own set of problems. By focusing on com-mon ideals, idealism is weighted towards universalism. That clearly has tensions with the cultural relativist approach to human rights and with post-colonial discourses.

19. See, for example, E. H. Carr, *The Twenty Years' Crisis, 1919–1939: An Introduction to the Study of International Relations* (New York: St Martin's Press, 1964).

20. M. J. Smith, *Realist Thought from Weber to Kissinger* (Baton Rouge: Louisiana State University Press, 1986), p. 13.

21. See, for example, H. J. Morgenthau, *Politics Among Nations: The Struggle for Power and Peace* (New York: McGraw-Hill, 1993).

22. See, for example, A. Roberts and B. Kingsbury (eds), *United Nations, Divided World* (2nd edn, Oxford: Oxford University Press, 1993).

23. A.-M. Slaughter, 'International Law and International Relations', 285 *Hague Academy of International Law* (2001), p. 32.

24. R. Freedman, *supra* Prologue note 13, pp. 93–101.

25. Nicholas Watt, Rowena Mason and Nick Hopkins, 'Blow to Cameron's authority as MPs rule out British assault on Syria', *The Guardian*, 30 August 2013, available at http://www.theguardian.com/politics/2013/aug/30/cameron-mps-syria

26. R. Freedman, *supra* Prologue note 13, pp. 174–5.

27. Chatham House interviews of European diplomats, January 2012, cited in S. Sceats and S. Breslin, 'China and the International Human Rights System', *Chatham House*, October 2012, p. 12, available at http://www.chathamhouse.org/sites/default/files/public/Research/International%20Law/r1012_sceatsbreslin.pdf

28. R. Freedman, *supra* Ch. 2 note 31.

29. Human Rights Council Resolution 21/3, 'Promoting human rights and fundamental freedoms through a better understanding of traditional values of humankind: best practices', 9 October 2012, UN Doc. A/HRC/RES/21/3.

30. See Chapter 5.

31. Angola, Bangladesh, Burkina Faso, Cameroon, China, Congo, Cuba, Djibouti, Ecuador, India, Indonesia, Jordan, Kuwait, Kyrgyzstan, Libya, Malaysia, Maldives, Mauritania, Philippines, Qatar, Russian Federation, Saudi Arabia, Senegal, Thailand and Uganda.

32. Austria, Belgium, Botswana, Costa Rica, Czech Republic, Hungary, Italy, Mauritius, Mexico, Norway, Poland, Romania, Spain, Switzerland and United States.

33. Note that seven countries abstained: Benin, Chile, Guatemala, Nigeria, Peru, Republic of Moldova and Uruguay. Those countries do not fit within one category. Some—for example Nigeria and Moldova—routinely discriminate against LGBT individuals, while others seek to implement rights for members of that vulnerable group.

34. See Chapter 6.

35. See Chapter 7.

36. See Chapter 8.

10. OUT OF SIGHT, OUT OF MIND: HIDDEN ABUSES ACROSS THE WORLD

1. Amnesty International, *supra* Ch. 5 note 23, pp. 36–8.

2. Office for Democratic Institutions and Human Rights, 'Republic of Belarus Parliamentary Elections 23 September 2012: OSCE/ODIHR Election Observation Mission Final Report', *ODHR*, 14 December 2012, available at http://www.osce.org/odihr/elections/98146

3. Amnesty International, *supra* Ch. 5 note 23.

4. Ibid.

5. Ibid.

6. Amnesty International Public Statement, 'Still behind bars: The plight of long-term prisoners in Belarus', 2 August 2012, AI Index: EUR 49/013/2012, pp. 3–4, available at http://www.amnesty.org/en/library/asset/EUR49/013/2012/en/c088ed34-f0ab-4367–949d-b1be8c93a4cc/eur490132012en.pdf

7. Ibid., p. 4.

8. 'World Press Freedom Index 2011–2012', *Reporters Without Borders*, 25 January 2012, p. 4, available at http://en.rsf.org/IMG/CLASSEMENT_2012/C_GENERAL_ANG.pdf

9. Foreign and Commonwealth Office, *supra* Ch. 7 note 26, pp. 127–31.

10. See, for example, Committee on the Rights of the Child, 'Concluding observations: Belarus', 8 April 2011, UN Doc. CRC/C/BLR/CO/3–4; Committee on the Elimination of Racial Discrimination, 'Concluding observations of the Committee on the Elimination of Racial Discrimination: Belarus', 10 December 2004, UN Doc. CERD/C/65/CO/2; Committee on the Elimination of Discrimination against Women, 'Concluding observations of the Committee on the Elimination of Discrimination against Women', 6 April 2011, UN Doc. CEDAW/C/BLR/CO/7; Committee Against Torture, 'Concluding observations of the Committee against Torture', 7 December 2011, UN Doc. CAT/C/BLR/CO/4.

11. International Service for Human Rights, 'Council creates a Special Rapporteur on Belarus following politicised debate', *ISHR*, 13 July 2012, available at http://www.ishr.ch/council/428-council-not-in-feed/1334-councils-politicised-engagement-on-belarus-continues-as-a-special-rapporteur-is-created

12. *World Report 2013: Events of 2012* (New York: Human Rights Watch, 2013), pp. 341–7, available at https://www.hrw.org/sites/default/files/wr2013_web.pdf

13. Amnesty International, *supra* Ch. 5 note 23, pp. 149–50.

14. BBC News, 'North Korea profile', *BBC News Online*, 23 July 2013, available at http://www.bbc.co.uk/news/world-asia-pacific-15256929

15. See, for example, Lucy Williamson, 'Delving into North Korea's mystical cult of personality', *BBC News Online*, 27 December 2011, available at http://www.bbc.co.uk/news/world-asia-16336991

16. Human Rights Watch, *supra* note 12.

17. Amnesty International, *supra* Ch. 5 note 23.

18. Rick Wallace, 'Plea to China on North Korea horror', *The Australian*, 22 August 2013, available at http://www.theaustralian.com.au/news/world/plea-to-china-on-north-korea-horror/story-e6frg6so-1226701567866

19. Ju-min Park and Michelle Kim, 'North Korean prison camp horror exposed at UN panel hearing', *Nambucca Guardian* (Australia), 21 August 2013, available at http://

www.nambuccaguardian.com.au/story/1720051/north-korean-prison-camp-horror-exposed-at-un-panel-hearing/?cs=12

20. Lucy Williamson, *supra* note 15.

21. See, for example, Committee on the Rights of the Child, 'Concluding Observations: Democratic People's Republic of Korea', 27 March 2009, UN Doc. CRC/C/PRK/CO/4; Committee on the Elimination of Discrimination against Women, 'Concluding comments of the Committee on the Elimination of Discrimination against Women: Democratic People's Republic of Korea', 22 July 2005, UN Doc. A/60/38, paras.19–76; Committee on Economic, Social and Cultural Rights, 'Concluding Observations of the Committee on Economic, Social and Cultural Rights: Democratic People's Republic of Korea', 12 December 2003, UN Doc. E/C.12/1/Add.95; Human Rights Committee, 'Concluding Observations of the Human Rights Committee: Democratic People's Republic of Korea', 27 August 2001, UN Doc. CCPR/CO/72/PRK.

22. For an exploration of DPRK's political history, see G. G. Chang, *Nuclear Showdown: North Korea Takes On the World* (New York: Random House, 2009).

23. See, for example, A. Scobell, *China and North Korea: From Comrades-in-Arms to Allies at Arm's Length* (Darby, PA: Diane Publishing, 2004), pp. 1–2.

24. Formalised through the Treaty of Friendship, Co-operation and Mutual Assistance (1961).

25. D. K. Nanto and M. E. Manyin, 'China–North Korea Relations', Congressional Research Service Report for Congress, 28 December 2010.

26. Security Council Resolution 1718 (2006), 'Non-Proliferation/Democratic People's Republic of Korea', 14 October 2006, UN Doc. S/RES/1718; and Security Council Resolution 1874 (2009), 'Non-Proliferation/Democratic People's Republic of Korea', 12 June 2009, UN Doc. S/RES/1874.

27. For an exploration of the sanctions against DPRK, see S. H. Kim and S. Chang, *Economic Sanctions Against a Nuclear North Korea* (Jefferson, NC: McFarland, 2007).

28. Human Rights Council Resolution 19/13, 'The situation of human rights in the Democratic People's Republic of Korea', 3 April 2012, UN Doc. A/HRC/RES/19/13.

29. UN Department of Public Information, 'Third Committee Approves Resolutions on Human Rights in Myanmar, Iran, Democratic People's Republic of Korea', 18 November 2010, UN Doc. GA/SHC/3998; and UN Department of Public Information, 'Third Committee Approves Draft Resolutions on Human Rights Situations in Iran, Democratic People's Republic of Korea, Myanmar', 21 November 2011, UN Doc. GA/SHC/4032.

30. Amnesty International, *supra* Ch. 5 note 23.

31. BBC News, 'Equatorial Guinea profile', *BBC News Online*, 25 June 2013, available at http://www.bbc.co.uk/news/world-africa-13317174

32. *Amnesty International Report 2010: The State of the World's Human Rights* (London: Amnesty International, 2010), pp. 15–137, available at http://report2010.amnesty.org/sites/default/files/AIR2010_EN.pdf

33. *Human Rights Watch 2012: Events of 2011* (New York: Human Rights Watch, 2012), pp. 110–16, available at http://www.hrw.org/sites/default/files/reports/wr2012.pdf

34. The World Bank, 'Equatorial Guinea', available at http://data.worldbank.org/country/equatorial-guinea

35. 'Equatorial Guinea: Account for Oil Wealth', *Human Rights Watch*, 9 July 2009, available at http://www.hrw.org/news/2009/07/09/equatorial-guinea-account-oil-wealth; and *Well Oiled: Oil and Human Rights in Equatorial Guinea* (New York: Human Rights Watch, 2009), available at http://www.hrw.org/sites/default/files/reports/bhr0709web_0.pdf

36. Human Rights Watch, *supra* note 33.

37. Amnesty International, *supra* note 32.

38. Human Rights Watch, *supra* note 33.

39. For example, Human Rights Council Working Group on Arbitrary Detention, 'Opinions adopted by the Working Group on Arbitrary Detention at its 64th session, 27–31 August 2012, no. 31/2012 (Equatorial Guinea)', 26 November 2012, UN Doc. A/HRC/WGAD/2012/31.

40. For example, Human Rights Council 19th Session: Agenda Item 3, 'Report of the Special Rapporteur on torture and other cruel, inhuman or degrading treatment or punishment, Juan E. Méndez, Addendum: Follow-up to the recommendations made by the Special Rapporteur visits to China, Denmark, Equatorial Guinea, Georgia, Greece, Indonesia, Jamaica, Jordan, Kazakhstan, Mongolia, Nepal, Nigeria, Paraguay, Papua New Guinea, the Republic of Moldova, Spain, Sri Lanka, Togo, Uruguay and Uzbekistan', 1 March 2012, UN Doc. A/HRC/19/61/Add.3.

41. For example, Human Rights Council 18th Session: Agenda Item 3, 'Report of the Working Group on the use of mercenaries as a means of violating human rights and impeding the exercise of the right of peoples to self-determination Chair-Rapporteur: Amada Benavides de Pérez, Addendum: Mission to Equatorial Guinea (16–20 August 2010)', 4 July 2011, UN Doc. A/HRC/18/32/Add.2.

42. For example, Human Rights Council 13th Session: Agenda Item 3, 'Report of the Working Group on Enforced or Involuntary Disappearances', 21 December 2009, UN Doc. A/HRC/13/31.

43. For example, Human Rights Council 14th Session: Agenda Item 3, 'Report of the Special Rapporteur on the promotion and protection of the right to freedom of opinion and expression, Frank La Rue, Addendum: Summary of cases transmitted to Governments and replies received', 1 June 2010, UN Doc. A/HRC/14/23/Add.1.

44. For example, Human Rights Council 11th Session: Agenda Item 12, 'Report of the Special Rapporteur on the independence of judges and lawyers, Leandro Despouy, Addendum: Situation in Specific Countries Territories', 19 May 2009, UN Doc. A/HRC/11/41/Add.1.

45. T. G. Weiss, *supra* Ch. 2 note 4, p. 61.

46. Ibid.

47. Amnesty International, *Annual Report 2007* (London: Amnesty International, 2008), pp. 333–6.

48. T. G. Weiss, *supra* Ch. 2 note 4, p. 62.

49. Human Rights Watch, *supra* note 33.

50. Ibid.

51. Amnesty International, 'Gambia: Climate of fear continues: Enforced disappearances, killings and torture in Gambia', 22 June 2011, Index Number: AFR 27/001/2011, p. 6, available at http://www.amnesty.org/en/library/info/AFR27/001/2011

52. Ibid.

53. Foreign and Commonwealth Office, *supra* Ch. 7 note 26, pp. 45–8.

54. Monica Mark, 'Gambian tourist paradise conceals local misery and human rights abuses', *The Guardian*, 16 June 2013, available at http://www.theguardian.com/world/2013/jun/16/gambian-tourist-paradise-misery-human-rights

55. *Amnesty International Report 2012: The State of the World's Human Rights* (London: Amnesty International, 2012), pp. 152–3, available at http://files.amnesty.org/air12/air_2012_full_en.pdf

56. Amnesty International, 'The Gambia: Hundreds accused of "witchcraft" and poisoned in government campaign', *Press Release*, 18 March 2009, available at http://www.amnesty.org/en/for-media/press-releases/gambia-hundreds-accused-%E2%80%9Cwitchcraft%E2%80%9D-and-poisoned-government-campaign-20

57. Adam Nossiter, 'Witch Hunts and Foul Potions Heighten Fear of Leader in Gambia', *New York Times*, 20 May 2009, available at http://www.nytimes.com/2009/05/21/world/africa/21gambia.html?pagewanted=all&_r=1&

58. The Gambia ratified the International Convention on Civil and Political Rights in 1979; the International Convention on Economic, Social and Cultural Rights in 1978; the Convention on the Elimination of All Forms of Racial Discrimination in 1978; the Convention on the Elimination of All Forms of Discrimination against Women in 1993; the Convention Against Torture in 1985; and the Convention on the Rights of the Child in 1990.

59. The African Charter on Human and Peoples' Rights; the African Charter on the Rights and Welfare of the Child; the Convention Governing Specific Aspects of Refugee Problems in Africa; and the Protocol to the African Charter on Human and Peoples' Rights.

60. Monica Mark, 'Gambian tourist paradise conceals local misery and human rights abuses', *The Guardian*, 16 June 2013, available at http://www.theguardian.com/world/2013/jun/16/gambian-tourist-paradise-misery-human-rights

61. Aryn Baker, 'Qatar's Leadership Shake-Up: Powerful Emir to Step Down for 33-Year-Old Son', *TIME*, 24 June 2013, available at http://world.time.com/2013/06/24/qatars-leadership-shakeup-powerful-emir-to-step-down-for-33-year-old-son/#ixzz2co2lOlSw

62. Ian Black and Agencies, 'Emir of Qatar hands power to his son in peaceful transi-

tion', *The Guardian*, 25 June 2013, available at http://www.theguardian.com/world/2013/jun/25/qatar-emir-hands-power-son

63. Associated Press, 'Qatari poet jailed for life after writing verse inspired by Arab spring', *The Guardian*, 29 November 2012, available at http://www.theguardian.com/world/2012/nov/29/qatari-poet-jailed-arab-spring

64. 'The plight of Qatar's migrant workers', *Al-Jazeera Online*, 14 June 2012, available at http://www.aljazeera.com/programmes/insidestory/2012/06/201261472812737158.html

65. 'Building a Better World Cup: Protecting Migrant Workers in Qatar Ahead of FIFA 2022' (New York: Human Rights Watch, 2012), p. 1, available at http://www.hrw.org/sites/default/files/reports/qatar0612webwcover_0.pdf

66. Al-Jazeera, *supra* note 64.

67. Law no. 14 of the year 2004 promulgating the Labor Law sets maximum weekly working hours, paid annual leave, and mandates strict health and safety regulations for the workplace. Employers are banned from confiscating passports and required to provide workers with accommodation that meets certain minimum standards.

68. Human Rights Watch, *supra* note 65, p. 5.

69. Human Rights Watch, *supra* note 65.

70. For example Committee on the Rights of the Child, 'Concluding observations: Qatar', 14 October 2009, UN Doc. CRC/C/QAT/CO/2; and Committee Against Torture, 'Concluding observations on the second periodic report of Qatar, adopted by the Committee at its 49th session (29 October–23 November 2012)', 31 January 2013, UN Doc. CAT/C/QAT/CO/2.

71. Some recent examples include Human Rights Council, 'Opinions adopted by the Working Group on Arbitrary Detention at its 62nd session, 16–25 November 2011— No. 68/2011 (Qatar)', 22 June 2012, UN Doc. A/HRC/WGAD/2011/68; Human Rights Council 19th Session, 'Report of the Special Rapporteur on torture and other cruel, inhuman or degrading treatment or punishment, Juan E. Méndez—Addendum—Observations on communications transmitted to Governments and replies received', 29 February 2012, UN Doc. A/HRC/19/61/Add.4; General Assembly 66th Session, 'Protection of migrants—Report of the Secretary-General', 3 August 2011, UN Doc. A/66/253; and Human Rights Council 17th Session, 'Report of the Special Rapporteur on the promotion and protection of the right to freedom of opinion and expression, Frank La Rue—Addendum—Summary of cases transmitted to Governments and replies received', 27 May 2011, UN Doc. A/HRC/17/27/Add.1.

72. Kingdom of Saudi Arabia, 'Basic Law of Governance', Royal Order No.(A/91), 27 Sha'ban 1412H—1 March 1992, published in *Umm al-Qura Gazette* no. 3397, 2 Ramadan 1412H—5 March 1992.

73. Ibid., Article 5(b).

74. Amnesty International, *supra* Ch. 5 note 23, pp. 224–7.

75. Ibid.

76. Hadeel Mohammed, 'Saudi Arabia Continues to Fight Human Rights Organizations',

Global Voices, 10 August 2013, available at http://globalvoicesonline.org/2013/08/10/saudi-arabia-continues-to-fight-human-rights-organizations/

77. Kevin Sullivan, 'Saudi Arabia's riches conceal a growing problem of poverty', *The Guardian*, 1 January 2013, available at http://www.theguardian.com/world/2013/jan/01/saudi-arabia-riyadh-poverty-inequality

78. For example, 'Millions of Saudi's below poverty line, report', *YaLibnan*, 4 December 2012, available at http://www.yalibnan.com/2012/12/04/millions-of-saudis-below-poverty-line-despite-welfare-programs/

79. For example, 'Censored! There are no poor people in Saudi Arabia', *France 24*, 7 November 2011, available at http://observers.france24.com/content/20111107-there-are-no-poor-people-saudi-arabia-poverty-video-prison-bloggers-firas-buqna-Al-Jaradiya

80. Foreign and Commonwealth Office, *supra* Ch 7. note 26, pp. 209–14.

81. Nabila Ramdani, 'Saudi women are allowed to cycle—but only around in circles', *The Guardian*, 3 April 2013, available at http://www.theguardian.com/lifeandstyle/the-womens-blog-with-jane-martinson/2013/apr/03/saudi-women-allowed-to-cycle

82. Rachel Shabi, 'Wadjda and the Saudi women fighting oppression from within', *The Guardian*, 7 August 2013, available at http://www.theguardian.com/commentisfree/2013/aug/07/wadjda-saudi-women-fighting-oppression

83. Katha Pollitt, 'Saudi Human Rights Activist Wajeha Al-Huwaider Sentenced to Prison', *The Nation*, 19 June 2013, available at http://www.thenation.com/blog/174894/saudi-human-rights-activist-wajeha-al-huwaider-sent-prison#axzz2Wrzn6XRw

84. Joshua Muravchik, 'Case of jailed women's activists symbolizes Saudi Arabia's regression on rights', *Washington Post*, 21 June 2013, available at http://articles.washingtonpost.com/2013–06–21/opinions/40119716_1_international-women-s-day-two-women-few-dozen-women

85. Katha Pollitt, *supra* note 83.

86. Ibid.

87. Some recent examples include Committee on the Elimination of All Forms of Discrimination Against Women, 'Concluding observations', 8 April 2008, UN Doc. CEDAW/C/SAU/CO/2; Committee on the Elimination of All Forms of Discrimination against Women, Summary record of the 816th meeting', 27 February 2012, UN Doc. CEDAW/C/SR.816; and Committee on the Elimination of All Forms of Discrimination against Women, 'Reports provided by specialized agencies—UNESCO', 2 November 2011, UN Doc. CEDAW/C/2008/I/3/Add.3.

88. Some recent examples include Committee Against Torture, 'List of Issues', 4 August 2009, UN Doc. CAT/C/SAU/Q/2; Committee on the Rights of the Child, 'Concluding Observations', 17 March 2006, UN Doc. CRC/C/SAU/CO/2; and Committee on the Elimination of Racial Discrimination, 2 June 2003, UN Doc. CERD/C/62/CO/8.

89. Press Release, 'Pillay says Saudi Arabian executions violate international standards', OHCHR, 14 March 2013, available at http://www.ohchr.org/en/NewsEvents/Pages/DisplayNews.aspx?NewsID=13139&LangID=E

90. Press Release, 'Saudi Arabia: UN human rights experts outraged at execution of seven men by firing squad', OHCHR, 13 March 2013, available at http://www.ohchr.org/en/NewsEvents/Pages/DisplayNews.aspx?NewsID=13135&LangID=E

91. Press Release, 'Saudi Arabia: UN experts outraged at beheading of a Sri Lankan domestic worker', OHCHR, 11 January 2013, available at http://www.ohchr.org/en/NewsEvents/Pages/DisplayNews.aspx?NewsID=12922&LangID=E

92. Some recent examples include Human Rights Council, 'Report of the Working Group on Arbitrary Detention—Addendum—Opinions adopted by the Working Group on Arbitrary Detention—Corrigendum', 28 August 2013, UN Doc. A/HRC/16/47/Add.1/Corr.1; Human Rights Council 17th Working Group of the Universal Periodic Review, 'Compilation prepared by the Office of the High Commissioner for Human Rights in accordance with paragraph 15 (b) of the annex to Human Rights Council resolution 5/1 and paragraph 5 of the annex to Council resolution 16/21—Saudi Arabia', 6 August 2013, UN Doc. A/HRC/WG.6/17/SAU/2; Human Rights Council 23rd Session, 'Report of the Special Rapporteur on the rights to freedom of peaceful assembly and of association, Maina Kiai—Addendum—Observations on communications transmitted to Governments and replies received', 30 May 2013, UN Doc. A/HRC/23/39/Add.2; Human Rights Council 23rd Session, 'Report of the Special Rapporteur on extrajudicial, summary or arbitrary executions, Christof Heyns—Addendum—Observations on communications transmitted to Governments and replies received', 27 May 2013, UN Doc. A/HRC/23/47/Add.5.

93. Amnesty international, *supra* note 55, pp. 345–6.

94. European Bank for Reconstruction and Development, 'Turkmenistan', available at http://www.ebrd.com/pages/country/turkmenistan.shtml

95. Central Intelligence Agency, *The World Factbook* (CIA, 2013), available at https://www.cia.gov/library/publications/the-world-factbook/geos/tx.html#top

96. Transparency International, 'Corruption by Country', 2013, available at http://www.transparency.org/country#TKM

97. David Trilling, 'Oil, Gas and Poverty: What does Turkmenistan Really Have to Offer Tourists', 20 January 2011, available at http://oilprice.com/Geopolitics/Asia/Oil-Gas-And-Poverty-What-Does-Turkmenistan-Really-Have-To-Offer-Tourists.html

98. Foreign and Commonwealth Office, *supra* Ch. 7 note 26, pp. 239–44.

99. Some recent examples include Committee on the Elimination of All Forms of Discrimination against Women, 'Concluding observations on the third to fourth periodic report of Turkmenistan adopted by the Committee at its fifty-third session (1–19 October 2012)', 21 November 2012, UN Doc. CEDAW/C/TKM/CO/3–4/CORR.1; Committee on the Elimination of Racial Discrimination, 'Concluding observations', 13 April 2012, UN Doc. CERD/C/TKM/CO/6–7; and Committee

on Economic, Social and Cultural Rights, 'Concluding observations', 16 December 2011, UN Doc. E/C.12/TKM/CO/1.

100. Press Release, 'Turkmenistan has long way to go in ensuring human rights, says UN official', *UN News Centre*, 28 May 2013, available at http://www.un.org/apps/news/story.asp?NewsID=45022#.Uhx9DG2wUrA

101. Ibid.

102. Ibid.

103. Foreign and Commonwealth Office, *supra* Ch. 7 note 26.

104. Amnesty International, 'Turkmenistan: Human rights violations continue as recommendations made during previous review go unheeded—Amnesty International Submission to the UN Universal Periodic Review', AI Index EUR 61/006/2012, October 2012, available at http://www.amnesty.org/en/library/asset/EUR61/006/2012/en/661b7a87-f445–4dab-b9db-af1c5531745b/eur610062012en.pdf

11. THE 'GOOD GUYS'

1. *Those Who Take Us Away: Abusive Policing and Failures in Protection of Indigenous Women and Girls in Northern British Columbia, Canada* (New York: Human Rights Watch, ISBN 1–56432–985–2, 2013), available at http://www.hrw.org/sites/default/files/reports/canada0213webwcover_0.pdf

2. Ibid.

3. M. Rhoad, 'Native Women Deserve a National Inquiry on Violence', Human Rights Watch, 31 January 2014, available at https://www.hrw.org/news/2014/01/31/native-women-deserve-national-inquiry-violence

4. Ibid.

5. See, for example, UPR-Info, 'Recommendations and Pledges: Canada, 2nd Review', 2013, available at http://www.upr-info.org/IMG/pdf/recommendations_and_pledges_canada_2013.pdf

6. M. Blanchfield, 'Canada Says No To UN Call For Review Of Violence On Aboriginal Women', *Huffington Post*, 19 September 2013, available at http://www.huffingtonpost.ca/2013/09/19/canada-un-aboriginal-women_n_3952425.html

7. A. Humphreys, 'A spectacle of hypocrisy and farce': North Korea, Iran attack Canada's human rights record at UN forum', *National Post*, 26 April 2013, available at http://news.nationalpost.com/2013/04/26/north-korea-iran-attack-canadas-human-rights-record-at-un-forum/

8. Amnesty International, 'Canada Gives Human Rights the Cold Shoulder: Disgraceful Response to UN Human Rights Review Contains No New Commitments', 19 September 2013, available at http://www.amnesty.ca/news/news-releases/canada-gives-human-rights-the-cold-shoulder-disgraceful-response-to-un-human-righ

9. Ibid.

10. Committee on the Elimination of Racial Discrimination, 'Concluding Observations: Canada', 4 April 2012, UN Doc. CERD/C/CAN/CO/19–20.

11. Ibid., para. 9.
12. Ibid., paras. 11 and 12.
13. Ibid., para. 19.
14. Ibid., paras. 14 and 20.
15. For example, CESCR 36th Session, 'Concluding observations of the Committee on Economic, Social and Cultural Rights: Canada', 22 May 2006, UN Doc. E/C.12/CAN/CO/4; HRCttee 85th Session, 'Concluding observations of the Human Rights Committee: Canada', 20 April 2006, UN Doc. CCPR/C/CAN/CO/5.
16. For example, HRC 13th Session, 'Report of the independent expert on minority issues: Mission to Canada', 8 March 2010, UN Doc. A/HRC/13/23/Add.2; CHR 61st Session, 'Report of the Special Rapporteur on the situation of human rights and fundamental freedoms of indigenous people, Rodolfo Stavenhagen: Mission to Canada', 2 December 2004, UN Doc. E/CN.4/2005/88/Add.3.
17. Irish Family Planning Association, 'Comments of the Irish Family Planning Association in respect of the Third Periodic Report of Ireland under the International Covenant on Civil and Political Rights (ICCPR)', June 2008, available at *www2. ohchr.org/english/bodies/hrc/docs/ngos/IFPA_Ireland93.doc*
18. Ibid.
19. Ibid.
20. HRCttee General Comment, 'General Comment No. 28: Equality of rights between men and women (article 3)', 29 March 2000, UN Doc. CCPR/C/21/Rev.1/Add.10, para. 10.
21. HRCttee General Comment, 'General Comment No. 20: Replaces general comment 7 concerning prohibition of torture and cruel treatment or punishment (Art. 7)', 10 March 1992, UN Doc. CCPR/C/20/Rev.1, para. 5.
22. According to the IFPA, *supra* note 17, 'A national survey of the population (ages 18–45), conducted by the State's Crisis Pregnancy Agency in 2003, found that 51% thought that a woman should always have a choice to have an abortion, regardless of the circumstances, 8% felt woman should never have this choice, 2% had no opinion and the remaining proportion (39%) of participants felt there should be choice in certain circumstances. A 2007 survey of public opinion on abortion conducted by the Safe and Legal Abortion Campaign indicated that 43% agreed with the proposition that termination should be available on the basis of a woman's right to choose, 69% in situations of rape, and 75% in the case of fetal anomaly incompatible with life. Agreement with the availability of a termination in each of the specified situations tends overall to be higher than average amongst the younger age cohorts (the under 35s). In addition, an *Irish Times* Behaviour & Attitudes poll on women published in September 2007 reported that a total of 54 per cent of women believe the Government should act to permit abortion. While support was found to be highest among young and single women, a majority of most age groups were found to favour allowing abortion.'
23. E. O'Toole, 'The midwife who told the truth in the Savita Halappanavar abortion

case', *The Guardian*, 19 April 2013, available at http://www.theguardian.com/com-mentisfree/2013/apr/19/savita-halappanavar-abortion-midwife

24. *A., B. & C. v. Ireland*, no. 25579/05 [2010] E.C.H.R. 2032 (16 December 2010).
25. See, for example, F. de Londras and L. Graham, 'Impossible Floodgates and Unworkable Analogies in the Irish Abortion Debate', 3(3) *Irish Journal of Legal Studies* (2013), pp. 54–75.
26. *A.G. v. X* [1992], 1 I.R. 1.
27. Human Rights Watch, 'Ireland: Abortion Law Fails Women', *HRW Dispatches*, 13 July 2013, available at http://www.hrw.org/news/2013/07/12/ireland-abortion-law-fails-women
28. Ibid.
29. HRC 19ᵗʰ Session, 'Report of the Working Group on the Universal Periodic Review: Ireland', 6 March 2012, UN Doc. A/HRC/19/9/Add.1.
30. Women's Human Rights Alliance, 'Follow-up Report to the United Nations Committee against Torture', *National Women's Council of Ireland*, July 2012, available at http://tbinternet.ohchr.org/Treaties/CAT/Shared%20Documents/IRL/INT_CAT_NGS_IRL_12079_E.pdf

12. IT IS NOT ALL DOOM AND GLOOM

1. Universal Declaration of Human Rights, *supra* Ch. 3 note 18.
2. International Covenant on Civil and Political Rights, *supra* Ch. 3 note 20.
3. International Covenant on Economic, Social and Cultural Rights, *supra* Ch. 3 note 21.
4. International Convention on the Elimination of All Forms of Racial Discrimination (1965); Convention on the Elimination of All Forms of Discrimination against Women (1979); Convention against Torture and Other Cruel, Inhuman or Degrading Treatment or Punishment (1984); Convention on the Rights of the Child (1989); International Convention on the Protection of the Rights of All Migrant Workers and Members of Their Families (1990); International Convention for the Protection of All Persons from Enforced Disappearance (2006); Convention on the Rights of Persons with Disabilities (2006); and the relevant Optional Protocols.
5. See Chapter 1, particularly text accompanying note 39.
6. E.g. *Al-Adsani v. United Kingdom* (2002), 34 EHRR 273, para. 61; *Caesar v. Trinidad and Tobago*, IACtHR Series C No. 123 (11 March 2005); Human Rights Committee, General Comment 29, HRI/GEN/1/Rev.9 (Vol. I) 234, para. 3; Committee Against Torture, General Comment 2, HRI/GEN/1/Rev.9 (Vol. I) 376, para. 1; and *Prosecutor v. Furundzija* (1998), No. 17–95–17/1, Trial Judgement, paras. 153–7; International Law Commission, Draft Articles on State Responsibility, A/56/10, ch. IV.E.2.
7. See text accompanying notes 39 and 49, and M. Cherif Bassiouni, *supra* Ch. 1 note 35.
8. International Covenant on Civil and Political Rights, *supra* Ch. 3 note 20, Articles 7 and 10.

9. European Convention on Human Rights, Article 3; American Convention on Human Rights Article 5; and African Charter on Human and People's Rights, Article 5.

10. The most famous of which is Amnesty International, *Report on Torture*, 1 January 1973, AI Index Number: ACT 40/001/1973 available at http://www.amnesty.org/en/library/info/ACT40/001/1973/en

11. Ibid.

12. Ibid.

13. Ibid.

14. General Assembly Resolution 3452 (XXX), 'Declaration on the Protection of All Persons from Being Subjected to Torture and Other Cruel, Inhuman or Degrading Treatment or Punishment', 9 December 1975, UN Doc. A/RES/30/3452.

15. Ibid., Articles 3–6.

16. Ibid., Articles 7–9.

17. C. Ingelse, *United Nations Committee Against Torture: An Assessment* (Martinus Nijhoff Publishers, 2001), p. 72.

18. Amnesty International, *supra* note 10, pp. 26–7.

19. Convention Against Torture and Other Cruel, Inhuman or Degrading Treatment or Punishment, *supra* Ch. 1 note 29.

20. Alan Travis, 'Abu Hamza and other four terror suspects face 'clean version of hell'', *The Guardian*, 5 October 2012, available at http://www.theguardian.com/world/2012/oct/05/abu-hamza-terror-suspects

21. As of 2013, states that have not ratified the Convention Against Torture include Angola, Bahamas, Barbados, Bhutan, Brunei Darussalam, Central African Republic, Comoros, Cook Islands, Democratic People's Republic of North Korea, Dominica, Eritrea, Fiji, Gambia, Grenada, Haiti, India, Iran, Jamaica, Kiribati, Malaysia, Marshall Islands, Micronesia, Myanmar, Niue, Oman, Palau, Papua New Guinea, Saint Kitts and Nevis, Saint Lucia, Samoa, São Tomé and Príncipe, Singapore, Solomon Islands, South Sudan, Sudan, Suriname, Tonga, Trinidad and Tobago, Tuvalu, United Republic of Tanzania, Vietnam, Zimbabwe.

22. Convention Against Torture, *supra* Ch. 1 note 29, Article 17.

23. Albania, Argentina, Algeria, Azerbaijan, Bangladesh, Belize, Bolivia, Bosnia and Herzegovina, Burkina Faso, Cape Verde, Chile, Colombia, East Timor, Ecuador, Egypt, El Salvador, Ghana, Guatemala, Guyana, Guinea, Honduras, Indonesia, Jamaica, Kyrgyzstan, Lesotho, Libya, Mali, Mauritania, Mexico, Morocco, Mozambique, Nicaragua, Niger, Nigeria, Paraguay, Peru, Philippines, Rwanda, Senegal, Seychelles, Sri Lanka, Saint Vincent and the Grenadines, Syria, Tajikistan, Turkey, Uganda and Uruguay.

24. Human Rights Committee (CCPR); Committee on Economic, Social and Cultural Rights (CESCR); Committee on the Elimination of Racial Discrimination (CERD); Committee on the Elimination of Discrimination against Women (CEDAW); Committee against Torture (CAT); Subcommittee on Prevention of Torture (SPT);

Committee on the Rights of the Child (CRC); Committee on Migrant Workers (CMW); Committee on the Rights of Persons with Disabilities (CRPD); Committee on Enforced Disappearances (CED).

25. Also known as 'General Recommendations' when issued by CEDAW or CERD.

26. ICCPR may consider individual communications alleging violations by States parties to the First Optional Protocol; CEDAW may consider individual communications alleging violations by States parties to the Optional Protocol; CAT may consider individual complaints alleging violations by States parties who have made the necessary declaration under Article 22 of the Convention; CERD may consider individual petitions alleging violations by States parties who have made the necessary declaration under Article 14 of the Convention; CRPD may consider individual communications alleging violations by States parties to the Optional Protocol; CED may consider individual communications alleging violations by States parties who have made the necessary declaration under Article 31 of the Convention; CESCR may consider individual communications alleging violations by States parties to the Optional Protocol. CMW and CRC have individual complaint mechanisms that have not yet entered into force.

27. Committee on Economic, Social and Cultural Rights, 'General Comment No. 15 (2002): The right to water (arts. 11 and 12 of the International Covenant on Economic, Social and Cultural Rights)', 20 January 2003, UN Doc. E/C.12/2002/11.

28. Commission on Human Rights Resolution 2001/25, 'The right to food', 20 April 2001, UN Doc. E/CN.4/RES/2001/25, para. 9.

29. Human Rights Council Resolution 7/22, 'Human rights and access to safe drinking water and sanitation', 28 March 2008, UN Doc. A/HRC/RES/7/22.

30. See, for example, World Health Organization, *Safer Water, Better Health: Costs, benefits, and sustainability of interventions to protect and promote health* (Geneva: WHO, 2008), available at http://whqlibdoc.who.int/publications/2008/9789241596435_eng.pdf; and United Nations Development Programme, *Human Development Report 2006, Beyond Scarcity: Power, poverty and the global water crisis* (Geneva: UNDP, 2006), available at http://hdr.undp.org/en/media/HDR06-complete.pdf

31. See Prologue.

32. Israel is the only country to have refused to attend its review session (in January 2013), but later rescinded and attended a rescheduled review; see, for example, Rosa Freedman, 'UPR and Israel', *IntLawGrrls*, 21 October 2013, available at http://ilg2.org/2013/10/21/upr-and-israel/

13. ALTERNATIVES: A RADICAL PROPOSAL

1. M. Scheinin, 'Swiss Initiative to Commemorate the 60th Anniversary of the UDHR. Protecting Dignity: An Agenda for Human Rights. Research Project on a World Human Rights Court: COURT: "Towards a World Court of Human Rights"', June 2009, European University Institute (Florence, Italy).

2. See Chapter 13.

3. M. Nowak, 'It's Time for a World Court of Human Rights', in *New Challenges for the UN Human Rights Machinery: What Future for the UN Treaty Body System and the Human Rights Council Procedures?* (M. C. Bassiouni and W. A. Schabas, eds) (Mortsel, Belgium: Intersentia Uitgevers, 2011).

4. On the international criminal tribunals and hybrid courts, see *supra* Ch. 3 notes 12, 13, 14 and 15.

5. F. De-Londras and L. Dzehtsiarou, 'The European Court of Human Rights and the Burden of Constitutionalism' (2014, draft on file with author.)

6. S. Trechsel, 'World Court for Human Rights', *Northwestern Journal of International Human Rights* 1(1) (2004), para. 70: 'neither desirable, nor necessary, nor probable'.

7. J. Kozma, M. Nowak and M. Scheinin, *A World Court of Human Rights: Consolidated statute and commentary* (Viennna: Neuer Wissenschaftlicher Verlag, 2010).

8. M. Scheinin, *supra* note 1, p. 6.

9. Algeria, Angola, Armenia, Azerbaijan, The Bahamas, Bahrain, Belarus, Bhutan, Brunei, Cameroon, China, Cuba, Egypt, El Salvador, Equatorial Guinea, Eritrea, Ethiopia, Guinea-Bissau, Haiti, India, Indonesia, Iraq, Iran, Israel, Jamaica, Kazakhstan, Kiribati, Kuwait, Kyrgyzstan, Laos, Lebanon, Libya, Malaysia, Mauritania, Federated States of Micronesia, Monaco, Morocco, Mozambique, Myanmar, Nepal, Nicaragua, North Korea, Oman, Pakistan, Palau, Papua New Guinea, Qatar, Russia, Rwanda, Saudi Arabia, São Tomé and Príncipe, Singapore, Solomon Islands, Somalia, South Sudan, Sri Lanka, Swaziland Sudan, Syria, Thailand, Togo, Tonga, Turkey, Turkmenistan, Tuvalu, Ukraine, United Arab Emirates, United States, Uzbekistan, Vietnam, Yemen, Zimbabwe.

10. M. Scheinin, *supra* note 1, p. 25.

11. See, for example, M. Scheinin, *supra* note 1, p. 8; M. Nowak, 'The Need for a World Court of Human Rights', 7(1) *Human Rights Law Review* (2007), pp. 251–9.

12. M. Scheinin, *supra* note 1, p. 5.

13. Ibid., p. 22.

14. For a more detailed critique of the proposal, see P. Alston, 'Against a World Court for Human Rights', *Ethics and International Affairs* (forthcoming, 2014).

14. ALTERNATIVES: A LESS RADICAL ALTERNATIVE

1. See, generally, S. Greer, *The European Convention on Human Rights: Achievements, Problems and Prospects* (Cambridge: Cambridge University Press, 2006).

2. European Convention on Human Rights, *supra* Ch. 3 note 19.

3. O. Bowcott, 'Conservatives clash over European court ruling on prisoner voting rights', *The Guardian*, 20 November 2013, available at http://www.theguardian.com/politics/2013/nov/20/prisoners-vote-european-court-human-rights

4. F. De-Londras and L. Dzehtsiarou, *supra* Ch. 13 note 5.

5. O. Bowcott, *supra* note 3.

6. See, generally, Harris and Livingstone (eds), *The Inter-American System of Human Rights* (Oxford: Oxford University Press, 1998).

7. *Velasquez Rodriguez Case*, Judgment of July 29, 1988, Inter-Am.Ct.H.R. (Ser. C) No. 4 (1988).

8. Ibid.

9. Ibid., para. 147.

10. See, generally, Burgenthal, 'Remembering the Early Years of the Inter-American Court of Human Rights and Beyond', 2 *New York University Journal of International Law and Politics* (2008), p. 37.

11. For example, *Sawhoyamaxa Indigenous Community v. Paraguay* IACtHR, Judgement of 20 March 2006.

12. See, generally, J. Pasqualucci, 'The Evolution of International Indigenous Rights in the Inter-American Human Rights System', 6 *Human Rights Law Review* (2006), p. 281.

13. B.O. Okere, 'The Protection of Human Rights in Africa and the African Charter of Human and Peoples' Rights: A Comparative Analysis with the European and American Systems', 6(2) *Human Rights Quarterly* (1984), p. 148.

14. C. Heyns and M. Killander, 'Africa', in D. Moeckli, S. Shah and S. Sivakumaran (eds), *International Human Rights Law* (Oxford: Oxford University Press, 2010), p. 488.

15. ALTERNATIVES: REFORM

1. Human Rights Council Resolution 5/1, *supra* Ch. 6 note 39.

INDEX

INDEX

Azerbaijan 2, 100

Bahrain 14, 52, 100, 110
Balkan States 22
Balkars 20, 61
Baltic peoples 20, 61
Ban Ki-Moon 49
Bashir, Halima 69–70
Al-Bashir, Omar 73
Beijing 2008 Summer Olympics
    88–9
Belarus 2, 98–100, 120
Belgium 2
Berdymukhamedov, Gurbanguly
    Mälikgulyýewiç 114
Blunt, Crispin 154
Bosnia and Herzegovina 2, 25–6
Botswana 93
Boutros-Ghali, Boutros 88
Brazil xv, 83, 89
BRIC nations (Brazil, Russia, India
    and China) 83
Bubi people 103
Buqna, Firas 112
Burkina Faso 49
Burma 19, 20, 62, 64
Bush, George Walker 30, 84

Cairo University 109
Cambodia 29
Canada 2, 61, 62, 113, 119–22,
    126, 135, 138
Catholicism 122–6
Chad 27, 71, 137
Chechnya 4, 16, 20, 57–9, 61,
    62–3, 65
China 14, 16–17, 19, 77, 89–90,
    92–3, 94, 95, 97, 100, 108, 137,
    166
  arms exports 16
  Beijing 2008 Summer Olympics
      88–9

and cultural relativism 42
and International Convention on
    the Protection of the Rights
    of All Migrant Workers and
    Members of Their Families 83
and Israel 66
and Japan 22
and Non-Aligned Movement 61,
    92
and Rome Statute 8
and Sudan xv, 16–17
and Tibet 4, 16, 17, 20, 61, 62,
    65, 66
and Turkmenistan 115, 117
and Uighurs 20, 61
veto power 17–18, 24, 90–1
Christianity 7, 122–6
Church of England 7
CIA (Central Intelligence Agency)
    15
circumcision 45
Civil and Political Rights 32, 102,
    105, 107, 111, 115, 122–3, 125,
    129, 130, 152–3, 158, 165
civil society 51, 54, 86, 88, 89, 92,
    99, 100, 104, 108, 110, 112,
    115, 117, 118, 137, 139, 148
CND (Campaign for Nuclear
    Disarmament) 12
'Coalition of the Willing' 11
Cold War 14, 15, 16, 18, 23, 61,
    66, 129
Collective Rights 32, 152, 158
colonialism 13, 23, 39, 42, 58, 61,
    63, 72, 73–4, 75, 77–8, 93, 105,
    108, 159, 164–5
Commission on Human Rights 35,
    58, 62–3, 94, 129, 135, 164
Committee on Economic, Social
    and Cultural Rights 135
Committee on the Elimination of
    Racial Discrimination 121

INDEX

INDEX

international human rights law 28,
   31–4, 50–1, 97–8, 127–40, 142,
   143, 152–60
   African system 158–60
   Convention against Torture and
      Other Cruel, Inhuman or
      Degrading Treatment or Pun-
      ishment 8, 108, 114–15, 123,
      125, 130, 131
   Convention on the Elimination
      of All Forms of Discrimination
      against Women 6–7, 38, 102,
      107, 114, 115, 123, 125, 130,
      133
   Convention on the Rights of the
      Child 6, 102, 105, 108, 114,
      115, 123, 129
   and cultural relativism 38–46
   European system 152–5
   idealism 90, 143, 148
   Inter-American system 155–8
   International Convention on the
      Elimination of All Forms of
      Racial Discrimination 8, 107,
      114, 130
   International Convention on the
      Protection of the Rights of All
      Migrant Workers and Mem-
      bers of Their Families 83, 86,
      130, 133
   International Covenant on Civil
      and Political Rights 32, 102,
      105, 107, 115, 122–3, 125,
      129, 130
   International Covenant on
      Economic, Social and Cultural
      Rights 32, 102, 105, 107, 115,
      129, 135
   realism 90–1, 95
   Third Generation Rights 32–3,
      152

Universal Declaration of Human
   Rights (UDHR) 31–2, 74, 90,
   129–30, 133–4
international humanitarian law
   26–8
   and obligation 28
International Labour Organisation
   110
international law 4–10
   customary 9
   peremptory norms 6
   treaties 7–8
International Monetary Fund (IMF)
   164
International Olympic Committee
   (IOC) 88, 89
intifada 63
Iran 2, 14, 16,100, 103, 108, 120
   cultural relativism 74
   and Iraq 22
   and Organisation of Islamic
      Cooperation (OIC) 24
   and Russia 16
   and United States 92
Iraq
   and Iran 22
   Kurds 47, 60
   Iraq War (2008–2011) 11, 92
Ireland 2, 122–6, 153
irregular migrants 79–86
   non-refoulement 131, 132
Isaev, Zelimkhan 57
Islam 15, 20, 43, 52–3, 59, 61, 111
   Shariah law 7, 52–3, 114
   Shia 112
   Sunni 53
Israel 16, 20, 21, 21, 23, 52, 62–4,
   66–7, 73, 85, 94, 95, 165
   disproportionate scrutiny of
      62–4, 66–7
   intifada 63

INDEX

INDEX

#INDEX

INDEX

INDEX